Politics of Catastrophe

'This book advances our understanding of the complex and often paradoxical terrain of the catastrophe as a field of knowledge and target of anticipatory governance. In doing so, its authors stand at the forefront of new thinking about contemporary regimes of security, power and governmentality.'

Mitchell Dean, University of Newcastle, Australia

'This excellent volume is the first book-length engagement with the implications of catastrophe for contemporary practices of security governing. It is an important contribution to our current understandings of the politics of preemption, and it is indispensable reading for anyone interested in the contemporary logic of security and securitization.'

Marieke de Goede, University of Amsterdam

This book argues that catastrophe is a particular way of governing future events – such as terrorism, climate change or pandemics – which we cannot predict but which may strike suddenly, without warning, and cause irreversible damage.

At a time where catastrophe increasingly functions as a signifier of our future, imaginaries of pending doom have fostered new modes of anticipatory knowledge and redeployed existing ones. Although it shares many similarities with crises, disasters, risks and other disruptive incidents, this book claims that catastrophes also bring out the very limits of knowledge and management. The politics of catastrophe is turned towards an unknown future, which must be imagined and inhabited in order to be made palpable, knowable and actionable. *Politics of Catastrophe* critically assesses the effects of these new practices of knowing and governing catastrophes to come and challenges the reader to think about the possibility of an alternative politics of catastrophe.

This book will be of interest to students of critical security studies, risk theory, political theory and International Relations in general.

Claudia Aradau is Senior Lecturer in International Relations at King's College London. She is the author of *Rethinking Trafficking in Women: Politics out of Security.*

Rens van Munster is Senior Researcher at the Danish Institute for International Studies (DIIS). He is the author of *Securitizing Immigration: The Politics of Risk in the EU.*

PRIO New Security Studies

Series Editor: J. Peter Burgess, PRIO, Oslo

The aim of this book series is to gather state-of-the-art theoretical reflexion and empirical research into a core set of volumes that respond vigorously and dynamically to the new challenges to security scholarship.

Politics of Catastrophe

Genealogies of the unknown

Claudia Aradau and Rens van Munster

Routledge
Taylor & Francis Group

LONDON AND NEW YORK

First published 2011
by Routledge
2 Park Square, Milton Park, Abingdon, Oxon OX14 4RN

Simultaneously published in the USA and Canada
by Routledge
711 Third Avenue, New York, NY 10017

Routledge is an imprint of the Taylor & Francis Group, an informa business

First published in paperback 2013

British Library Cataloguing in Publication Data
A catalogue record for this book is available from the British Library

Library of Congress Cataloging-in-Publication Data
A catalog record has been requested for this book

ISBN13: 978-0-415-49809-8 (hbk)
ISBN13: 978-0-415-62738-2 (pbk)
ISBN13: 978-0-203-81579-3 (ebk)

Typeset in Baskerville by
Pindar NZ, Auckland, New Zealand

Contents

Acknowledgements

Many ideas have a way of transforming between their early inception and their final materialization. This project is no exception. It has changed shape many times since we began writing a few years ago. Originally, we thought of this book as an expansion of our earlier thoughts on precautionary risk and the war on terror. However, as we went along, we became increasingly interested in the idea of catastrophe as a signifier of the unknown future and the styles of reasoning deployed to make these futures actionable. Many colleagues and friends have been part of this transformative process and we have incurred many debts while writing the book. Although it would be impossible to personally mention everyone who influenced us, a few people stand out. We would like to thank Jef Huysmans, Engin Isin and Casper Sylvest for conversations, ideas, thoughts, suggestions and, not least, encouragement. On a train commute from Milton Keynes to London, Engin came up with the idea of 'genealogies of the unknown', which we chose to adopt as the book's subtitle. His phrasing also opened new directions for our thinking about the rendition of catastrophe as a historical object of security knowledge.

The Department of Politics and International Studies at the Open University offered generous support for a 'critical reader workshop' in London, where Peter Burgess, Jef Huysmans, Engin Isin, Vivienne Jabri and Mark Neocleous carefully read and discussed most of the chapters. Their comments and suggestions not only re-energized us at the beginning of a long summer but have also proven invaluable as we revised the manuscript. Louise Amoore, Didier Bigo, Marieke de Goede, Anna Leander and Wouter Werner have all heard several versions of some of the chapters and offered us many comments and ideas. The Pavis Centre for Social and Cultural Research and the Centre for Citizenship, Identities and Governance at the Open University have supported this research through a pilot project on 'Governing through the future' and we would like to thank Victoria Basham for her enthusiastic research on Project ARGUS. We also benefited greatly from Columba Peoples who kindly shared with us his knowledge on nuclear strategy and thinking during the Cold War. We are grateful to many colleagues at the Danish Institute for International Studies who have read and commented on various book chapters. We would also like to thank Vincent Antonin Lepinay for suggesting the work of Carlo Ginzburg as a possible way to think about 'speculation'. Ginzburg's notion of conjectural knowledge also provided important clues for our thinking about the styles of reasoning through which catastrophic futures are made knowable.

The ideas in the book have been aired to audiences in various venues: the ISA Annual Conventions in San Francisco (2008), New York (2009), New Orleans (2010) and Montreal (2011); the ATACD conference 'Changing Culture: Cultures of Change' at the University of Barcelona; the workshop on 'Premediation, Anticipation, Speculation: Futures in Security and Finance', organized by PRIO and the University of Amsterdam; the 'Another Politics, Another Subject' workshop at the University of Aberystwyth; the 'Mobilisations of Uncertainty and Responsibility in International Politics and Law' workshop at the Netherlands Defence Academy; and the 'The Cultural Life of Catastrophes and Crises' summer school at the University of Copenhagen. Interlocutors have grappled with earlier versions during invited talks at the University of Newcastle, University of Nottingham, University of Southern Denmark and the VU University Amsterdam. We would like to thank all the participants, discussants and especially the hosts at these institutions: Tanja Aalberts, Nina Boy, Wout Cornelissen, Matt Davies, Marieke de Goede, Jenny Edkins, Isak Winkel Holm, Tom Lundborg, Simon Philpott, Simona Rentea, Oliver Richmond, Erna Rijsdijk, Frederik Tygstrup and Andreja Zevnik.

The editor of the PRIO New Security Studies series, Peter Burgess, has been the ideal editor: offering both support and critical engagement. Andrew Humphrys and Rebecca Brennan at Routledge have been equally supportive during the long process of writing and patiently endured our ever-shifting deadlines. For financial support for this project we are grateful to The Open University, the Centre for Citizenship, Identities and Governance, the Pavis Centre for Social and Cultural Research, and the Danish Institute for International Studies. Earlier versions of some of the material appeared in 'Governing Terrorism through Risk: Taking Precautions, (Un)knowing the Future', *European Journal of International Relations* 13(1), 2007, pp. 89–115; 'Insuring Terrorism, Assuring Subjects, Ensuring Normality: The Politics of Risk Post-9/11', *Alternatives* 33(2), 2008, pp. 191–210; and 'Exceptionalism and the "War on Terror": Criminology Meets International Relations', *British Journal of Criminology* 49(5), 2009, pp. 686–701. We thank the publishers for their permission to reprint parts of these articles here. All articles have been substantially revised and the arguments have been inevitably transformed, particularly as we have come to realize the importance of epistemological questions for the governance of catastrophic events. The heterogeneity of modes of knowledge has led us to think shifts in security practices beyond precautionary risk and exceptionalism.

We are also grateful to the following institutions that have given us permission to use the visual materials in Chapter 5: RMS (Risk Management Solutions), Swiss Re, AKG Images, MoMA, FEMA, Association of Chief Police

Officers and the Metropolitan Police Service in the UK, and WEF (World Economic Forum),

Every effort has been made to contact copyright holders for their permission to reprint material in this book. The publishers would be grateful to hear from any copyright holder who is not here acknowledged and will undertake to rectify any errors or omissions in future editions of this book.

No acknowledgement is complete without thanking those who made the project possible in the most fundamental sense. We would therefore like to thank our families for their love, encouragement and support.

1 Introduction

Catastrophes to come

In the process of writing this book, a spate of Hollywood films kept churning imaginaries of disaster. *The Road, 2012, The Book of Eli, 9, Watchmen, The Day after Tomorrow, I am Legend* and *Children of Men* are all recent productions that have capitalized on disaster and catastrophe. Of course, imaginaries of disasters, calamities, emergencies and catastrophes are not new: fears of apocalypse, dreams of catastrophic transformation and occurrences of disaster punctuate the history of mankind. However, the construction of catastrophic events as objects of anticipatory governance appears to be of more recent extraction, although here too it is possible to trace multiple origins depending on the field of application. In the domain of security, which is the main focus of this book, many experts have associated the emergence of catastrophe as a peculiar and challenging object of governance with the introduction of nuclear weapons after World War II or with recent suspicions of terrorist or so-called rogue actors – states or otherwise – getting access to nuclear material in the post-Cold War or post-9/11 era. Most of these arguments tend to emphasize the particularity of catastrophes as types of events that remain shrouded in uncertainty, confound expectation and challenge the predictive, preventive and protective knowledge of security experts. They are seen as 'rare, if not unique, and as striking rarely and without warning' (Clarke 2005: 6). They are unexpected and unknown both in their scope and their singular actualization.

The Hollywood movies nicely capture this. Not only do they show a world where threats have taken on disastrous, catastrophic or even apocalyptic proportions, they also make present a post-catastrophic future that changes the way in which the temporality of security threats and risks unfolds. The cause of the event often remains unknown and unknowable – as in Cormac MacCarthy's *The Road* – and the narrative instead enacts a future that invites audiences to inhabit a world where the catastrophic event has already happened. Humans are not seen as acting in the pre-evental present but in a post-evental future. As an article in the *Wall Street Journal* puts it, '[t]he story line of what happens after an inevitable disaster permeates nearly all the new projects, in contrast to movies like "Armageddon", which showed humanity warding off an impending threat' (Jurgensen and Brophy-Warren 2009). If at first sight the post-catastrophic Hollywood worlds of social breakdown, struggle for survival and violence appear reminiscent of Hobbes's fictional state of nature where the creation of the Leviathan served to guard civilization through 'a system of preventive defence against the mass movements that forms the basis of civil wars (of classes and of religions) and of revolutions' (Balibar 1994: 16), these films also convey the altogether different message that today catastrophes cannot be prevented. They explode both within and beyond the remit of the Leviathan.

This book inquires into how the potential catastrophic event – be it global warming, a terrorist attack or global pandemics – that cannot be prevented, neutralized or contained but nevertheless needs to be inhabited has fostered new modes of knowledge and styles of reasoning about security. The catastrophe to come induces new problematizations and modes of questioning that are related but not reducible to problems of dangers, risks, accidents, crises, emergencies or disasters. In distinction to these other terms, catastrophe probably captures best the sense of the limit or 'tipping point' invoked by an unexpected future that introduces a temporal disruption with the present. Its etymology (as opposed to those of disaster, crisis or emergency) hints at this sense of rupture, surprise and novelty. This book examines the regime of practices that emerges at the limit of anticipatory knowledge and entails new modes of governing that do not reduce the unknown and unexpected to what is familiar and predictable but works from the recognition that the future catastrophe cannot be known. How can we 'think the unthinkable', 'know the unknowable' or 'expect the unexpected'? In other words, what modes of knowledge and practices are deployed to act on an event that cannot be known, has not yet taken place but may radically disrupt existing social structures?

To answer this question, the book explores the rationalities and forms of knowledge through which the catastrophe to come is rendered actionable. It concludes that the concern with catastrophic futures has given rise to a new mode of governing where imagination and sensorial experience play an increasing role, alongside more traditional forms of knowledge, in our attempts to access and inhabit unknown futures. Unpacking what it means to imagine or experience the future, our purpose is not simply to question conventional beliefs about the catastrophe to come and concomitant injunctions to be prepared and ready for the future, but also to explore the political investment into the problematization of the future as catastrophic. To this purpose, we place catastrophe in relation to exceptions and events, two modes of disruption and reconstitution that have raised questions about political transformation, emancipation and the temporal relationship between past, present and future. Is the catastrophe to come simply an exceptional event? Diagnoses of exceptionalism have been rife in international relations and security studies, particularly after 9/11. Yet this book takes issue with the generalized diagnostic of exceptionalism by questioning the politics deployed to think, tame and live through catastrophic events.

Catastrophe, what do you mean?

In a seminal article titled *Security! What Do You Mean?*, Jef Huysmans (1998) observed that the all-pervasive talk of security – human security, societal security, environmental security, military security, individual security, global security – had not been matched by an in-depth exploration of security as an organizing concept that constitutes a field of knowledge, practices and technologies through which certain events are rendered intelligible and governable as security issues. His article was part of a wave of publications that dealt with the question of security as a specific way of problematizing social issues, or what Barry Buzan *et al.* (1998) have referred to as a process of securitization.[1] This book makes a similar observation about the concept of catastrophe. Despite its increasing role in public and professional discourse, catastrophe needs yet to be unpacked as a specific problematization of securing the future. Security scholars have paid scant attention to catastrophe. According to some, for instance, catastrophe is simply interchangeable with disaster, calamity and emergency – a quota filled with a series of other dangers, risks, uncertainties and anxieties:

> Even in a state of considerable peace there will still be plenty about which to complain and worry: the catastrophe quota will always remain comfortably full. Even though the chances of a global thermonuclear catastrophe (a humongous war on Carter's scale, presumably) have diminished to the point where remarkably few even worry about it anymore, one can concentrate on more vaporous enemies like trouble, chaos, uncertainty, unpredictability, instability, and unspecified risks and dangers.
>
> (Mueller 1994: 372)

Mueller also appears to suggest that catastrophe is, in a sense, a master signifier of the future, defined through a constant 'catastrophe quota'. However, if in this case catastrophe may be used simply as a hyperbole of insecurity, others carefully avoid the language of catastrophe, which would seem to pass an a priori judgement on governmental efforts. In public discourse, catastrophe often appears as the limit of management and frames the occurrence of an event as the failure of its prevention. Although for a long time catastrophe carried a theatrical meaning in English, by the mid-twentieth century, this had been forgotten and its negative meaning was well in place and related to the lack of action: 'UN calls for urgent action to prevent catastrophe in Cyprus' (The Times 1974). Catastrophe increasingly emerged as something that did not lend itself to control. 'Nuclear catastrophe' renders this meaning most poignantly. No longer situated in the processual development of time, catastrophe becomes associated with the radical moment of interruption. Tellingly, catastrophe does not become an attribute of management ('catastrophe management') alongside 'crisis management', 'emergency management', 'risk management' and 'disaster management'. It also does not name a profession – there are no 'catastrophe planners' like, say, 'emergency planners'. In taxonomies for disaster managers, such as the United Nations Terminology for International Disaster Reduction (2009), catastrophe is not even mentioned as a category. The UK government similarly uses the terminology of 'major disasters' or 'major incidents' rather than 'catastrophe' to refer to 'any emergency (including any known or suspected acts of terrorism) that requires the implementation of special arrangements by one or all of the Emergency services and will generally include the involvement, either directly or indirectly, of a large number of people' (Metropolitan Police 2008: 3). An incident is that occurrence, happening or event which literally 'falls upon' (from Latin *cadere*) somebody and which therefore passes no prior judgment upon governmental policy and initiatives.[2]

It is of course important to inquire how the presence or absence of the language of catastrophe has important political effects for our judgement of the present. Language is never innocent. As Andrew Lakoff argues in relation to Hurricane Katrina, it is crucial to consider to what extent the response by the US government played a role in turning Katrina from disaster into catastrophe (Lakoff 2006). At the same time, if we are to understand the governmental regime that emerges in our encounter with an unknown and unexpected future, it is equally important to move beyond discursive differences. Even when naming an event as 'catastrophe' is carefully avoided, unknown, unpredictable and worst case scenario events are added to the knowledge of disasters, risks, crises, emergencies and dangers. The subject description of disaster management courses in the UK is indicative of the constitution of this new field of knowledge around catastrophic events:

> Bombs in Bali, hurricanes in Florida, Guatemalan mud slides, earthquakes in Kashmir, Asian tsunami, famine in Africa: a week rarely passes without scenes of disasters flashing around the world. It's not just climate, geology and human beings that cause disasters: their causes can be technological, scientific or biological too. Refinery fires, factory explosions, train crashes, HIV Aids, and perhaps even a mutating avian or swine flu virus can also be disasters, sometimes with worldwide impact. Disaster management is a rapidly emerging subject and professionals

with academic qualifications and practical experience have key roles in lessening the impact of human and ecological catastrophe.[3]

(The Complete University Guide 2010)

Crisis, emergency and disaster management incorporate, realign and invent modes of knowledge adequate to the task of dealing with a calamitous future. They all share a similar field of intervention: how to govern unknown and unexpected future catastrophes. As Michael Rich, Executive Vice President of the RAND Corporation notes, particular modes of knowledge are more adept in tackling the catastrophe to come:

> Today's security environment is no longer bipolar, of course. But the risk of catastrophe is no less. It is generally believed that nine states have detonated and currently possess nuclear weapons. At least three others are strongly suspected of actively pursuing the development of nuclear weapons. We know that more than one terrorist group, most notably Al-Qaeda, has tried to acquire a nuclear weapon, and at least one, Aum Shinrikyo, has tried to build one. In this world, it is more essential than ever to generate and apply cutting-edge methods in systems analysis and modeling to manage these new catastrophe risks.

(Rich 2010)

Our choice for catastrophe (rather than risk, emergency or disaster) as a *concept* through which to think about the problematization of a calamitous future in security governance is based on two considerations. The first is that catastrophe induces a sense of the limit. Catastrophe, we suggest, functions as a 'tipping point', to use the language made current by climate change experts and adopted by nuclear war experts.[4] Indeed, when it is mentioned, catastrophe is generally seen as the intensification of disaster on a gradual continuum of destruction. Catastrophes are worst case scenarios. For example, the US Federal Emergency Management Agency (FEMA) training on risk and disaster management locates events on an emergency-disaster-catastrophe-extinction scale. Catastrophe is defined as 'any natural or manmade incident, including terrorism, that results in extraordinary levels of mass casualties, damage, or disruption severely affecting the population, infrastructure, environment, economy, national morale, and/or government functions' (US Department of Homeland Security 2008). Unlike emergencies and disasters which can be tackled with existing local and national resources, catastrophes appear to radically challenge existing technologies and processes (Quarantelli 2006). The 'next catastrophe' is the catastrophe that can radically disrupt and destroy our way of life.[5] Or, as Frédéric Neyrat puts it, we need to think catastrophe as situated in-between the accident (that which simply happens and does not disrupt historical continuity) and apocalypse (the ultimate discontinuity) (Neyrat 2008: 35). Catastrophe also speaks to the limit of knowledge and radical unknowability. It allows us to consider how knowledge and its limits (not just silences) intervene in practices of governing and subjectification.

The second reason is related to the etymological meaning of catastrophe as 'overturning'. Whereas disaster and crisis are associated with undesirable events, catastrophe was a term associated with theatre: it referred to a moment in the progress of the play. In theatre, the moment of 'overturning' is integrated into a processual understanding of the spectacle. At the beginning of the nineteenth century catastrophe in its theatrical meaning of 'overturning' dramatic actions was still sporadically used. An article from *The Times* comments about a theatre play: 'It is from commencement to catastrophe a finished piece of acting' (The Times 1803). When used in other contexts than the theatrical one, the meaning of catastrophe thus needed to be qualified through the adding of adjectives, as for example in 'sad catastrophe' (The Times 1803), 'melancholy catastrophe' (The Times 1805b) or 'shocking catastrophe' (The Times 1805a). An 'unexpected catastrophe' names an MP's resignation in 1848 (The Times 1848). Even later on, when the uncertainty of everyday life was increasingly linked with a growing awareness of uncertainty and risk as part of social and political life and the term became largely synonymous to disaster and accident,[6] catastrophe still retained its notion of overturning. As Henry Kissinger pointed out in 1977, catastrophe was both a moment of fear and closure and a generative moment, one of the 'brief moments when an old order is giving way to a pattern new and unseen; these are times of potential disorder and danger, but also of opportunity for fresh creation' (Kissinger 1977: 182). Catastrophes are unexpected, unforeseen and may radically break with the present. This break, however, need not necessarily be rendered as something negative but could also provide a new beginning. More than disaster or risk, catastrophe brings out the political issues that surround the invocation of imaginaries of the future.

Unknowns

Confronted with the catastrophic event, expert knowledge needs to tackle its very limit: the unknown. Natural and social sciences have often represented the unknown through the opposition between risk and uncertainty. Translated as an opposition between 'known unknowns' and 'unknown unknowns', former US Secretary of Defense Donald Rumsfeld has done much to popularize this distinction:

> The message is that there are no knowns. There are things that we know that we know. There are known unknowns. That is to say there are things we now know we don't know. But there are also unknown unknowns – things we don't know we don't know.
>
> (Rumsfeld 2002)

Rumsfeld's formula of the unknown unknowns has been simultaneously derided and embraced in the social sciences. Although it famously earned him the Campaign for Plain English Foot in Mouth Award in 2003, he did not coin the term. In international relations, nuclear strategists were well aware of the need to distinguish known unknowns and unknown unknowns back in the 1980s (Carter 1987: 637). Computer scientists had been interested in unknown unknowns long before Rumsfeld used the term (Okashah and Goldwater 1994). The terminology had also already been well established in environmental sciences to refer to the mysteries and surprises not yet imagined about the earth's ecosystems. Thus, a year before Rumsfeld's usage, 'unknown unknowns' were mentioned in a paper written by the Chair of Greenpeace UK, Robin Grove-White (see Durodie 2004). In 1993, the British environmentalist Norman Myers wrote in an article on biodiversity and the precautionary principle:

> The reader might object that unknown unknowns are a contradiction in terms: how can we know what we do not know? But consider; while we know all too little about global warming, and still less about the time when it will arrive in full scope and with whatever regional variations, we know for all practical intents and policy purposes that it is on its way sooner or later.
>
> (Myers 1993: 77)

How are the limits of knowledge tackled for the purposes of governance? The 'discovery' of unknown unknowns as a separate field of intervention has led security experts to invent new modes of knowledge by redeploying, recalibrating and interlinking old ones in slightly different manner. The proliferation of emergency, disaster, crisis or contingency planning across governmental, private and academic organizations has gone hand in hand with the proliferation of expert knowledge about catastrophic events in traditional security institutions such as the military, the intelligence services and the police as well as private sectors such as the insurance industry. Although a range of analyses have described how traditional governmental strategies have always sought to reduce, tame and calculate the unknown through practices of risk, we argue that it is important to consider the challenge posed by catastrophe as a separate field of security interventions, irreducible to risk calculations or the opposition between risk and uncertainty.

Although the current concern with catastrophic futures draws inspiration from the ways in which nuclear war, natural disasters and other events have been made actionable as risks, knowledge about the catastrophe to come could be best described, we argue, as conjectural. Alongside other styles of reasoning about catastrophic events, a conjectural style aspires to access the invisible and unknowable and adopts an aggregative model of knowledge drawn from computing approaches where knowledge is extracted from 'raw' data.

This conjectural epistemology is not simply an internal reshuffling of old lines of knowledge and expertise but also depends on particular forms of subjectivation. Imagination and aesthetic sensorial experience are not just indispensable to knowledge production in general, but are problematized as modes of knowledge *sui generis*. If imagination and sensorial experience had been disavowed in security knowledge, they now appear as essential supplements to more traditional forms of security knowledge. Imagination and aesthetics, we argue, also foster particular subjects of catastrophe. Referring to catastrophic terrorism, Ashton Carter *et al.* invite their readers to

> ... imagine the possibilities for themselves, because the most serious constraint on current policy is lack of imagination. An act of catastrophic terrorism that killed thousands or tens of thousands of people and/or disrupted the necessities of life for hundreds of thousands, or even millions, would be a watershed event in America's history. It could involve loss of life and property unprecedented for peacetime and undermine Americans' fundamental sense of security within their own borders in a manner akin to the 1949 Soviet atomic bomb test, or perhaps even worse.
> (Carter *et al.* 1998)

This injunction shows that imagination already emerged as an epistemic category before 9/11. Yet, imagination took centre stage for security professionals and bureaucracies, when the 9/11 Commission Report reproached the intelligence agencies for their failure to imagine the future – particularly the future catastrophe – and recommended that these therefore should 'find a way of routinizing, even bureaucratizing the exercise of imagination' (National Commission on Terrorist Attacks upon the United States 2004: 344). Today, imagination has been translated into new organizational set-ups, as emergency planners are now integrated in many private organizations and emergency planning is legally required in central and local government organizations. This organizational imaginary is turned particularly upon the possibility of catastrophic futures although it shares with 'futures studies' or foresight the desire to achieve a 'thorough understanding and analysis of the subject in its broadest perspective and identify different ways the future could develop' (UK Foresight Programme 2010). As a result, security professionals are increasingly engaged in imagining scenarios and creating simulations of the unexpected. Unexpected catastrophic events have led to increases in new professions, centres of training and academic knowledge focused on emergency or contingency planning:

> Emergency planning officers play a major role in planning, protecting and maintaining public safety in the event of a major catastrophe. Emergency planning professionals work as part of a team to anticipate and respond to threats to public safety, so their work in an ideal world will never come to fruition, but all too often it does and the swift and

coordinated response of all the emergency services and other government agencies will often be down to their hard work.

(Police Jobs 2010)

Imagination leads to the creation of new forms of knowledge, as evinced in scenario planning. Scenarios do not simply develop trends and causes of insecurity and potential disaster, but attune imagination to the unexpected, the rare and the uncertain. The reports produced by the National Intelligence Council (NIC), a centre of strategic thinking within the US government that provides the president and senior policymakers with analyses of foreign policy issues that have been reviewed and coordinated throughout the intelligence community, have recently offered a series of fictional scenarios for the future (National Intelligence Council 2004). These are inserted at the end of discussions of trends. They stand on their own, separated both in terms of their formal presentation (font and format are different) and in terms of their access to knowledge. The message conveyed is that knowledge of unexpected future events cannot be derived from trends, only from imagination. As Mathew Burrows, counsellor to the NIC and principal author of the reports, argues, developing worst case scenarios about the future is closer to art than science.[7] What are the political effects of the inclusion of particular forms of imagination and aesthetics within expert security knowledge?

Scenarios, simulations and large-scale exercises ask citizens to inhabit the catastrophic event and prepare themselves for it. According to Burrows, scenarios are also like theatre, designed to get the audience out of their comfort zone and into the script.[8] This book investigates the depoliticizing effects of conjectural knowledge and the problematization of imagination and aesthetics within an anticipatory regime of securing the future. As Wendy Brown has aptly put it, depoliticization involves 'construing inequality, subordination, marginalization, and social conflict, which all require political analysis and political solutions, as individual and personal, on the one hand, or as natural, religious, and cultural on the other' (Brown 2006: 15).

If we understand catastrophe as an anticipatory regime of organizing the social, with its attendant forms of power, knowledge and subjectivation, it is important to also raise the question of the implications of governing subjects through their senses. Whereas the disciplinary effects of power have been well described in the literature on risk and governmentality,[9] our conclusion is that the disciplining at stake in governing through the senses works in more subtle and insidious ways, as bodily regimenting is aligned with subjective experiences of pleasure and excitement.

Temporality

Catastrophe is 'a figure of time, a figure of eventfulness' that raises anew the question of temporality (Juengel 2009). Understood in its etymological sense of an overturning point, the catastrophic event is the moment of radical interruption and novelty. The catastrophic event comes by surprise. As Ben Anderson has put it, 'the assumption is that to think "the event" is to think an open future that cannot be secured' (Anderson 2010a: 228). Ulrich Beck had also noted a changing relationship to time in a society defined by catastrophic risks:

> The concept of risk reverses the relationship of past, present and future. The past loses its power to determine the present. Its place as the cause of present-day experience and action is taken by the future, that is to say, something non-existent, constructed and fictitious. We are discussing and arguing about something that is *not* the case, but *could* happen if we continue to steer the same course we have been. (Emphasis in original.) (Beck 2005: 214)

However, if risk and probability introduce an array of finite possibilities for the future, catastrophe challenges the limits of possibility. Catastrophe is a temporal concept that points towards an unexpected future and, as such, breaks with the ways in which the future has been apprehended in modernity. According to Peter Osborne (1995), modernity is characterized by its valorization of the present over the past. He argues that in the decades around 1800 there was a turn to the present, understood to be in constant transition and renewal, as a 'fleeting moment'.[10] At the same time, the future remained an 'indeterminate future characterized only by the prospective transcendence of the historical present and its relegation of this present to a future past' (Osborne 1995: 14). For Hannah Arendt (1958) too, modernity established processual thought, be it evolutionism, historical materialism, life philosophy, or the belief in progress. This process was made possible on the one hand by a biological understanding of life and, on the other, by the capitalist colonization of the future through the credit system and risk management. Capitalism uses the future to secure the present – in that sense the future becomes an 'extended present' (Nowotny quoted in Adam 2003: 73). Whether repeating the past through the iteration of statistical laws and regularities or repeating the present through the abstract temporality brought about by money and capitalism, the future does not have an existence of its own. It is incessantly folded back upon the present or the past. Catastrophe also breaks, at least to some extent, with the understanding of temporality that Michel Foucault (2007) assigned to biopolitics. Biopolitics takes hold of collective, serial and probabilistic phenomena, whereas the 'biopolitics of catastrophe' would imply a radical reconsideration of temporality, a temporality that cannot be directly subsumed to the repetitive and the serial of statistical predictability.[11]

What counts for the governance of catastrophe is the 'next' event, which comes unexpectedly yet brings about large-scale destruction and radical change. Raising questions about these different modes of temporality, catastrophic events also intensify the problem of the 'new'. Catastrophe, even when it adopts a negative meaning of destruction and fear, is still informed by the idea of radical disruption, exceptional events, unexpectability and spectacle. Although exceptionalism has been mostly associated with illiberal and sovereign practices, catastrophe can also be the moment of radical change. History is replete with catastrophic events that irremediably change the world as we know it and social and political transformation has been often associated with catastrophic events. Catastrophe, we argue, also requires us to think an event, not just calculations of risk and uncertainty. Both Marxism and social movements – from the anti-nuclear campaigns during the Cold War to the ecological politics of the end of the twentieth and beginning of the twenty-first centuries – have elaborated the need to imagine the future for political praxis. In the sociological literature, these more radical forms of praxis have been incorporated within the regime of democratic participation (see e.g. Beck 1992, 1999, Dupuy, 2005). Radical change can emerge out of the self-destruction of the system as exposed by Beck's and Jean-Pierre Dupuy's discussions of catastrophe. In this perspective, the catastrophe is inscribed within the very system of technological governance; it is the result of the accident which is no longer insurable. Catastrophic events emerge from the break-down of modern systems of risk management. For Beck (1992), the catastrophe can lead to a radical subpolitics which questions political decisions.[12] For Marxism and critical theory, the future can be reclaimed and deployed at the horizon of humanity changing the world and making history. The future becomes the realm of political subjectivity, the real domain of the unforeseeable and the unexpected. In an utopian Marxist approach such as Ernst Bloch's (1995 [1959]), concrete utopias complement historical materialism. They are apparent in fables, fairy tales, religion and literature and give materiality to the hope for the future. Focusing too much on the present, humanity can lose what Bloch calls the *novum* – the unexpectedly new (Moylan 1982).

However, one needs to approach the language of the 'new' carefully. As argued above, new styles of reasoning are never completely new and any ascent towards the future catastrophic event requires a genealogical descent towards earlier events and their governmental appropriation. For instance, Stephen Collier and Lakoff (2008) have traced the continuity of preparedness practices to civil defence exercises during the Cold War, while Didier Bigo and others have shown how these practices – designed by security experts pre-9/11 and then considered necessary by the changes brought about by 9/11 – had already been in the waiting for a considerable time (Bigo and Tsoukala 2008). Just as '[t]he reoccupation of a prophesied future by a predicted future [did not] fundamentally rupture the plane of Christian expectations' (Koselleck 2004: 18), the new introduced by the catastrophic event does not necessarily rupture radically with the language of prophecy, prediction and prevention.

The tension between the injunction to imagine the future and the governmental destruction of novelty has been astutely expressed by Frederic

Jameson in his analysis of literary utopias. According to Jameson, what is important about science fiction literature is not its capacity to imagine the future but its demonstration of our incapacity to imagine the future. We are unable to imagine the utopia 'not owing to any individual failure of imagination but as the result of the systemic, cultural, and ideological closure of which we are all in one way or another prisoners' (Jameson 1982: 153). He therefore draws a distinction between the content and form of utopia, arguing that 'the attempt to establish positive criteria of the desirable society characterizes liberal political theory from Locke to Rawls, rather than the diagnostic interventions of the Utopians' (Jameson 2005: 12). It is not the substance of the future, but the form of imagining the future that matters. Jameson cautions on the use of the concept of utopia as positivity and upholds a concept of utopia as negativity, as ultimately defined in relation to the failures of the present:

> We do not use this concept properly unless we grasp its critical negativity as a conceptual instrument designed, not to produce some full representation, but rather to discredit and demystify the claims to full representation of its opposite number. The 'moment of truth' is thus not a substantive one, not some conceptual nugget we can extract and store away with a view towards using it as a building block of some future system.
>
> (Jameson 2005: 175)

For Jameson, therefore, the utopia is a fundamentally negational principle (Pizer 1993: 132).[13] Can critical engagement with temporality and catastrophe to come follow a similar strategy? Should we, as significant parts of the ecological or anti-nuclear movement have done, appropriate the catastrophic imaginary for political purposes? How can we think the political investment in the concept of radical rupture or transformation? We approach these questions in the final chapter through a discussion of the politics of catastrophe in relation to theories of exception and event.

Genealogy

To analyse how future catastrophic events are rendered actionable at the limits of knowledge, this book deploys a broadly genealogical approach. Genealogy, as Foucault has it, is an inquiry into the 'past of the present' with the objective to destabilize what we know and do not or no longer question. Genealogy requires a descent into history rather than a search for origins, its detailed documentary work serving the critical goal of defamiliarization, of rupturing that which is taken for granted.

But if the objective of genealogy is defamiliarize the *present*, how can this method be put to work in relation to the *future*? After all, the catastrophic event is not located in the present but addresses a future that is unpredictable, elusive and disruptive rather than a present that is known, familiar and taken for granted. It supports a discourse of the new, of discontinuity and rupture, of a future threshold that will be passed. How can we critically interrogate catastrophic events which have not yet and perhaps may never take place? Although not present yet, the future of catastrophic events seems taken for granted in current discourse: the catastrophe *will* happen. Today, the terminology of 'catastrophic events' has become widely used in relation to an array of potentially threats – from climate change to terrorism and global pandemics – and intervenes in a field of power struggles in which expert knowledge and authorities of governance must recalibrate and redeploy. This book suggests that a genealogy of catastrophic events requires an analysis of past events alongside present invocations of future events. The objective remains to defamiliarize the present, but this is done through the conjoint descent towards the past and ascent towards the actualization of the event in the future.

In this book, we take genealogy's aim at defamiliarization to inquire into how past and present invocations of the catastrophic event arrange relations between knowledge, power and subjectivity. The relation between knowledge and power is at the heart of Foucault's formulation of a genealogical approach, which analyses how systems of knowledge foster particular forms of subjectivity (they literally 'make up' subjects, in Ian Hacking's famous terminology) and how these function in relation to particular power relations:

> In a specific form of discourse, appearing historically and in specific places … what were the most immediate, the most local power relations at work? How did they make possible these kinds of discourses, and conversely, how were these discourses used to support power relations? How was the action of these power relations modified by their very exercise, entailing a strengthening of some terms and a weakening of others, with effects of resistance and counterinvestments …?
>
> (Foucault 1998 [1976]: 97)

The close relationship between power and knowledge also means that a genealogical study of extradiscursive relations of power should not be exclusive of epistemological and archaeological discussions. Despite some attempts to see Foucault's concerns with the status of knowledge as pre-genealogical,[14] Foucault never lost interest in these questions. Rather, as argued by Arnold Davidson, Foucault 'had to develop an analysis of power to go along with his analysis of discursive practices so that ultimately he would have the conceptual resources to pose the question of the kinds of relations that exist between systems of knowledge and networks of power' (Davidson 2004: 204). Following Davidson, we are interested in the conditions of validity and conditions of possibility of the knowledge of catastrophe. We inquire into how certain statements about how to govern the future obtain the status of expert knowledge and scientific validity, how these modes of making the catastrophic event governable have emerged and changed over time, and how these systems of knowledge have been strategically mobilized for political ends.

To this purpose, we analyse particular objects of knowledge, methods and ways of assessing what is true and false, plausible or implausible as the result of particular 'styles of reasoning' (Hacking 2004). In Hacking's formulation, these imply particular ways of assessing truth and methods of establishing evidence that are not reducible to power relations. Drawing on the work of the historian A. C. Crombie, Ian Hacking has located six such styles:

(a) the simple postulation established in the mathematical sciences,
(b) the experimental exploration and measurement of more complex observable relations,
(c) the hypothetical construction of analogical models,
(d) the ordering of variety by comparison and taxonomy,
(e) the statistical analysis of regularities of populations and the calculus of probabilities, and
(f) the historical derivation of genetic development (Hacking 1992, Hacking 2004: 161).

Thus, a probabilistic style of reasoning (e) would be different from an experimental style (c), although the two need not be mutually exclusive, as computer modelling shows. What characterizes a style is that it introduces new 'objects, evidence, sentences (new ways of being a candidate for truth or falsehood), laws, or at any rate modalities, [and] possibilities' (Hacking 2004: 189). Although styles of reasoning have emerged at different moments in history and have gradually become stabilized, they differ from both Foucault's epistemic regimes and Thomas Kuhn's paradigms. Styles of scientific reasoning are not mutually exclusive as paradigms nor do they disappear as particular epistemic regimes. Hacking also warns that the analysis of styles should not lead to a continuist view that disallows space for historical change.

The emergence of catastrophe as an object of governance entails particular styles of reasoning about the future developed by different disciplines. Our analytical focus on styles of reasoning adds to more sociological approaches to security that have tended to focus on experts' interests in producing a particular 'regime of truth'. In particular, Bigo and his colleagues – the so-called Paris School of security studies – have approached security as a professional struggle between experts (military, police, intelligence services, private military companies and other actors) to define insecurity.[15] Part of this struggle, of course, is to couch arguments in a style that is recognizable and acceptable by other players in the field. Nevertheless, the accent of these studies has been on mapping the extradiscursive strategies of actors. In this book, we ask the related but slightly different question of what makes particular statements, technologies, modes of knowledge candidates for truth or evidence. We thus add the question of conditions of validity of knowledge to analyses of the conditions of possibility and the power struggles over the formation of an epistemic regime.

Our analysis interrogates the proliferation of discourses about the unknown on two levels: that of 'tactical productivity' (or their relation of modes of knowledge and practices of power) and that of 'strategical integration' (what makes their utilization necessary) (Foucault 1998 [1976]: 102). If the criteria for what constitutes truthfulness and evidence in relation to the unknown future are subject to change and modification, what effects does this have upon the constitution of subjects and possibilities for political action? Following Foucault's methodological prescriptions, we look at the 'multiplicity of discursive strategies that can come into play in various strategies' (Foucault 1998 [1976]: 100). This focus also takes us beyond governmentality studies of risk that have stressed the role of statistics and probabilistic reasoning at the heart of 'regimes of truth', but only recently have begun to ask how that style of reasoning is brought together and mixed with other styles.[16] In the field of security studies, our analysis adds new insights about styles of reasoning that can be deployed in the management of danger. Although a growing body of literature has unpacked the implications of probabilistic reasoning in the case of migration, terrorism, human trafficking and other issues,[17] this book shows that the regime of knowledge constituted to govern future catastrophic events does not depend only on calculations of risk and uncertainty. Faced with the unexpected, the unconventional and the improbable, different modes of knowledge need to be deployed:

> Experts combining experience in every quadrant of the national security and law enforcement community all consider this catastrophic threat perfectly plausible *today*. Technology is more accessible, society is more vulnerable, and much more elaborate international networks have developed among organized criminals, drug traffickers, arms dealers, and money launderers: the necessary infrastructure for catastrophic terrorism. Practically unchallengeable American military superiority on the conventional battlefield pushes this country's enemies toward the unconventional alternatives. (Emphasis in original.)
>
> (Carter *et al.* 1998)

The unexpected event irrupting in the future – which could moreover become catastrophic – prompts us to inquire into the emergence of more heterogeneous modes of knowledge and their effects alongside existing knowledge about threats and risks. In the context of claims about changes brought about by the 'war on terror' and anticipations of the 'next terrorist attack', it is important to bring to light continuities that challenge the 'myth of origin' for new styles of reasoning. Rather than discontinuity or continuity, perhaps the language that best characterizes our line of interpretation is that of an 'inflexion of the curve' (Foucault 1998 [1976]: 115) – neither rupture not uninterrupted continuity.

Chapter outline

Beginning with the question of the unknown, the first three chapters unpack how the challenges of the unknown have been tackled through the redeployment of old modes of knowledge. Starting from the field of security studies, Chapter 2 examines how catastrophic futures of nuclear war and large-scale disasters have been made governable in the past and considers the challenges posed to these regimes of truth by the catastrophic event. Chapter 3 moves on to consider the imbrication of different modes of expertise in taming the 'unknown' by the state. It focuses on the ways in which existing forms of knowledge and styles of reasoning identified with the four Ps of counter-terrorism governance (pursuit, protect, prevent, prepare) are deployed in response to the problematization of the unknown. The chapter also locates a particular style of reasoning, which we name 'conjectural', and interrogates it political effects. Chapter 4 continues this line of inquiry into political effects by focusing on the knowledge and practices deployed by insurance companies in the governance of catastrophe risks. Placing catastrophe risk in the history of insurance, this chapter traces how after 9/11 the insurance industry has appropriated catastrophe both as an object of governance and opportunity for profit. Chapters 5 and 6 turn to the often disavowed elements of knowledge production: imagination and aesthetics. Chapter 5 considers the problematization of imagination in knowledge acquisition about catastrophes to come and traces its integration with existing modes of security expertise. Chapter 6 inquires into aesthetics as a form of sensorial knowledge about catastrophic futures. Finally, Chapter 7 analyses the relations between catastrophe, exceptions and events, and the implications for what can be done about the future. Although other analyses of counter-terrorism have mainly approached the politics of catastrophe through sovereign decisions and exceptional practices, this chapter also explores the political implications of thinking catastrophe as a *political* event.

2 Securing catastrophic futures

The threat as such is nothing yet – just a looming. It is a form of futurity, yet has the capacity to fill the present without presenting itself. Its future looming casts a present shadow, and that shadow is fear.

Brian Massumi (2005)

Catastrophe and the Cold War

In his seminal history of the world, the British historian Eric Hobsbawn (1996) refers to the first half of the twentieth century – characterized by two World Wars, genocide, the rise of totalitarian regimes and a crumbling of the world economy – as the age of catastrophe. As the previous chapter suggested, however, today the label 'catastrophe' is increasingly used in a prospective rather than retrospective sense: the catastrophic event increasingly captures our problematization of the future rather than our understanding of the past. Drawing attention to the steadily growing governmental apparatus aimed at the assessment, prevention and governance of a wide variety of man-made and natural catastrophes, Ben Anderson captures the prevailing mood when he argues that today 'bombs are dropped, birds are tracked, and carbon is traded on the basis of what has not and may never happen: the future' (Anderson 2010b: 1).

Although risk management now is a *sine qua non* of many political, social and economic activities and disciplines (economics, environmental studies, sociology, geography, anthropology, health and so on), this trend has arguably been most explicit in the field of security. In the post-9/11 literature on security, the notion of 'catastrophe' has been added to 'risk' to capture the radical uncertainty, eventfulness and potential destruction that future terrorist events harbour. The 'next terrorist attack' has become one of the main fixtures of the collective imagination of catastrophe. 'Next Terrorist Attack on U.S. Not Matter of If, But When' headlines an insurance news journal (Jakes Jordan 2006); 'Another Terrorist Attack Coming Soon?' asks the media (Page 2006). In short: 'Are We Ready for the Next Terrorist Attack?'

(Cote 2007). The following chapters explore the 'next terrorist attack' as a problematization which entails the deployment and strategic assemblage of different knowledges into a 'new' regime of truth about how to secure catastrophic futures.

Before turning to the new styles of reasoning that have emerged in relation to the unknown and catastrophic future, this chapter first traces some of the historical lineages of the project of securing catastrophic futures. In spite of its novelty in strategic thinking, the terminology of catastrophe also draws on a parallel vocabulary that, with its attendant *dispositif* of power and knowledge, can be located in the 'traditional' history of Cold War security.[1] This often remains unacknowledged in much of the security literature, which all too willingly has posited a radical break between the Cold War and the post-Cold War or post-9/11 period. Several authors have developed Christopher Coker's work based on the premise that after the fall of the Berlin Wall war has become risk management in all but name (Coker 2009: viii). These analyses argue that strategic thinking in the Cold War period was considered within the management of predictable and well-known threats, whereas after the Cold War, with the demise of the Soviet Union, states were faced with a plethora of threats that could not be known, predicted and prevented. For example, Mikkel V. Rasmussen has argued that since the end of the Cold War 'Western governments simply are much less certain of whether and when they are secure' (Rasmussen 2004: 382), while another commentator has claimed that, compared to the Cold War, '[t]oday's world is far from predictable ... Risk and uncertainty are the hallmarks of world politics at the dawn of the twenty-first century' (M. J. Williams 2008: 58).[2]

By contrast, this chapter argues that the question of how to secure the present against catastrophic futures has been central to security experts since the development of nuclear weaponry and interballistic missiles. Strategists did not assume a world of certainty where threats could be known or predicted, let alone neutralized. It is also worth remembering that uncertainty had been key to understandings of security dilemmas (see Glaser 1997, Roe 1999, Cerny 2000, Booth and Wheeler 2007) and did not enter security studies with post-Cold War debates about risk and uncertainty. Herman Kahn, probably the most flamboyant of RAND intellectuals, claimed that understanding nuclear war required 'thinking about the impossible, the improbable, the implausible, and the unlikely' (Kahn 1962: 18).[3] Bernard Brodie, another RAND scholar and a founding father of strategic studies, argued that nuclear weapons 'have transformed all recognition with the past', the 'change being so unprecedented that historical comparisons fail us almost completely' (Brodie 1949: 475, 478). This is nicely summed up by Jacques Derrida, who argued that the phenomenon of nuclear war 'is fabulously textual ... [I]t has existence only through what is said of it, only where it is talked about. Some might call it a fable, then, a pure invention: in the sense in which it is said that a myth, an image, a fiction, a utopia, a rhetorical figure, a fantasy, a phantasm, are inventions' (Derrida 1984).

Even if the language of catastrophe has not been taken up directly in strategic studies during the Cold War and often remains unnamed as such, the anticipation of the possibility of nuclear war, natural hazards and other events can be viewed as expressions of the wish to tame the possibility of a calamitous future. Two concepts have been particularly central in the problematization of an unknown, catastrophic future: crisis and disaster. In as far as each has given rise to separate, yet related, regimes of practices through which the unknown future has been captured and rendered intelligible, both concepts represent important historical moments in a genealogy of the 'unknown'. The regimes of 'crisis' and 'disaster' move strategic thought, understood as a way of acting out the future through calculation in order to gain control over it, to its very limit. They mobilize and apply forms of knowledge that oscillate between the possible instead of the probable and the plausible instead of the true. Rather than postulating that the Cold War period was characterized by a future that was known and predictable, the interesting question to ask from a governmental perspective is what forms of discourses, methods and forms of knowledge are legitimized and deployed for governing an unknown future? What kind of actions in the present are made possible on the basis of worst case scenarios of nuclear war and natural hazards? And in which ways do these regimes inform the novel regime of practices identified with the concept of catastrophe? What are the connections between 'crisis', 'disaster' and 'catastrophe' in the government of security?

In an attempt to deal with these questions, the chapter begins with a brief account of risk and uncertainty, two concepts that have recently spawned a number of analyses on continuities and discontinuities in security governance and the unknown future. On the basis of that discussion, the chapter then explores 'crisis' and 'disaster' as two different regimes of security governance, each with their own set of discourses, experts, technologies and knowledge. Arguing that today these concepts and their associated modes of knowledge and practices have come to function around the same problematization of catastrophic irruptions, the final section explores the novel elements catastrophe introduces to these regimes. Despite important continuities between these concepts, 'catastrophe' also redeploys and intensifies the anticipatory logics at work in 'crisis' and 'disaster'. In doing so, 'catastrophe' brings together familiar styles of reasoning about securing the future in a regime of governing the unknown and potentially catastrophic event.

Governing risks

For a long time, the concept of risk, which has been thought to be coextensive with the insurable (Ewald 1986), has been shunned by security studies. Traditional security studies could not fit a logic of insurance within their definition of danger and the military techniques to neutralize these dangers. Constructivist approaches such as the Copenhagen School of security studies have looked at the performative naming of security and could not therefore identify techniques and rationalities of risk if not explicitly named as such.[4] Risk was seen as a term most closely related to issues of welfare and social security but of little significance for security studies. Governmentality scholars, too, have tended to see security and risk as separate domains. Michel Foucault (2000) and especially François Éwald (1986) have viewed insurance as a social technology of justice that holds the promise of solidarity – a far cry from practices of national security that are generally associated with exclusion, emergency measures and the exercise of violence (Buzan *et al.* 1998). Even though some observers have noted that social security has historically been paired with the objectives of national security, few authors question that, in principle, social security operates as a rationality of social solidarity.[5]

Defined by Nikolas Rose as a 'family of ways of thinking and acting, involving calculations about probable futures in the present followed by interventions into the present in order to control that potential future' (Rose 2001: 7), the concept of risk has the important advantage that it establishes a direct relation to time. It draws attention to a 'wager on the future' that is left somewhat implicit in security studies. For instance, the Copenhagen School's understanding of securitization as a speech act that calls for urgent decisions to counter existential threats does not exclude the possibility of framing the future as something catastrophic, but its logic nonetheless remains wedded to a vocabulary of war, urgency and defence rather than prevention (Buzan *et al.* 1998).

The concept of risk, in turn, shifts the analytical focus from utterances referring to threats to the technologies and strategies by means of which the future is produced as calculable and renders the problem of strategy more explicitly as one of securing an 'unknown' future. Didier Bigo (2004) has introduced considerations of risk in security studies through the question of security knowledge by analysing how managers of unease – the police, intelligence services, military or private security agencies – have used the 'authority of statistics' to classify and prioritize threats to determine what exactly constitutes a security issue. For example, when the police make use of insurance knowledge, statistics and profiling for the purposes of prevention, risk enters the remit of security. Moreover, risk management is not only about particular technologies, but speaks of the expansion of model of knowledge – constituted by its experts, power relations, technologies and rationalities – that increasingly permeate security practices such as intelligence, border control and military deployment.

If the concept of risk has only recently been 'discovered' by security studies, others have argued that, particularly after the attacks of 9/11, the concept may well be on its way out again as a useful way of capturing what is at stake in security governance. In the security imagination after 9/11, these authors argue, risk has given way to modes of apprehending the future that, based on imagination, premediation and intuition, are said to go beyond the calculative modality of risk.[6] In security studies, this change is often captured through the distinction between risk and uncertainty as two different ways in which the present is connected to the future (Daase and Kessler 2007, Kessler and Werner 2008, Best 2009).[7] As Jacqueline Best has pointed out, '[u]ncertainty is ... a conceptual category that defines the unknown in different terms from risk' (Best 2009: 359). If risk is an attempt to make the future calculable, uncertainty is a principle that stimulates thinking about the plausible or possible rather than the probable:

> [U]ncertainty is not a type of risk, and a governmental analysis needs to recognize this. This is not meant to suggest that we accept ... claims that the distinction reflects divergent properties of real events or situations. From a governmental standpoint, risk and uncertainties are neither real nor unreal. Rather, they are ways in which the real is imagined to be by specific regimes of government, in order that it may be governed.
>
> (O'Malley 2004: 15)

This governmental view of uncertainty is clearly distinguished from the way it is used by Ulrich Beck and his followers in security studies. For Beck, uncertainty is merely the residual of risk, the incalculable leftover of risk management. It is a term related to the lack of control and management. In Beck's optic, 9/11 did not usher in novel technologies for managing catastrophic futures but was merely another reminder that we now live in a society defined by uncontrollable dangers that move us 'beyond rational calculation into the realm of unpredictable turbulence' (Beck 2002: 43).[8]

Whereas for Beck 'the hidden central issue in world risk society is how to *feign* control over the uncontrollable – in politics, law, science, technology, economy and everyday life' (Beck 2002: 41, emphasis added), in a governmental analysis the concept of uncertainty indicates a type of knowledge about the unknown that belongs to a different epistemic class than risk. Rumsfeld's expository of the unknown mentioned in the previous chapter gets at the heart of this difference. His 'known knowns' and 'known unknowns' are the forms of uncertainty that can still be calculated and integrated by technologies of risk. They refer to the unknown future that can be governed through statistical probabilities and other forms of computation. By contrast, the 'unknown unknowns' can be said to include worst case scenarios of the future that disturb existing, risk-based modalities of taming the unknown future. As Patrick O'Malley concludes, uncertainty 'involves techniques of flexibility and adaptability, requires a certain kind of "vision" that may be thought of as intuition but is nevertheless capable of being explicated at great length in terms such as "anticipatory government" and "governing with foresight"' (O'Malley 2004: 5).

Uncertainty, however, is not just a hallmark of governing security post-9/11; regimes of uncertainty can be traced in the ways in which the catastrophic future of nuclear war was made actionable during the Cold War. The concept of crisis emerged as a way of governing the catastrophic future of nuclear war and constituted a regime of knowledge and practice that created a relationship to the future that can be located somewhere between risk and uncertainty, probability and plausibility. Without the possibility to extrapolate from past events (a nuclear war had never taken place), the future of nuclear war was made accessible through the use of scenarios and models that legitimized actions taken in the present. Sharon Ghamari-Tabrizi, among others, has noted that nuclear weapons 'swallowed up the personal wisdom of senior officers rooted in combat experience in favour of intuitions arising from repeated trials of laboratory-staged simulations of future war' (Ghamari-Tabrizi 2005: 48). These scenarios did not attempt to predict the future but merely outlined a range of possible or plausible futures. Herman Kahn (1962) famously referred to this non-probabilistic mode of capturing the unknown as 'thinking the unthinkable': without historical data on the basis of which the likelihood of nuclear war could be forecast, strategic analysts relied on different modes of knowledge such as war gaming, simulations and scenario planning to produce a 'synthetic history' to help statesmen exploit and control the risk of future nuclear war. As US Secretary of State John Foster Dulles put it in 1956, at the peak of the Cold War: 'The ability to get to the verge without getting into war is the necessary art. If you cannot master it … if you are scared to go to the brink, you are lost' (cited in Wight 1991: 194).

In distinction to crisis, disaster is not primarily about decision-making in a situation before reaching the threshold, but covers the knowledge and actions deployed to manage a dangerous irruption as it occurs. With disaster, one can say the threshold has been crossed. The sociologist Thomas Drabek defined a disaster as '… an event in which a community undergoes such severe losses to persons and/or property that the resources available within the community are severely taxed' (Drabek 2004). Crises raise issues of prevention and recovery; disasters imply a more complex cycle of preparedness, response, recovery and mitigation. Drawing an analogy to the use of the Richter scale, Henry Fischer has proposed a 'disaster scale' based upon 'the degree of disruption and adjustment a community(s)/society experiences when we consider scale, scope and duration of time' (Fischer 2003: 99–106). The representation of an event as 'disaster' demands from security experts not so much that they are able to imagine plausible futures in order to help prevent them from becoming real but rather urges them to inhabit, rehearse and exercise the event in order to devise adequate responses should the event ever materialize.

Crisis and disaster management

Crisis and disaster, then, can be said to formulate different discourses about securing the future which evolve around particular referent objects of security, and which gain validity through different styles of reasoning about the unknown future. For many observers, what characterizes both crises and disasters – in contradistinction to risk management – is their so-called '"un-ness": unexpected, unscheduled, unprecedented, and almost unmanageable' (Rosenthal *et al.* 1989: 5). The concepts of crisis and disaster mobilize and apply forms of knowledge that oscillate between the probable and the possible. Despite their differences, both concepts share a common history and were developed in response to the same question: how to secure society against extreme events and emergencies, in particular nuclear war?

The concept of crisis was fundamental to governing the catastrophic future of nuclear war. Couched in the vocabulary of risk, uncertainty and chance, nuclear strategists for instance considered their task as one of dealing with future contingencies.[9] To this end, they often deployed the notion of insurance in a context that was different from probabilistic calculation. In this view, 'planning is a prudential exercise, like taking out insurance against an accident. You hope you don't need it, but you've taken reasonable precautions just in case' (Kahn 1984: 55). Obviously, important differences exist between insurance and nuclear strategy. Insurance generally deals with recurring accidents of a non-catastrophic nature, which means that losses and damage are tolerable as long as they can be compensated for on a routine basis. Nuclear war, clearly, does not allow that luxury. Rather than risk compensation, nuclear strategists focused predominantly on war planning and civil defence as means of decreasing the probability of nuclear war. Using the analogy of insurance, however, rendered planning as an insurantial technology through which the incalculability of a nuclear attack was made actionable.

Concerned with the question of the threshold, the notion of crisis refers not just to the actual moment of decision but includes the broader prior strategic choices and actions that move or prevent a situation from moving in the direction of the decisive moment of victory or defeat (Koselleck 1982: 625).[10] As is illustrated most evidently by the Cuban Missile Crisis, a crisis was understood as a protracted period of interdependent conflict that had not yet reached the critical point of war. The task of security analysts and experts was to strategically plan, based on the rational and conscious estimation of possible advantages and disadvantages, a given course of action whose consequences could nevertheless be never known in full (Allison 1971).[11] The continuum crisis-disaster-catastrophe draws attention not just to the modes of knowledge mobilized to secure the future beyond computations of risk, but also to the knowledge of events, pre-evental processes and post-evental effects. Crises, disasters, catastrophes can be understood as *dispositifs* of governance, deployed in response to particular problematizations of the future.

Technologies and forms of knowledge developed to prevent a nuclear war – such as deterrence, mutually assured destruction, second strike capabilities and civil defence – only make sense when these are looked at through the concept of crisis as a distinct style of reasoning about catastrophic futures. Deterrence, in particular, functioned as a practice of crisis management through which the likelihood of a full-blown nuclear war could be reduced, if not completely prevented. At the same time, the idea of a threshold enabled the development of knowledge about how to approach the extreme point of no return without actually passing it. Crises were to be managed and prevented from developing; they also provided an opportunity to gain political or military advantage over the adversary through competitive risk-taking (Schelling 1960). Crisis management was about the 'controlled loss of control' where the risk of war is deliberately made more likely through policy actions and choices. Schelling referred to this strategy of manipulating risk as 'the deliberate creation of a recognizable risk of war, a risk that one does not completely control. It is a tactic of letting the situation get somewhat out of hand, just because its being out of hand may be intolerable to the other party and force his accommodation' (quoted in Freedman 2003: 208). Kahn's description of a complex escalation ladder that, infamously, involved over forty different steps also conveyed the basic idea that a limited war could and should get out of hand by degrees (Kahn 1960).

Crisis, then, is not so much a decisive turning point as the process leading up to that critical and extreme situation; it is not triggered by a decision but the outcome of multiple causes that work together over time to produce an existential threat. A security crisis embraces 'those situations that threaten basic values through perceptions of a heightened risk of military violence' (Stern 2003: 188). Here, the concept of crisis thus denotes a different temporal relation than securitization which, dealing with the extreme moment of decision only, tells us little about the strategies deployed to avert, manage or even exploit the future possibility of nuclear war. As Michael C. Williams has argued in a different context,

> to focus too narrowly on the search for singular and distinct *acts* of securitization might well lead one to misperceive *processes* through which a situation is being gradually intensified, and thus rendered susceptible to securitization, while remaining short of the actual securitizing decision. (Emphasis in original.)
>
> (M. C. Williams 2003: 521)

The decisionism at the heart of theories of securitization misses the particular relationship that crisis establishes with the unknown future of nuclear war.

For some, similar forms of knowledge are thought to define both crisis and disaster management. Defining disaster as the negative outcome of crisis, the failure to prevent a crisis from passing the threshold, these authors do not consider disaster as constituting a separate field of knowledge and practices (Rosenthal 1998, Boin 2005). Nevertheless, the focus on non-military disasters taking place during peace time, even if only selected for their presumed resemblance to air raids, introduces a significant shift. Moving away from a view of external agents as a cause, disaster focuses on the vulnerability of social structures only. Even as the etymological roots of 'disaster' (ill-starred, *des* + *astro*) point towards outside circumstances such as the positioning of the stars, fate, God's will or the laws of nature as the cause for harm, in the modern world they have been governmentalized as vulnerabilities as part of and built into social structures:

> [D]isasters are inherently social phenomena. It is not the hurricane wind or storm surge that makes the disaster; these are the sources of damage. The disaster is the impact on individual coping patterns and the inputs and outputs of social systems … Vulnerability … is to be found in social structure and disruption is the outcome of vulnerability. There is some consensus, by inference, that the magnitude of a disaster should be measured not in lives or property lost, but by the extent of the failure of the normative or cultural system.
>
> (Perry 2007: 12, 13)

The focus is not on the cause of harm but on its impact. Although the phenomena of terrorism, hurricanes and floods may have different causes, disaster constitutes them as structurally similar in as far as they all represent 'the interdependent cascade of failure triggered by an extreme event that is exacerbated by inadequate planning and ill-informed individual or organizational actions' (Comfort 2005: 338). Disaster research also borrowed from the geography of natural hazards the idea that preparedness needs to span the entire hazard cycle and not just that of response.

Disaster research has emphasized the need to analyse disasters for the purposes of stimulating preparedness, resilience and recovery as valid objectives in and by themselves (Comfort 2005). Whereas crisis refers to a regime that works through gradual escalation and competitive risk-taking, the epistemic regime of disaster inscribes a range of policies, laws and practices that are to strengthen readiness and preparedness in all kinds of sectors. Although response and recovery are important elements of disaster management, these are subordinate to the objective of creating disaster-resistant communities through fostering preparedness and readiness in individuals, families and households, organizations and communities. Under the telling title *Are You Ready?*, the US Department of Homeland Security (2004) has published a guide that helps US citizens and families to be prepared against all types of hazards and disasters.

Disaster management does not rely primarily upon maintaining a competitive advantage against an adversary but on reducing vulnerability in one's own society, organization or subjectivity to be able to withstand disastrous events. The acting-out of catastrophe serves the objective of mitigating and absorbing the catastrophic event by improving preparedness and readiness. Through preparedness exercises, vulnerabilities in the milieu can be mapped, and hypothetical scenarios and imagined futures can be made physically present in specific ways that allow the future to be rehearsed: 'In staging, an "in-between" opens up between the present and the future in which the consequences of the event can be experimented with. The scenario is therefore best conceptualised as a theatrical device that enables an "as if" future to be made present' (Anderson 2010a: 233).

Unlike in a crisis, scenarios do not primarily serve the function of imagining alternative futures, but to make the future present as a bodily experience through staging, playing and performance (Davis 2007, Collier 2008, Anderson 2010b). The knowledge generated by disaster studies strongly depends on experiential knowledge generated through exercises and the bodily embracement of an unknown future. Stephen Collier (2008) refers to this as 'acting out' the future; the unknown future is not just imagined but also actualized through a governing of the senses which are regimented to experience reality in a certain way.[12] In Anderson's apposite formulation, '[t]he space of the exercise becomes an occasion for experiencing how a future event might feel' (Anderson 2010b: 10). Acting out the catastrophic event serves the objective to mitigate and absorb the catastrophic event by improving preparedness and readiness.

The distinctions we have drawn between crisis and disaster management should not be taken to mean that similar forms of knowledge, discourses, practices and technologies cannot be seen at work in both regimes. The two are not the same regime, but neither do they constitute wholly separate tracks: they circulate in a constant back-and-forth movement of practices and schemas of knowledge. Discourses and technologies developed in one regime were put to a different strategic use in the other. For example, governing the future through crisis also required the collection of knowledge about systemic vulnerabilities. Yet, this knowledge was strategized in a different way in as far as it was inserted within a rationality of crisis escalation and competitive risk-taking, which also required some sort of appreciation of complex systems, their functioning and proneness to disruption: the more resilient social structures were, the higher the chance that a possible attack could be countered, and the more likely that a possible aggressor would be deterred (Wohlstetter 1958). Thus, within the regime of crisis, national space was reinterpreted as an interconnected field of potential targets and vulnerabilities forcing a process of de-urbanization and the diffusion of critical industries throughout the nation (Galison 2001). Similarly, strategists 'discovered' civil defence and preparedness as useful practices for promoting deterrence and prevention.[13]

Moreover, during the Cold War, the focus of research on natural disasters resonated with the interests of security experts given their focus on impact and organization and public responses. Questions of how the public would react to a nuclear attack could be answered by researching the 'laboratories' of natural disasters (Tierney 2007: 504). Claude Gilbert depicts these analogies in relation to disaster studies as a separate field of knowledge:

> The scientific approach to disaster is therefore a reflection of the nature of the *market* in which disaster research became an institutional demand. Bombs fitted easily with the notion of an *external agent*, while people

harmed by floods, hurricanes, or earthquakes bore an extraordinary resemblance to victims of air raids. (Emphasis in original.)

(Gilbert 1998: 13)

Yet, the rationalities underpinning the utilization of these technologies can nonetheless be distinguished. For those concerned with the management of crisis, the rationality behind civil defence, preparedness and vulnerability reduction was first and foremost to cancel out the enemy's advantage of a first strike. It was a way of preventing or minimizing the risk of a military attack. Therefore, when crisis management is discussed in organizational studies today, the focus is that of maintaining a competitive advantage.

More recently, however, the regimes of crisis and disaster have become increasingly merged in securing catastrophic futures. This is driven both by institutional changes such as the inclusion of FEMA under Homeland Security in the US, which are themselves enabled by modes of knowledge that consider a continuum of future incidents that are attributable to an external agent and those that are not immediately so. For example, the European Union programme for critical infrastructure protection takes an 'all hazards' approach rather than a 'terrorism' one (European Commission 2004). Expert knowledge, from academic expertise in disaster management to insurance professionals, has redefined terrorism as intentional disaster. Sociologists such as David Alexander or Jean-Pierre Dupuy have placed 9/11 in the continuity of historical disasters or catastrophes such as the Lisbon Earthquake of 1755 (Alexander 2002, Dupuy 2002b). A series of analogies are thereby established:

> Both disasters affected great commercial cities with extensive networks of influence abroad. Both dealt a body blow to trade and postage, though not a fatal one. On a smaller scale, some of the physical parallels are remarkable … Both events represent a symbolic victory of chaos over order.
>
> (Alexander 2002: 5–6)

Moreover, the knowledge developed in sociology and geography about disasters has also informed this merging. Drabek, for instance, has prepared literature summaries for instruction on FEMA courses focused on the social dimensions of disasters (Drabek and Evans, 2005: 3). Even if the interpenetration of these practices has gained more attention after 9/11, the knowledge of crisis and disaster management shows that the concern with unknown, catastrophic futures predates 9/11 and the end of the Cold War.

At the same time, the field has paid scant attention to the problem of the event and the continuum crisis-disaster-catastrophe. We suggest that the concept of catastrophe can capture both elements: unknowability and eventfulness. If the unknowns that plague security experts today can no longer be satisfactorily captured through the regimes of crisis and disaster management alone, one can speak of a strategic reintegration, recalibration and enveloping of these practices into a new epistemic regime that appears at the very *limit* of these forms of management. This style of reasoning is best captured by the concept of catastrophe, which to some extent surpasses the concepts of both crisis and disaster. Although 'disaster' and 'catastrophe' are often used interchangeably – this is, to an extent, the result of a double etymology to render similar events: disaster derives from Latin, while catastrophe is of Greek origin – a qualitative distinction separates these concepts:

> Hurricane Katrina has reinforced the view of some researchers that the scale of any collective crisis has to be taken into account in any analysis. To them, just as 'disasters' are qualitatively different from everyday community emergencies, *so are 'catastrophes' a qualitative jump over 'disasters'*.
> (Quarantelli 2006, emphasis added)

The FEMA training on risk and disaster management also differentiates catastrophes from disasters, which are considered less destructive (US Department of Homeland Security 2008). The Lisbon Earthquake in 1755, Hurricane Mitch in 1998 and the famine in India in 1965–1967 are given as historical examples of catastrophe. Natural and human-caused events are seen to cause catastrophic effects affecting the well-being of whole nations, while disaster management emergency tools are seen as inadequate to tackle catastrophe. Whereas crisis implies a diagnostic and prognostic intent, representing the point of no return and the possibility to transform and manage the crisis successfully, catastrophes appear beyond our ability to resolve them. Barack Obama recently cautioned in relation to the economic crisis that 'A failure to act, and act now, will turn crisis into a catastrophe' (Krauthammer 2010). Unlike crises, catastrophes must be prevented at all costs, both pre-eventally and in the course of the event itself to minimize its disruptions. Catastrophes can be diagnosed and prognosticated but not solved. Behind the issues of scale that are increasingly seen to differentiate emergencies, crises, disasters and catastrophes, the question of the unknown thus needs to be posed anew: how to manage events that are difficult, if not impossible, to predict and that could have potentially catastrophic consequences? What epistemic regime emerges when security professionals can no longer solely rely on the controlled manipulation of risk or be sure if such events can be absorbed or mitigated?

Knowledge of the future

Confronted with the problem of the unknown, security studies have had recourse to debates about risk and uncertainty to conceptualize what is at stake in securing the future against catastrophic events. Catastrophes appear to bring that undefined extra, an element of 'un-ness' that crisis and disaster do not capture. But what is this 'un-ness' of catastrophe? For Beck, the answer is relatively simple. Catastrophes are incalculable, uncontrollable and ultimately ungovernable. They do not just seem unmanageable, they *are* unmanageable. As he argues, 'it makes no sense to insure against the worst-case ramifications of the global spiral of threat' (Beck 1999: 142). What catastrophe brings out is an idea of the event as extraordinary or exceptional. Catastrophes radically challenge existing technologies and processes. One of the characteristics of catastrophe is that '[m]ost, if not all, of the everyday community functions are sharply and concurrently interrupted' (Quarantelli 2006).

However, thinking catastrophes as unmanageable would be to ignore the modes of knowledge deployed to govern potential catastrophes as well as the practices developed and institutions mobilized to anticipate and inhabit future events. At the same time, this does not mean that the language of catastrophe is simply similar to that of risk and danger. Inserting 'catastrophe' in debates about security raises questions of political effects that are slightly different from those of practices of risk, crisis, disaster or emergency. Others have pointed out that against the backdrop of radical contingency institutions have attempted to devise means to minimize or avoid the catastrophic promise of the future, seeking for alternative ways to master it (Bougen 2003, O'Malley 2003: 276). Collier (2008) has argued that there has been a move away from the archival-statistical knowledge involved in risk prevention to an 'enactment knowledge' that is produced by acting-out future threats in order to understand their societal impact. Lee Clarke (2005) has named it 'possibilistic knowledge', whose basis in the imagination of the unthinkable supplements the probabilistic knowledge of risk management. Anderson (2010a) talks about three types of knowledge practices that function in relation to anticipation: calculation, imagination and enactment. Calculation is based on the power of numbers, imagination on that of fabulation and enactment on that of drama or theatre. Melinda Cooper (2008) sees speculation as the driver of new forms of knowledge. Speculation is a technology of calculating the uncertainties of the future, which is different from statistical prognosis and forecasting. It is about data mining, simulations and modelling. As in globalized capitalism, where circulation appears to increasingly rely on speculative financial practices (Comaroff and Comaroff 2000, Lee and LiPuma 2002), speculation appears to have become a rationality and mode of knowledge for governing the unexpected event (de Goede 2008b, Braun 2007, Cooper 2006).

'Enactment knowledge', 'possibilistic knowledge', 'anticipatory knowledge', 'speculative knowledge' – these are all different labels to refer to modes of knowledge deployed to capture the non-calculable. Yet, the modes of knowledge deployed to tackle the emergence of catastrophic events constitute a more heterogeneous amalgam. Although they draw on the rationalities, practices and forms of knowledge that have underpinned the governance of uncertainty during the Cold War, the governance of catastrophe depends upon a new *dispositif* of heterogeneous practices, knowledges, institutions and authorities. This emerging *dispositif* is not so much defined solely by enactment, speculation or possibility. Catastrophe recreates a govern-mental *dispositif* at the limits of knowledge. The challenge posed by the limit appears clearly in the cautionary note offered by a commentator of risk: post-September 11, prevention has entailed a 'series of expensive Maginot lines against risk, each of which does a wonderful job at protecting secur-ity against a known risk, while doing nothing to protect society from the unknown' (Baker 2002: 356).

As an object of knowledge and governance, catastrophes are made know-able and amenable to action through the deployment of particular styles of reasoning. The problematization of potential catastrophe has elicited new modes of knowledge and promises of managing dangerous irruptions, which are neither entirely new nor simply continuations of risk, uncertainty, crisis or disaster management. Rather, we see both a realignment of different styles of reasoning and the reconfiguration of a particular style which we in the next chapter, following Carlo Ginzburg, will call 'conjectural'.

3 Conjectures of catastrophe
The 'next terrorist attack'

Conjecture: The interpretation of signs or omens; interpretation of dreams; divining; a conclusion as to coming events drawn from signs or omens; a forecast, a prognostication. *Obs.* Conclusion as to facts drawn from appearances or indications. *Obs.* The formation or offering of an opinion on grounds insufficient to furnish proof; the action or habit of guessing or surmizing; conclusion as to what is likely or probable.

Oxford English Dictionary

Conjectural reasoning

This chapter unpacks the heterogeneous assemblage of modes of knowledge constituted around the question of unknowability about the 'next terrorist attack'. How does one govern what one does not know? What are the unknowns which must be made actionable through the creation and deployment of knowledge and what are the conditions of validity for truthful statements about the unknown? How are unpredictable and unexpected events made knowable? These questions are not new and by no means exclusive to the problematization of future catastrophic events. Yet, as the previous chapter has shown, worst case scenarios of catastrophic events have been taken to have caused a series of mutations in governmental and security knowledge. If labels such as speculation, premediation, imagination or enactment capture important elements of what is at stake in the governance of the 'next terrorist attack', the central claim of this chapter is that the term 'conjecture' allows us to understand the particularity of a style of reasoning which does not function through analogy with financial practices as implied by speculation, in denial of evidence as premediation would hold, or at a distance from scientific knowledge, as uses of imagination and fantasy in this context intimate.

A conjectural style of reasoning, we argue, constructs an explanation out of apparently insignificant details. It links the smallest and most inconsequential details to a larger context which cannot be directly observed or experienced. In particular, Carlo Ginzburg has noted the connections between the art historian trying to correctly attribute a painting to an artist, detective work and analysis of psychoanalytic symptoms. In all these, 'tiny details provide the key to a deeper reality, inaccessible by other methods' (Ginzburg 1980: 11). Where Ian Hacking (2004) has analysed styles of reasoning in natural sciences, Ginzburg (1979, 1980) associates the clue or the conjectural style with a particular modality of reasoning in historical research as opposed to Galilean science. Thus, argues Ginzburg, medicine, law, history share a common epistemology with divinatory practices that focus on practical cases and derives proof through traces, clues and hints. For instance, Giovanni Morelli, the typical art historian, developed a new method of recognition based on minor details such as ear lobes or nails. Sigmund Freud, whom Ginzburg claims to have been influenced by Morelli, relied on slips of tongue or fragments of dreams to get access to the unconscious. Similarly, Arthur Conan Doyle's Sherlock Holmes traced the proofs of murder through details that escaped others. What interests us is the particular use of a modified conjectural style in relation to the 'next terrorist attack' as a catastrophic event to be known.

The conjectural style of reasoning as outlined by Ginzburg is underpinned by a model of reality as double: some trivial details from reality, invisible to all but to the eyes of specialists, offer access to a hidden reality underneath. In this chapter, we understand conjectural reasoning in terms of what Michel Foucault has called the logic of strategy (Foucault 2004b).[1] Unlike dialectics, which valorizes contradictory styles with the promise of resolution through unity, the logic of strategy establishes the possible connections among different elements which nonetheless remain disparate (Foucault 2004b: 44). The logic of strategy allows us to consider how the conjectural style of reasoning brings together different and disparate (at times perhaps even contradictory) forms of knowledge that function together, without presupposing or necessitating homogeneity (Hacking 1992, 2004). Rather than assuming, as Karl Popper does, that there is a universal rationalist way of arriving at truth from conjectures, each style of scientific reasoning has different criteria for establishing what counts as truthful and how its evidence can be refuted. Statements about the 'unknown' of a future, terrorist attack become comprehensive and appear truthful as they draw upon and invoke a conjectural style of reasoning, which makes various modes of knowledge appear as cumulative, mutually reinforcing and bridging each other's gaps. At the same time, through the mediation of computing technologies, the conjectural style acquires new dimensions that render it quite different from its use in history or psychoanalysis.

This chapter begins by unpacking the different ways in which the unknown is made sense of in order to become actionable. The unknown of a terrorist attack in the future has led to a seemingly endless addition of various 'Ps' (e.g. protection, prevention, precaution, preparedness, pursuit, persecution), each naming a different epistemic and practical response to the problematization of the unknown of terrorism. Each of the 'Ps' has its own *modus operandi* and entails different combinations of styles that cannot be synthesized, yet have come to function around the same problematization of the 'next terrorist attack'. This chapter explores how all these different Ps are reconciled and made to function in a conjectural style of reasoning about the novelty of the 'next terrorist attack'.

Adding the Ps

The UK counter-terrorism strategy (CONTEST 2009) is interesting for the detailed way in which it presents each of the P-streams and redeploys them into a counter-terrorism *dispositif*. Here, under the motto 'the more the better', the Ps appear as different but cumulative responses to the 'next terrorist attack'. Or rather, the more 'P-modes of knowledge' can be named, the safer we will be! More specifically, the document is structured around four Ps: pursue, prevent, protect and prepare. *Pursuit* refers to the investigation, disruption and prosecution of terrorist networks. *Prevention* refers to stopping people from becoming terrorists or embracing violent extremism. *Preparation* concerns the consequences of an event and the mitigation of the effects of an attack and has led to emphasis on business continuity arrangements and recovery. Besides being an overarching rationale of the report, *protection* is also one of the particular work streams in the document and tautologically defined as 'strengthening protection against attack'. The CONTEST document is arguably the most explicit crystallization of the forms of action and modes of knowledge that also inform many other counter-terrorism strategies and plans of action. The EU counter-terrorism strategy, for instance, has also categorized the actions to tackle terrorism into four main categories: prevention, protection, prosecution and response (Council of the European Union 2005), where the EU term 'response' (the only 'non-P') resonates with the rationality of preparedness in the UK strategy. Even though our dominant focus on the UK thus cancels out some differences in particular national contexts (see Lentzos and Rose 2009) and the different struggles through which these strategies have come into being, the focus on the UK report serves our main purpose of unpacking the ways in which the unknown is problematized and how epistemological uncertainties about the future are tackled.

The P-modes of knowledge have a longer history, in which the unknown received more or less attention. For example, war raises questions of the protection of civilian populations; crime-related risks require prevention; potentially catastrophic events ask for the application of precautionary measures; and nuclear attacks entail prevention and preparedness arrangements. Each, moreover, has its own particular emergence, forms of authorization and specification (Foucault 2002 [1969]). Security studies have focused on the politics of protection and the role of states in protecting populations (Huysmans *et al.* 2006). Risk management has emphasized the rationality of prevention. Precaution, in turn, has been mostly associated with environmental risks and hazards, while preparedness, one of the cornerstones of Cold War civil defence, has been intrinsic to disaster and crisis management.

Each P, then, establishes different knowledge constructions and gives rise to different problematizations of the limits of knowledge. How do these different forms of expertise and knowledge problematize the unknown? Not-knowing is not simply an absence, a gap, but a relation between knowledge and non-knowledge. As Foucault has pointed out, what constitutes knowledge, what is to be deemed as unknown or unworthy of the pursuance of knowledge, and who is designated as having the authority to know, involves acts of power (Foucault 1984). It is thus important to consider the techniques of power/knowledge in relation to the techniques of weakness/non-knowledge. The power of expert knowledge is dependent upon the experts' capacity to subsume and tame the unknown and to offer particular modes of knowledge as the answer to the problematization of the unknown (Smithson 1989, Gross 2007). It is also dependent upon their capacity to produce non-knowledge as an actionable limit of their knowledge. In his lectures on the 'Abnormal' at Collège de France, Foucault argued that psychiatry entered the legal field exactly by presenting its expertise as a response to the unknowns of crime:

> When crime suddenly irrupts, unprepared, implausibly, without motive and without reason, then psychiatry steps forward and says: Even though no one else is able to detect in advance this crime that suddenly erupts, psychiatry, as knowledge, as science of mental illness, as knowledge of madness, will be able to detect precisely this danger that is opaque and imperceptible to everyone else.
>
> (Foucault 2004a: 121)

The various Ps that have entered the governing of terrorism can be seen as part of a strategy of authorization, of legitimizing a series of responses as offering privileged access to the problem of catastrophic irruptions in the future. The distinction between what counts as known and unknown needs to be understood, then, in relation to particular epistemic regimes, which authorize certain modes of knowledge and make possible the simultaneous production of unknowns. If knowledge is 'a way of defining an idea of the thinkable, an idea of what the objects of knowledge themselves can think and know' (Sedgwick 1990: 6), non-knowledge can be similarly thought of as a way of defining an idea of the unthinkable, of what cannot be thought and known.[2] Non-knowledge functions in heterogeneous ways, allying itself with particular modes of knowledge and their limits. Ignorances 'are produced by and correspond to particular knowledges and circulate as part of particular regimes of truth' (Sedgwick 1990: 8).[3] Unpacking unknowns beyond ignorance allows us to understand the modes of knowledge and regimes of truth and objectivity within which they circulate.

In this sense, the CONTEST report can be viewed as the surface upon which the effects of such authorization have been inscribed. The plural knowledges it describes also give rise to plural limits of knowledge. Our interest in this document, therefore, lies thus not so much in the political and bureaucratic struggles and routines through which it was produced, but rather in the ways the document allows us to unpack the challenges posed by the unknowns to which the different Ps appear to provide a strategic answer. What, in other words, are the unknowns articulated through pursuit, prevention, precaution and protection?

Secrecy and ignorance

Associated with the Ps of 'pursuit' and 'prevention', stopping terrorist attacks is named as the 'most immediate priority' for the UK government. Categorized under the strategy of 'pursuit', stopping terrorist attacks is ultimately a pro-active strategy that attempts to tackle the risk of attack before its irruption in the future. The other element associated with stopping terrorist attacks is grouped under the label of 'prevention' and concerns 'stopping people from becoming terrorists'. Although categorized under pursuit and prevention respectively, stopping terrorist attacks and stopping people from becoming terrorists are in fact both preventive strategies that depend on pre-evental knowledge. Both imply that at some level prediction is possible, as violent behaviour can be seen to follow patterns or trends. Just as the law of large numbers in probability calculations assumed that individual irregularities become regular over 'large numbers', data mining and predictive analytics operate on the basis that patterns and regularities emerge from analyzing large swathes of data:

> While behavioural analysis might not be able to identify a specific individual or suspect, it frequently can provide investigators additional knowledge or insight regarding what type of person might be associated with a particular crime or series of crimes. Perhaps more importantly, this type of analysis also can provide some insight regarding what type of behavior might predict or foreshadow violence.
>
> (McCue 2005: 51)

Yet, acquiring pre-evental knowledge under the headings of 'pursuit' and 'prevention' brings into play and seeks to eradicate two different kinds of unknowns. The unknown related to the issue of pursuit is the unknown of secrecy. As the CONTEST report puts it: 'Terrorists operate in secret' (Home Office 2009b: 13). The modality of knowledge that is fostered in response to the unknowns created by secrecy is preventive intelligence, which is deemed vital to detect and disrupt terrorist activities and plans before they are brought to fruition.[4] The secret is simultaneously the 'nature' of terrorist activity and the limit of intelligence knowledge. Thus, the Report on the 7 July attacks in London cautions that 'the limitations of intelligence coverage, and the possibility of attack planning going on without detection, must be made clear' (Intelligence and Security Committee 2006: 22). The diagnostic of 'secrecy' associated with terrorist operations has fostered techniques of dis-concealment as well as techniques of mimesis in the governance of terrorism. In order to respond to the unknown of secrecy, knowledge needs to penetrate beyond appearances and dispel concealment, while creating its own secret. Intelligence becomes 'like a classified encyclopaedia of the world, knowledge about everything, but not for everyone' (Horn and Ogger 2003: 66). Although secrecy has been a long-standing concern for intelligence professionals, constituting its own regime of knowledge through spying, contra-espionage and double agents, the assumption that 'terrorist plots and activities will leave an *information signature*, albeit not one that is easily detected' (emphasis added) (Popp *et al.* 2004: 38) has led intelligence services to draw on detection instruments from the information sciences. Dispelling secrecy is increasingly seen in terms of transparency of networks – making transparent means locating connections, links and movements, from money laundering to travel patterns (Amoore 2009).

Secrecy can be dispelled through the use of algorithms that attempt to detect 'secret' patterns beyond the manifest reality. Patterns emerge in a sort of alternative reality, which is connected to, yet different from, the 'real' reality. Access to data that can be processed by algorithms and predictive models is seen as key for stopping terrorist attacks. For instance, the founders of the Terrorism Early Warning Group (TEW) in the US state that 'TEW members and analysts now speculate on future threats and run war games designed to gauge Los Angeles' vulnerability to terrorism' (Sullivan and Bauer 2008: 24). The TEW group makes use of advanced social network analysis and related tools such as non-obvious relationship awareness or analysis (NORA), for the purposes of 'knowledge discovery'. Knowledge discovery, a new concept widely used in computer science, is based on the assumption that data visualization tools and data mining software will not only reveal particular patterns but might also 'discover' unexpected relationships among data. The purpose of many of the algorithms and data mining technologies is to identify terrorism-related patterns out of heterogeneous data. A report for the US Congress describes data mining as a potential means to identify terrorist activities, such as money transfers and communications, and to identify and track individual terrorists themselves, such as through travel and immigration records (Seifert 2007).

As knowledge discovery becomes defined as an interdisciplinary area focusing upon methodologies for identifying valid, novel, potentially useful and meaningful patterns from data, often based on underlying large data sets, academic and business research is called upon to offer better algorithms and mathematical models for extracting patterns from data. In the UK, in April 2009, the Office for Security and Counter-Terrorism started the INSTINCT programme (INnovative Science and Technology IN Counter-Terrorism) to harness science and technology to respond to the unknowns of terrorism. Unravelling secrecy was to be achieved through the use of artificial intelligence (AI) – for example to spot hostile situations in crowded places such as airports and railway stations –, data mining or modelling. In the US, the University of Arizona's Artificial Intelligence Lab has Web-based counterterrorism knowledge portals that are seen to support 'the analysis of terrorism research, dynamically model the behavior of terrorists and their social networks, and provide an intelligent, reliable, and interactive communication channel with the terrorized (victims and citizens) groups' (Reid *et al.*: 127). Similarly, the Counter-Terrorism Lab at the University of Southern Denmark is specialized in developing mathematical models and data processing tools that can help security agencies identifying key persons in terrorist networks.[5] Another project at Cornell University, DARPA (Distributed Mining and Monitoring System) supports 'the development and integration of information fusion technologies such as data mining, biometrics, collaborative and knowledge discovery technologies that identify and display links among people, content, and topics to counter "asymmetric threats" such as those found in terrorist attacks' (Reid *et al.* 2004: 129).

Besides secrecy, the strategy of prevention problematizes ignorance as a second vital unknown to be confronted. Ignorance and lack of communication appear as the 'root causes' that preventive action is increasingly asked to counter by involving a wide range of actors (Council of the European Union 2010). According to the European Commission, possible factors that contribute to radicalization are terrorist propaganda in the media, youth vulnerability, and integration failure (European Commission 2006). Similarly, the UK government emphasizes that its strategy 'needs the support of communities and community organisations in this country to protect vulnerable people from radicalisation, and recruitment to terrorism' (Home Office 2009b). If the unknown of secrecy implies the need for disclosing what has always been there through discovery, the growth of knowledge about ignorance is governed by a form of progress and enlightenment that leads to the reduction of uncertainty. Just as the secret presupposed the existence of two worlds, one manifest but false and another real but hidden, ignorance assumes that there are more worlds, coexisting in parallel. However, only one is 'real'. This real world can be accessed if knowledge is revealed to the ignorant and false ideas are rectified – or so we are told. The unknown of ignorance is the 'not yet known' awaiting the spread of knowledge. In the UK government's strategy, the unknown of ignorance is false consciousness or misrecognition which can be progressively corrected:

> Vulnerability is not simply a result of actual or perceived grievances. It may be the result of family or peer pressure, the absence of positive mentors and role models, a crisis of identity, links to criminality including other forms of violence, exposure to traumatic events (here or overseas), or changing circumstances (e.g. a new environment following migration and asylum).
>
> (Home Office 2009b: 89)

The reduction of ignorance therefore works on a model of revelation different from the disclosure of secrecy. The unknown of secrecy constitutes the model of knowledge as revelation through discovery, while the unknown of ignorance presupposes an idea the role of knowledge as revelation through enlightenment. One of the strategies promoted by the 'prevention' strand is to 'challenge the ideology that supports violent extremism and support those who develop positive alternatives' (Home Office 2009b: 88). When faced with better knowledge and possibility of integration, extremist views are supposedly dispelled.

Ironically, however, responding to the unknowns of secrecy and ignorance effaces the active production of secrecy and ignorance in the processes of governance itself. Mark Hobart has suggested resurrecting the obsolete English word 'obliviate' to capture the active ignoring of others' views and the prosecution of one's own ideas (Hobart 1993: 16). Theirs is an 'ideology', ours are 'shared values'. Secrecy in particular is so often taken for granted as a characteristic of terrorism that discussions about the dynamics of concealment and revelation often remain limited to terrorism. As a result, the affinity between the secrecy located as a characteristic of terrorism and the lack of trust (read: secrecy) associated with intelligence often goes unnoticed.

However, secrecy is constitutive of intelligence action; it is what sets it apart from other forms of knowledge and legitimizes its claims to authority (Horn and Ogger 2003).[6] Just as psychiatric knowledge assumed privileged access to the 'opaque and the imperceptible', access to secrecy and the unravelling of its mystery has become the claim of intelligence agencies. While data mining and predictive analytics technologies of intelligence work on a given body of data, the question that emerges is how the data has been assembled: advanced passenger information, airline bookings, biometric passport data, immigration, identity and border records, criminal records, as well as governmental and private sector data. In the presentation of a documentary film about the US government's use of secrecy, directed by the well-known philosopher of science Peter Galison, in collaboration with Ross Moss, the increase in secrecy is made clear:

> In a single recent year the U.S. classified about five times the number of pages added to the Library of Congress. We live in a world where the production of secret knowledge dwarfs the production of open knowledge. Depending on whom you ask, government secrecy is either the key to victory in our struggle against terrorism, or our Achilles heel.
>
> (Galison and Moss 2008)

At the same time, the secret creates the possibility of a 'second world alongside the manifest world' (Wolff 1950: 330). While these two worlds are inter-related and influence each other, the latter does not offer access to the former except through revelation by experts who are authorized to seek and expose the secret. The challenge of knowledge is to establish links between the manifest world and the secret world, where everything is not what it seems. Reframing the unknown as a question of secrecy risks blurring the latter with privacy: 'The term private usually establishes that the other person does not have a right to some knowledge because of his or her social distance. A secret, on the other hand, concerns information that the other person may have rights to, but that the possessor chooses, is told to, or is obligated to withhold' (Bellman 1981: 4).[7] If privacy was the area of personal knowledge where only intimates can have access, the problematization of secrecy in relation to personal knowledge renders the injunction to knowledge of the unknown as an injunction to access to this knowledge:

> From secrecy, which shades all that is profound and significant, grows the typical error according to which everything mysterious is something important and essential. Before the unknown, man's natural impulse to idealize and his natural fearfulness cooperate toward the same goal: to intensify the unknown through imagination, and to pay attention to it with an emphasis that is not usually accorded to patent reality.
>
> (Wolff 1950: 333)

The problematization of terrorism as secrecy delegitimizes claims about privacy – 'this is private data' is reframed as 'this is secret data' and therefore data that belongs to another, potentially dangerous, reality.

Secrecy and ignorance do not exist separately from the modes of knowledge that create them and make them possible. Their problematization draws heavily on analogical styles of reasoning, attempting to establish parallels, correlations and links between the worlds it postulates as existing. It also experiments and models likelihood within these worlds. To this purpose, making correlations and associations is an important technique of establishing evidence and creating an object of knowledge – the identity of the suspected terrorist, the one who conceals the secret of potential catastrophic irruptions (Amoore 2009, Amoore and de Goede 2008, 2005).

The problematization of secrecy and ignorance as the unknowns to be revealed is not without political consequences. By privileging analogies between what is and what is 'real', it entrenches their separate existence and justifies measures that are taken to access the clue, the information signature.[8] The relation between secrecy and ignorance also creates an important division: there are those who can know and expose secrets and those who don't know. It reminds us that '"knowledge" [*savoir*] is always double: it is an ensemble of knowledges [*connaissances*] and an organized distribution [*partage*] of positions' (Rancière 2006: 3). Non-knowledge becomes a distribution of positions in which some can know by being able to detect secrecy and others remain ignorant and vulnerable to 'extremist ideologies'.

Risk and uncertainty

The model of knowledge through disclosure and revelation is, however, limited. As a former analyst with the National Security Agency notes: 'You definitely need to do it, because it gives you warning of major storms. But it's not going to tell you about individual raindrops' (Vijayan 2010). If the 'next terrorist attack' cannot be stopped and the unknown of secrecy and ignorance cannot be exposed, knowledge is mobilized to reduce vulnerability. In the CONTEST strategy, the question of high vulnerability and uncertainty is tackled through the 'P' of protection. Protection covers the 'protection of critical national infrastructure (CNI), crowded places, the transport system, our borders, and our interests overseas; and protection against threats from insiders and from the misuse of hazardous substances' (Home Office 2009b: 15). The European Commission clarifies the meaning of protection by adding action on 'chemical and biological threats'. Or as the UK Home Office argues:

> Terrorist organisations will have access to more lethal technology. Scientific training and expertise will have even greater significance for terrorist organisations because technology will be able to compensate for the vulnerabilities they will have. Terrorists will continue to aspire to develop or steal and then to use chemical, biological, radiological and nuclear weapons.
>
> (Home Office 2009b: 49)

The main focus of 'protection' is on 'preferred terrorist targets' (Home Office 2009b: 107). Among these, critical infrastructure is seen to be one of the targets of predilection for terrorist attacks. The general argument about the necessity to protect critical infrastructure is framed along the following lines (with little variation from one report or author to another):

> Our modern society and day to day activities are dependent on networks of critical infrastructure – both physical networks such as energy and transportation systems and virtual networks such as the Internet. If terrorists attack a piece of critical infrastructure, they will disrupt our standard of living and cause significant physical, psychological, and financial damage to our nation.
>
> (Bennett 2007: 9)

The UK's Centre for the Protection of National Infrastructure (CPNI) defines the effects of any failure in national infrastructure as leading to 'severe economic damage, grave social disruption, or even large scale loss of life' (CPNI 2009).

The protection associated with the vulnerability of critical infrastructures is not used here in the more familiar sense of offering protection to those caught in catastrophic events. It does not ask the traditional question 'Who is to be made secure?' and it is not primarily about sheltering, offering help and protecting life.[9] What defines the unknown of the 'next terrorist attack' is not just ignorance or secrecy, but radical uncertainty and unpredictability. Protection emerges as a form of knowledge that responds to the two elements that appear to differentiate terrorism from other catastrophic risks: (i) its potential to escalate into catastrophic events through the use of weapons of mass destruction and (ii) its radical uncertainty as a result of human intent:

> Terrorism risk shares features with other forms of catastrophe risk, including a time series of historical events, yet goes beyond them with an extra layer of impenetrability. Defensive studies of terrorism risk resemble risk analyses of complex engineering systems (nuclear power plants, satellite launches, etc.). A particular scenario can be analyzed in terms of the probability of failure of critical subsystems. However, unlike natural disasters, it features human intelligence, and unlike industrial disasters it features human intent.
>
> (Major 2002)

According to François Éwald (2002: 282), situations of scientific uncertainty and irreversible damage are generally targeted through precautionary measures.[10] In contrast to risk management, which is associated with the rationale of risk and its numerical calculability, precaution has been seen as a rationality of uncertainty that defies probabilistic models of management. As Andreas Klinke and Ortwinn Renn have remarked: 'With the denotation of "risk" it becomes clear that risk management relies on the numerical assessment of probabilities and potential damages, while the denotation of "precaution" implies prudent handling of uncertain or highly vulnerable situations' (Klinke and Renn 2002: 1074).

The precautionary principle has entered the realm of governance through the imaginary of environmental catastrophic risks. More specifically, the precautionary principle has its roots in the German *Vorsorgeprinzip*, or foresight principle, which emerged in the early 1970s and developed into a principle of German environmental law. It has informed international policy statements and agreements and was initially recognized in the World Charter for Nature, which was adopted by the UN General Assembly in 1982 and subsequently adopted in the First International Conference on Protection of the North Sea in 1984. The European Commission, which used it for the first time in relation to the environment in the 1992 Maastricht Treaty, later extended it to other situations (European Commission 2000). The definition of the precautionary principle is however most often traced back to the 1992 Rio Declaration on Environment and Development: 'Where there are threats of serious or irreversible damage, lack of scientific certainty shall not be used as a reason for postponing cost-effective measures to prevent environmental degradation' (United Nations 1992). The precautionary principle asks us 'to take regulatory action on the basis of possible "unmanageable" risks, even after tests have been conducted that find no evidence of harm. We are asked to make decisions to curb actions, not on the basis of what we know, but on the basis of what we do not know' (Guldberg 2003). The European Commission's Communication puts in a nutshell the context for applying the precautionary principle: 'Whether or not to invoke the Precautionary Principle is a decision exercised where scientific information is insufficient, inconclusive or uncertain and where there are indications that the possible effects on the environment, or human, animal or plant health may be potentially dangerous and inconsistent with the chosen level of protection' (European Commission 2000: 10).

Precaution, which reframes the meaning of protection as reducing vulnerability in light of fundamental uncertainty and irreversible damage, has often been connected with pre-emption (see de Goede and Randalls 2009). But although there may be many affinities between the precautionary treatment of uncertainty in relation to climate change and that of terrorism, the principle is nevertheless translated differently in these contexts. At times, the difference between the two has been rendered through the distinction between 'passive' (precaution) versus 'active' (pre-emption) notions of governing (Cooper 2006). Yet, these distinctions are unstable, as precautionary governance entails forms of 'actionism' (Hannah 2010). Not acting is in that sense an active decision.

The difference is, rather, that in the environmental sphere, precaution implies that regulatory action must be taken even if scientific evidence concerning the imminence and precise nature of threats remains disputed (Sunstein 2005). Here, the precautionary principle advocates restraints on development on the basis of reasonable suspicion of possible environmental damage without waiting for scientific proof, and therefore, inevitably, without considering the costs and benefits (Tait 2001: 178). Problematizing the uncertainty of the 'next terrorist attack', by contrast, requires precautionary knowledge of a different kind. Unlike the juridicization of the precautionary principle in the field of environmental politics, counter-terrorism measures are aimed at zero risk. Graham Allison's comment that if countries 'lock down all nuclear weapons and bomb-usable material as securely as gold in Fort Knox, they can reduce the likelihood of a nuclear 9/11 to nearly zero' (Sanger 13 April 2010) indicates that stopping catastrophic terrorist attacks is about precautions to be taken to avoid the occurrence of risk.

Definitions of the precautionary principle assume the incompleteness of scientific knowledge, relying on a model of scientific knowledge that could – at least in principle – eliminate uncertainty. Thus, it assumes uncertainty to be a temporary lapse on the way to knowledge acquisition and production. At the same time, the precautionary model does not imply the suspension but rather the reinforcement of risk assessment. Matthias Kaiser has pointed out that one of the conditions that needs to be in place to invoke the precautionary principle is 'the existence of a science-based scenario of significant and/ or irreversible possible harm' (cited in van der Sluijs 2007: 592). Therefore, the creation of knowledge is necessary not to reduce unknowns, but for the purposes of early warning. Precautionary knowledge focuses on the production of 'early warnings', on detecting and isolating symptoms. Just as preventive knowledge uses data and attempts to discover patterns that might uncover the 'secret' of a terrorist network or plan, precautionary knowledge attempts to detect the invisible and intangible sign of potentially dangerous irruptions.

Even if these processes of 'discerning terrorist potentials' share many similarities with those of disclosing secrecy, early warning also involves the use of foresight and scenarios to surpass the limit of risk calculability (de Goede and Randalls 2009). Developed in the world of business by Peter Wack at Royal Dutch/Shell, scenario planning has increasingly became a necessary ingredient of organizational planning. Scenarios explore the possibility that something might happen and offer clues that may function as early warnings. They create analogies with the real world and attempt to replicate the conditions of early warnings for the purposes of decision-making. Scenarios do not have a predictive function, but entail an 'ordering of the world' (Anderson 2007: 163). They thereby construct alternative or parallel worlds. In that sense, they are similar to simulations and models. The unknowns of secrecy and ignorance presupposed the simultaneous existence of a 'real' and manifest world. Scenarios do not postulate such an existence but open up to alternative parallel worlds. As defined by Chermack and Lyndham:

> Scenario planning is a process of positing several informed, plausible and imagined alternative future environments in which decisions about the future may be played out, for the purpose of changing current thinking, improving decision making, enhancing human and organisation learning and improving performance.
>
> (2006)

Precautionary measures also require knowledge of materials, buildings, flows in space, routes and so on. They imply both taxonomical classifications and modelling of the 'real' world. For example, operational measures for critical infrastructure protection start with the delimitation of a site: 'State the location and purpose of the site or building and any background comments on its priority or importance. State the boundaries of the site or building under consideration. This is to ensure that it is clear what land around buildings can be used for security measures' (CPNI 2010: 6). Taxonomies concern not only types of materials and objects, but also measures to be taken to reduce vulnerability: demarcation of boundary; deterrence of entry into the area; protection against climbing over; protection against cutting through; outer and inner fences with sterile zone to support Perimeter Intruder Detection Systems; concealment of guards and/or activity (CPNI 2010).

Taxonomies are also hierarchical. The taxonomic style implies the distribution and division of spaces and places according to worth and value. As individuals were differentially distributed into kinds depending on the 'quotient' of ignorance, objects are differentially distributed as less or more vulnerable. In creating a parallel world, scenarios filter elements that are needed for decision-making from elements that would simply be 'noise', to use a computing term. The risks and uncertainties associated with the 'next terrorist attack' create parallel worlds as an intervention into the manifest world. Arguments about what could happen and how to reduce vulnerability are formulated and demonstrated within this parallel world, at a distance from the complexities and political decisions of the manifest world. The parallel world that supplements the hidden world of the secret does not exhaust responses to the problematization of the unknown. The 'next terrorist attack' is radically unknown not only in terms of risk and uncertainty, but also in terms of its eventfulness. Its occurrence remains shocking, surprising, unexpected. However much one goes over alternative futures, the untimeliness and unexpectedness of a catastrophic irruption entails a slightly different problematization.

Surprise and novelty

The 'Prepare' strand of the CONTEST document covers the knowledge and actions to be taken when a danger irrupts, i.e. 'where an attack cannot be stopped, to mitigate its impact' (Home Office 2009b: 13). Preparedness entails setting up capabilities to deal with a range of terrorist incidents, ensuring swift recovery, and training and equipping crisis management actors. The idea and knowledge of preparedness have emerged from the acceptance of the inevitability of nuclear attacks during the Cold War. From its application to nuclear preparedness, the concept migrated to 'all hazards' in the 1970s and is now used as a strategy of readiness for all forms of incidents, events, crises, disasters or catastrophes. Preparedness is generally taken to refer to a state of readiness to respond to unexpected and potentially catastrophic events. According to Lakoff, preparedness becomes 'an especially salient approach to perceived threats when they reach the limits of a rationality of insurance' (Lakoff 2007: 247). Even if insurance strategies are adapted to non-probabilistic, high-catastrophic risks, preparedness is seen as a technology complementary or supplementary to insurance. Preparedness, just like precaution, appears to offer a solution to the limits of probabilistic insurantial knowledge, by focusing on *inhabiting* the event.

Preparedness responds to the problematization of surprise and novelty, the unknowns that cannot be exhausted by secrecy, ignorance, risk and uncertainty. From floods and other weather disasters to the 'next terrorist attack' as a potential chemical, biological, radiological, and/or nuclear (CBRN) emergency, preparedness exercises create worst case scenarios in order to foster readiness for anything smaller. Preparing for the future is based on worst case scenarios because '[t]his helps the emergency services and all those who respond to incidents of this nature to prepare for similar events of smaller scale, which are more likely to occur, as well as for worst case scenario' (London Fire Brigade 2010). As potential disasters now appear as indeterminate, unpredictable and unexpected, preparedness exercises are placed at the heart of a mode of knowledge which challenges or replaces statistical calculability. In this sense, the future of unexpected events cannot be known or predicted, it can only be enacted. Uncertainty becomes an opportunity to 'speculate not just about "the future", but a *range of possible futures* that might arise from the uncertain course of the forces of change' (emphasis in original) (Ralston and Wilson 2006: 102).

Preparedness is closely entwined with the concept of 'planning' and the idea that planning for worst case scenarios would make subjects ready for responding to other events. As outlined in a document providing advice for businesses, 'Expecting the Unexpected', preparedness for a terrorist attack is key to any other form of future disruption: 'If your plan enables you to cope with a worst-case scenario, it will also help you deal more easily with lower-impact incidents' (National Counter Terrorism Security Office 2003: 11). Preparedness includes emergency plans, training, simulations and exercises. Simulations are supposed to test emergency management plans against the 'reality'. Unlike precautionary knowledge, which has been one response to non-probabilistic, catastrophic threats, preparedness does not depend upon the avoidance of catastrophe. Rather it entails a rationality of 'living with catastrophe', even if the catastrophe remains virtual, thrown forward into the future. It engages in the rehearsal of future terrorist attacks in order to bind future decisions to decisions in the present.

Through exercises, experts and citizens are trained to deal with real-life disaster situations. Computer simulations are used to assess possibilities of escape, model behaviours in crisis situations, access for emergency services and so on. Preparedness knowledge shifts risk assessment from the pre-evental temporality of prevention and precaution to the time of the event. Exercises simulate an emergency situation and aim to prepare organizations to respond to surprising and novel events:

> Exercises allow participants to 'practice' the performance of duties, tasks, or operations very similar to the way they would be performed in a real emergency. An exercise can test or evaluate emergency operation plans, procedures, facilities – or any combination thereof. The exercise should simulate a realistic event, and allow the company to evaluate how all participants performed.
>
> (Emergency Management & Safety Solutions 2010)

Or as a report by the British Standards Institute advises:

> Exercises can expose vulnerabilities in a weak organizational structure. They can start processes needed to strengthen both internal and external communication and can help improve management decision making during an incident.
>
> (Crisis Solutions 2008)

Exercises make use of an experimental style of reasoning – they analyse observables in a world that is as close to the manifest world as possible. They also draw analogies between the world enacted by the exercise – whether live or simulated – and the 'real' world of the event. Exercises experiment with the event in order to create new phenomena and 'make up' different subjects.

The goal of preparedness is not just to reduce vulnerability but to foster resilience. Vulnerability is a good indicator of risk, but is insufficient for analysing reactions to surprising events. Exercises do not just seek to create a sort of laboratory setting for risk assessment; they also seek to foster resilient subjects. 'Catastrophic failure' can be avoided through resilience:

> Efforts to prevent catastrophic events may fail. Preparedness refers to the pre-event actions that need to be rehearsed in order to reduce the impact of a 'real' catastrophic event. While preparedness has been connected with mitigation and adaptation, it is resilience that has become the passé-partout concept of emergency planning and preparedness. Resilience is defined as a 'system's ability to accommodate variable and unexpected conditions without catastrophic failure.
>
> (Litman 2006: 14)

Living through a surprising and novel – potentially catastrophic – event requires a different type of subject: not the prudential risk-calculating subject, but the resilient subject. Hence, to exercise an attack is to build resilience: 'The London First Security and Resilience Network galvanises business, security and police services to work together closely, to increase London's resilience and improve safety from crime for businesses and their employees.'[11] Resilience, as a metaphor, concept and practice, draws attention to taxonomies of preparedness and to the content of preparedness measures. It gives scientific weight to words like 'prepared' or 'preparedness', which have become tarred by the non-scientificity of everyday use:

> In the aftermath of Thursday's terror attacks, one word was repeated like a mantra. In his message from No 10 Tony Blair paid tribute to 'the stoicism and resilience of the people of London'. A couple of hours later, interviewed on Channel 4 News, Brian Paddick, Deputy Assistant Commissioner of the Metropolitan Police, assured viewers that the emergency services 'had sufficient resilience to cope'.
>
> If Mr Paddick's turn of phrase sounded a little awkward, his use of words was also highly significant. In the past few years, the idea of resilience has been elevated to the most important buzzword in defence policy-making circles. Since September 11, 2001, the Ministry of Defence has been busy commissioning all manner of research into the resilience of our big cities in the event of terrorist attack. Boffins in the Strategy Unit of No 10 have written countless turgid reports about what resilience

means. Universities have set up whole departments, such as Cranfield University's Resilience Centre, to teach and study it.

(Harkin 9 July 2005)

As a concept, resilience smoothly combines meanings derived from physics (the capacity of material to return to a previous state), psychology (the capacity of an individual to return to normal after a traumatic event), ecology (the capacity of systems to continue functioning and renew themselves after a disruptive event) and informatics (the capacity of a system to keep on functioning despite anomalies and design flaws).[12] In their definition of resilience, Filippa Lentzos and Nikolas Rose (2009: 243) have noted its widespread use and translatability: 'Resilience implies a systematic, widespread, organizational, structural and personal strengthening of subjective and material arrangements so as to be better able to anticipate and tolerate disturbances in complex worlds without collapse, to withstand shocks, and to rebuild as necessary.' It can refer to individuals or communities. It can signify the ability of society to absorb and resist the shocks and pressures caused by disaster or crisis, be it through external intervention or internal adaptation.

These various meanings of resilience make it an adept response to different types of unknowns: not just surprise and novelty, but also risk, uncertainty and even secrecy and ignorance. In the UK government's 2009 Counter-Terrorism Strategy, resilience characterizes three of the four strands of action envisioned. 'Prevent' is about supporting individuals who are vulnerable to recruitment by extremists and increasing the resilience of communities to violent extremism. In this strand, the psychological underpinnings of resilience make it a technology of the self through which agents come to see and govern themselves. Indeed, as the capacity of disaster-affected communities to '"bounce back" or to recover with little or no external assistance following a disaster' (Manyena 2006: 433), resilience fits the script of the entrepreneurial citizen who does not need intervention by the state or the emergency services to return to normal. Under 'Prepare', resilience is central as the UK government points out that '[w]e have studied every attack and plot against the UK to learn everything we can about how to improve our resilience'. 'Protect' implies resilience through the impact of technology, from e-border technology to design and construction materials. Security experts have taken up the concept of resilience to refer to 'the strengthening of the invisible but powerful systems that govern everyday life against catastrophic disruption' (Elkus 2007).

Resilience itself assumes the existence of invisible objects and relies on an epistemology of the invisible. While depending on experimental and experiential reasoning, it also assumes the existence of two worlds – the invisible powerful world which is resilient and the apparent world which appears vulnerable to catastrophic irruptions. The epistemology of resilience is based on the dichotomy between appearance and 'reality'. Through resilience, the invisible can be made visible not as a revelation of secrecy or discernment of risk, but as a discovery of new subjective capabilities.

At the same time, resilience also tells slightly different stories of continuity and change, routine and disruption, normality and abnormality. In psychology, resilience is defined as the ability to 'maintain relatively stable, healthy, levels of psychological and physical functioning' (Bonanno 2004: 21). In environmental studies, resilience implies that there are affinities between social and natural systems and that complexity theory is the best answer to social and ecological problems. It also suggests that the exceptional and unexpected occurrence of catastrophe can be thought and dealt with in unexceptional and ordinary terms. Ecological knowledge has emphasized the changing behaviour of ecological systems when confronted with random events. Ecological resilience has been associated with C. S. Holling's seminal paper, 'Resiliency and Stability in Ecological Systems', which opposes resilience to stability:

> One can be termed stability, which represents the ability of a system to return to an equilibrium state after a temporary disturbance; the more rapidly it returns and the less it fluctuates, the more stable it would be. But there is another property, termed resilience, that is a measure of the persistence of systems and of their ability to absorb change and disturbance and still maintain the same relationships between populations or state variables.
>
> (Holling 1973: 14)

Stability is concerned with fluctuation around equilibrium states; ecological resilience focuses on persistence. According to Holling, a resilience perspective accommodates unexpected future events and embraces the reality of unknowns. Unlike the concept of stability, which presupposes an equilibrium, and fluctuations around this equilibrium, the concept of resilience adopts a different view of complex systems (ecological, social or social-ecological). Holling is critical of the confusion between stability and systems' behaviour and argues that resilience is not dependent on stability. Systems can be resilient and still fluctuate greatly. Systems can retrieve a state of equilibrium, which can be one of multiple equilibria that systems can achieve.

Yet, what Holling tries to differentiate is collapsed together in the practices of counter-terrorism, which downplay or erase some of the elements present in one disciplinary modality of knowledge at the expense of others. What counts for the concept of resilience is not whether the system remains stable or unchanged – but that it undergoes change and reorganization while retaining essentially the same function, structure, identity and feedbacks (Walker *et al.* 2004). In the UK Civil Contingencies Act 2004 resilience is extensively used to refer to the 'ability of the community, services, an area or infrastructure to withstand the consequences of an incident' (Cabinet Office 2004). Building resilience entails developing capabilities. The UK government pursues its resilience-building programme under the heading of a 'Capabilities Programme'. Building resilience to disasters includes knowledge resources, relational resources and a capacity to mobilize. Capabilities can be developed across systems, encompassing individuals, organizations, or material infrastructures. In that sense, the psychological meaning of resilience allows it to travel across so many fields: creating capabilities can mean changing behaviour, adjusting governance arrangements, communication channels, cooperation or using different building materials. In a report on state-building and fragile states, the OECD recommends supplementing 'state fragility' with the concept of state resilience as 'the ability to cope with changes in capacity, effectiveness or legitimacy. These changes can be driven by shocks – sudden changes – or through long-term erosions (or increases) in capacity, effectiveness or legitimacy' (OECD 2008: 17).

Counter-terrorism is defined as the capacity of individual and community resilience to resist change, spring back to normal from the consequences of an attack or to resist radicalization. While Holling rejects assumptions of stability and return to an original equilibrium, others have defined resilience as the speed with which a system returns to its original state following a perturbation (Pimm 1984). Particularly through psychological knowledge, resilience is closely connected with stability and order. This second perspective has more in common with the psycho-physical approach to resilience and its assumptions of normality and a return to a state of normality. In contrast, psychological resilience presupposes the privileging of the normal and the everyday over the extraordinary and the abnormal. The *Independent* quotes one of the leaders of resilience as saying: 'Individuals are capable of astonishing resistance, coping, recovery and success in the face of adversity … The conclusion that resilience … arises from … ordinary adaptive processes rather than extraordinary ones provides an optimistic outlook for intervention' (Roberts 16 January 2010). A psycho-physical approach assumes that individuals, communities and systems can be resilient if the adequate capabilities are fostered. Here, resilience can refer to an observed behaviour, a hypothesis of an underlying psychic process and a personality characteristic. In this approach, resilience is focused on creating the capacity for recovery, for 'bouncing back' and returning to normal after a shock or trauma. Rather than ecology, it is psycho-physical knowledge that underpins resilience in its uses in preparedness knowledge.

Knowledge production assumes a dichotomy between the invisible and the visible, the real and the manifest. At the same time, different styles of reasoning are employed to establish what counts as truth, what remains unknowable and what unknowns can be domesticated and offered as evidence. Each style creates its own objects, criteria for objectivity and stipulates what counts as evidence and explanatory power. The problematization of the unknown by the four Ps has entailed various combinations of different styles: postulates in mathematical modelling, analogies in scenarios and exercises, taxonomies and comparisons, probabilistic calculations, correlations in data mining and historical derivations. Most experimental and theoretical systems create 'parallel worlds'. Computer modelling, data mining, algorithms, simulations, scenarios and exercises all create 'alternative' or proximate worlds analogous to the 'real' world. In their attempt to dispel the unknowns of secrecy and ignorance, the two Ps 'pursuit' and 'prevent' operate as tales of two worlds. Precautionary and preparedness knowledges also work with a model of two worlds: one is the world that is modelled and which can offer access to the functioning, vulnerabilities and uncertainties of the other, 'real' world of surprise and novelty. In trying to find out the secret, the kernel of ignorance, the risk, the uncertainty and timing of the 'next terrorist attack', counter-terrorism knowledge puts forward the discovery of details as a clue to the catastrophe to come as a mode of knowledge. To look for a clue can mean to look for a secret, for the symptom of vulnerability, ignorance or mal intent. It can also mean to look for the unexpected, the invisible and the unseen. Correlation, according to Hacking (2007: 309), is the 'fundamental engine of social sciences'. Because some correlations can be established in the absence of statistical analysis, knowledge simply relies on a quest for clues that may yield something important and 'connect the dots'.

These different styles of reasoning are not necessarily contradictory and they can coexist as part of the same project. They also function in a 'logic of strategy', as many can be called upon to respond to a particular problematization. Exposing secrets, dispelling ignorance, calculating uncertainty, computing risk, expecting surprise and preparing for novelty all aspire to 'connect the dots' and to be able to access the invisible and unknowable and, as such, appear to adopt an aggregative model of knowledge drawn from computing approaches where knowledge is extracted from 'raw' data. As Ilkka Tuomi (1999) argues, data is supposed to be objective, constituted of facts, while information and knowledge increasingly add interpretation and 'connect the dots'. As data is seen to precede information and knowledge, it has 'overtones of scattered, disjunct fragments of fact', appearing to constitute knowledge without a stable structure (Neocleous 2003: 52). For some, computer modelling and simulation, and in particular the modelling and simulation of complex systems, is seen as a newly emerging style of scientific reasoning that complements those identified by Hacking (Schweber 2009).

However, if computing technologies create strategic linkages between different modes of knowledge – or, in Hacking's terms, are the disunified unifiers of science – computing does not underpin the aspiration to tame the unknown and render the invisible visible and the unexpected manageable. The problematization of the unknown does not amount to one particular discipline having privileged access to the unknown – be it psychology or computer science – but to the ways in which disciplines deploy particular styles of reasoning. Rather, these modes of knowledge evince a particular conjectural style. This conjectural paradigm differs radically from Galilean science, which was based on experimental knowledge, repetitive events and measurement.

Unlike science, the 'historian's knowledge, like the doctor's, is indirect, based on signs and scraps, conjectural' (Ginzburg 1980: 16). The conjectural epistemology of sciences is ultimately a diagnostic one. It need not be orientated exclusively towards the past, but can work in relation to the past, present and future. After all, Ginzburg suggests, medicine as the science of symptoms was both diagnostic and prognostic, indicating likely or possible futures.[13]

Yet, the forms of knowledge deployed to govern the 'next terrorist attack' do not completely fit the conjectural reasoning that Ginzburg located in human sciences. For Ginzburg, conjectural knowledge takes as its point of departure the individual or the case (as in psychoanalysis or medicine). It is thus 'closely tied to the existence of a finite deposit of materials, an archive, from which such cases are drawn and which gives them epistemological support' (Osborne 1999: 58). By contrast, counter-terrorism knowledge attempts to find clues on the basis of styles of reasoning that look at regularities, patterns and correlations. The unknowns of secrecy, ignorance, risk, uncertainty, surprise and novelty are not tamed through patient engagement with the archive in each particular case; they are supposedly 'discovered' in a self-revelation of knowledge. On the one hand, preventive, precautionary and preparedness knowledges aspire to see through the irregularity in data and locate the detail that may yield the much-needed access to the invisible world. On the other, data itself is purged of inference and conjecture and not linked to any archive.

Thus, the reasoning based on the discovery of new patterns and clues among data uses conjectures in a quite different sense – they are seen as emerging not out of the individual case but out of the multiplicity of data. The parallel worlds are reminiscent of medical knowledge that according to Foucault '*develops* in accordance with a whole interplay of *envelopes*; the hidden element takes on the form and meaning of hidden content which means that, like a *veil*, it is *transparent*' (emphasis in original) (Foucault 1973: 204). However, as long as preventive, precautionary and preparedness knowledges establish truths, measure evidence and compute the future on the basis of styles of reasoning adapted to frequencies and regularities, they fail in the encounter with the irregular, the unexpected, radically uncertain and singular. As Ginzburg intimates in his analysis of the conjectural paradigm, to find the clue, to discover the unknown in the invisible reality one needs to consider the individual and particular case of the detective, the medical doctor, the art historian or those engaged in social science endeavours.[14] The failure, however, to access the irregular and uncertain events through indicating possible futures does not mean the end of such governmental regimes. Rather, it provides an impetus for the fabrication and invention of other modes of knowledge and practices (see Miller and Rose 1990). At the same time, the *dispositif* of governing catastrophic events is not simply characterized by failure. In the following chapter, we turn to a particular element of this *dispositif* – insurance – to explore both its effects of negation or limitation and its production of particular subjectivities.

4   Economies of catastrophe

> Every day, new risks develop and they are affecting not only the way we live,
> but the way we do business.
>
> Daniel Vetter (2010)

Insurance and terrorism

The previous chapter focused on how the 'next terrorist attack' was problematized through a series of different unknowns and the modes of knowledge
and styles of reasoning deployed to render these unknowns actionable. This
chapter considers how catastrophe risks are tackled by assurantial knowledge.
Because insurance was thought to function as an economic technology, it
has been removed from the disciplinary gaze of security studies and left
almost entirely outside the purview of studies on counter-terrorism strategy.[1]
Moreover, at first sight insurance appears inadequate for the task of taming
catastrophic events as it contradicts the main tenets of conjectural reasoning
discussed in the previous chapter. Where the latter focuses on the clue and
individual detail, insurance constitutes the quintessential model of regularity-
based knowledge based on probabilistic reasoning and statistical calculation:

> Like other sciences, that of Statistics seeks to deduce from well-established
> facts certain general principles which interest and affect mankind; it uses
> the same instruments of comparison, calculation, and deduction: but
> its peculiarity is that it proceeds wholly by the accumulation and com-
> parison of facts, and does not admit of any kind of speculation; it aims,
> like other sciences, at truth.
>
> (William Cooke Taylor quoted in Poovey 1993: 261)

Yet, even a quick search of some of the main insurance companies that under-
write terrorism post-9/11 inevitably comes across statements that directly
engage in threat construction:

The ongoing threat from terrorism means we have to face a stark reality, namely that this problem is here to stay. The indiscriminate nature of many Acts of Terrorism (AOT) means that we are all potentially at risk, regardless of whether we have been targeted.

(Jardine Lloyd Thompson 2009: 3)

Or:

Terrorism risk remains a critical concern for global companies. Recent attempted attacks in New York's Times Square and on a Detroit-bound flight on Christmas day 2009 remind companies of the importance of securing adequate financial protection against the possible catastrophic impact of terrorist events.

(Tucker 2010)

Insurance has entered the 'war on terror' as a complementary strategy in the prevention and management of terrorism to the extent that today terrorism insurance has become *continuous* with national security practices of knowing the unknown. By partnering up with the state, the insurance industry has entrenched the idea that state security practices are indispensable for the very existence of insurance. For instance, Joe Gunset, General Counsel for Lloyd's America, argued that 'this peril [terrorism] … is most uniquely linked to government policy and security measures and therefore is the proper focus on government role in this area of insurance' (Gunset 2006). The London-based company Risk Management Solutions (RMS), an independent risk analysis and modelling company, similarly calls for government to actively shape the risk of terrorism that insurance companies set out to cover:

Unlike the hazard of an earthquake or the occurrence of a hurricane making landfall, terrorism risk is not an absolute or a natural phenomenon. It can be changed by the actions of the government … Government action, through the resources and direction it provides to law-enforcement agencies and to counter-terrorism intelligence operations, can reduce the threat of terrorism by catching terrorists, making it harder for terrorists to operate and by interdicting increasing numbers of the plots they device. Improved counter-terrorism effectiveness reduces the overall risk.

(Risk Management Solutions 2005: 21)

What happens to insurance as it is modified and deployed in response to the problematization of the 'next terrorist attack'? Studies of terrorism insurance have mainly addressed this question in the context of US terrorism insurance post-9/11, which unlike countries in Europe (Spain, Germany, France and the UK) did not have a history of terrorist attacks – even after the Oklahoma bombings in 1995, terrorism was considered so improbable that it was never excluded from 'all-risk' policies (Kunreuther and Pauly 2009).

Although most of the losses of 9/11 were borne by re-insurers (Ericson and Doyle 2004a), barely a month after the attacks the Subcommittee on Capital Markets, Insurance and Government Sponsored Enterprises of the US House of Representatives met to deal with the financial fall-out of the attack in the insurance and reinsurance industries (Cooper 2004). In his congressional testimony, Richard J. Hillman of the US General Accounting Office claimed that 'both insurers and re-insurers have determined that terrorism is not an insurable risk at this time' (quoted in Kunreuther 2002: 427).[2] Nine years after the attack, the Insurance Information Institute, an organization dedicated to improving public understanding of insurance, still maintained that for many insurers the unknown of terrorism remained difficult, if not impossible, to insure:

> The fact that acts of terrorism are intentional and that the frequency and severity of attacks cannot be reliably assessed makes terrorism extremely problematic from the insurance standpoint. Many insurers continue to question whether terrorism risk is insurable. Large segments of the economy and millions of workers are exposed to significant terrorism risk, but the ability to determine precisely where or when the next attack may occur is limited.
>
> (Insurance Information Institute 2010: 7)

In 2002, therefore, the US Senate passed the Terrorism Risk Insurance Act (TRIA), which effectively regulates government involvement in the compensation of insured losses. Nevertheless, the private industry remains a significant insurer in the post-9/11 environment with the Act intended only as a temporary bailout measure.[3] Besides, in response to the incalculability of terrorism, the insurance industry has invented novel technologies to manage the future of potential terrorist attacks. These technologies include more complex probabilistic models for insuring against terrorism (Eqecat 2002) and attempts to model terrorism beyond actuarial knowledge by making use of game theory and scenario analysis (Risk Management Solutions 2004).[4]

Although these discussions provide significant insights into how insurance is redeployed to make the incalculable calculable and the unknown knowable, they leave unspecified an important element of insurance. Insurance is intimately connected not just with probability calculation, inference and modelling, but also with classification. Insurance depends on the description and enumeration of events as either insurable or uninsurable. As Ian Hacking (1992: 145) has pointed out, statistical reasoning produces new classifications by assuming that a class exists and is waiting to be counted. The insurance industry needs to define terrorism, create a calculable rendering of terrorism, and constitute the subject who is to be insured. For even when the mathematical calculus of probability finds itself surpassed by catastrophic events and other means of governing more akin to the game model are proposed, insurance still relies upon classifications and definitions of what and who are to be insured. As a classificatory technology, insurance 'makes up people' (Hacking 1995) while classifying events. To support its definition of terrorism, it simultaneously constitutes profiles for the 'terrorists' to support the process of underwriting and reproduces a 'we' that is to be insured against terrorism.

Assurantial knowledge is therefore underpinned by prior assumptions about terrorism, catastrophic events and, ultimately, society. It decides on key political issues pertaining to the question of who deserves protection from what or whom and at what price. Insurance classifies and hierarchizes that which is worthy of protection and needs to be insured and that which is not. September 11 insurance losses were estimated at about £30 billion and covered property, liability, workers' compensation and life insurance claims. In terms of loss of life, many of those killed on 9/11 were uninsured or underinsured (Levmore and Logue 2003). Moreover, many insurers needed to cover losses because terrorism had not been explicitly excluded from general insurance. Unknowable risks may not be on the insurers' radar and 'they may fail to exclude them explicitly, and the policyholder may be protected by default' (Kunreuther and Pauly 2009). In order to identify and calculate the chances of an event occurring, insurers classify the event, name it, and simultaneously classify the types of damages and losses its occurrence could entail. Insurers need to invent knowledge of uncertainty both in the probability of an event occurring and in the damages caused. To do so, they first need to know and name *what* these events and losses may be. Whereas insurance is generally associated with social solidarity, this chapter suggests that the assurantial capitalization of catastrophe has created divisions between propertied life and those without property. Insurance fosters capitalist subjects and enacts continuity as the key principle of social and political life.

Capitalizing on catastrophe

Inspired by the work of Michel Foucault, François Éwald (1986) has offered the most elaborate genealogy of insurance as a *dispositif* for governing the social. His work illuminates the central role of insurance for modern societies as a strategy through which subjects are made up and governed. In its early forms, he argues, insurance against accidents provided a solution to the otherwise insoluble question of responsibility. Who was responsible for industrial accidents? Was it capitalism, the corporations, or was it the worker? As the juridical answer was found to raise difficult questions in its negotiation of this question, insurance offered a solution that did away with legal responsibility through the creation of a form of solidarity. The particularity of insurance, Éwald argues, is that it no longer gives reparation on the model of charity, but on a model of justice given by a rule. The idea of risk, therefore, does away with causality; what matters is not the cause, but the rule according to which reparation is decided. For Éwald, insurance carries the promise of emancipation: it allows more freedom and autonomy to the working class and constitutes citizenship on a model of social solidarity.[5] Since the 1990s, governmentality scholars have expanded this genealogy by examining how neo-liberal schemes of private and individualized forms of insurance have transformed and reworked collective schemes based on the model of universal solidarity (see e.g. Baker and Simon 2002, Ericson *et al.* 2003, Ericson 2007).[6]

However, this trajectory of insurance against the work accident as it developed through the wage system overlooks how insurance has emerged in connection with the outbreak of catastrophic events, particularly large fires in cities and the occurrence of natural catastrophes (which often resulted in fire). Examining how insurance took off in relation to these events brings out a different lineage of insurance as a mode of knowledge and its attendant forms of power. What kinds of power relations and subjects do assurantial knowledge and practice constitute? To answer this question, we trace insurance back not to the statistical style of reasoning and calculations of regularities but to the context of unexpected events that posed a problem for insurers and assurantial knowledge.

Generally, the 1755 Lisbon Earthquake, followed by numerous aftershocks, a tsunami and five consecutive days of fire, is referred to as the first *modern* catastrophe in the sense that it heralded a risk approach to such events.[7] Before Lisbon, tornados, floods, fires and earthquakes were seen as forms of natural evil, i.e. God's punishment for sinful behaviour. However, for many, including the early Enlightenment philosopher Voltaire who wrote a poem on the Lisbon Earthquake, the latter was difficult to reconcile with the idea of natural evil in as far as it was hard to imagine a sin large enough to justify such indiscriminate suffering. As Susan Neiman puts it: 'If the Lisbon earthquake is a birthplace of modernity, it's because it demanded recognition that nature and morality are split. Lisbon ought not to have happened, but it did' (Neiman 2002: 267). The split between the natural and moral world enabled the classification of future catastrophic events as manageable and governable. Thus Kant, another great Enlightenment philosopher who commented on the Lisbon Earthquake, saw it first and foremost as 'a stimulus to scientific research and the development of technical instruments of measurement and prediction' (Ray 2004: 8, see also Benjamin 1999). Generally, however, the literature on the Lisbon Earthquake attributes the modern view on catastrophe to Rousseau (1992 [1756]) who, in a letter to Voltaire, argued that it was not so much the tremor that turned the earthquake into a catastrophe as the fact that it took place in one of the world's largest and most densely populated cities. His comment is often taken to imply that if only houses were built stronger, the catastrophe could have been avoided.[8]

If the Lisbon Earthquake signified for many the birth of the modern paradigm of risk, insurance had already emerged in relation to catastrophic events at other locations. In Copenhagen, for instance, the population was introduced to the idea and practice of insurance through fire insurance long before it was introduced through the wage system. The large fires that raged in Copenhagen in 1728 and again in 1795 propelled the introduction of formal insurance schemes (Feldbæk *et al.* 2007). In London, after the Great Fire of 1666, a number of schemes for permanent insurance replaced the pre-existing charity-based systems, a development which would eventually lead to the establishment of the first Fire Offices in 1680 (Pearson 2004: 62). In the US, where insurance came late and formal schemes were not introduced until the nineteenth century, insurance also played a significant part in the context of catastrophic events such as the 1906 San Francisco Earthquake (Swiss Re 2005). Here, insurance radically changed the ways in which Americans felt about disaster, economic development and urban planning (Rozario 2007).

Of course, fire no longer appears as something unpredictable or particularly catastrophic in its consequences today, but at the time fires destroyed a large part of cities, causing significant loss of life, industry and property. In addition, fires were often difficult to prevent due to the abundance of wooden buildings, regulatory gaps and the absence of actuarial data. On top of that, the occurrence of fire was thought to have disrupting effects on the social, political and economic order. Pearson notes that when the first fire insurance schemes were introduced in Britain, 'the meaning of fire and its impact upon society was ambiguous, and its predictability still uncertain' (Pearson 2004: 4). In the eighteenth century, data required for underwriting were not readily available or collected, and risks were still partly seen in non-probabilistic terms as '"genuine" and unquantifiable uncertainty' (Pearson 2004: 4). For instance, after the Great Fire of London, Charles II strongly advocated evacuation from London and resettlement elsewhere, because he feared a rebellion among the dispossessed (Reddaway 1940: 27).

Just like insurance against the work accident, insurance against catastrophic events had a solidaristic purpose. It offered compensation to a population that often lived in wooden houses and prevented the ruthless exploitation of those who had lost their homes and property. Solidarity through insurance could make up for the shortcomings of society and indemnity protected people against poverty. In Denmark, this was one of the main reasons for the establishment of mandatory fire insurance by the state in 1761 (Feldbæk *et al.* 2007: 168).[9]

Yet, insurance also served a different political and economic purpose. Catastrophic insurance is not interested simply in life, but in a particular form of life: propertied life. In this sense, Rousseau's comment on the catastrophic Lisbon Earthquake in 1755 also exposes a different understanding of catastrophic events. He asked: 'How many unfortunates perished in this disaster for wanting to take – one his clothing, another his papers, a third his money? They know so well that a person has become the least part of himself, and that he is hardly worth saving if all the rest is lost' (Rousseau 1992 [1756]). Rather than reading the earthquake as simply a natural event, Rousseau encouraged a perspective that stressed the social conditions, such as private property and inequality, which allowed natural events to take on catastrophic proportions. In short, life without property is worthless. Through insurance, certain forms of life could be guaranteed as propertied life, which in turn became the main condition for autonomy and self-ownership. According to Robert Castel:

> The valorization of private property ... ran the risk of maintaining a cleavage, or rather a fundamental antagonism, between property-owners and non-property-owners, which would have been still more serious than a class struggle, for it would have marked the opposition between social existence and non-existence, between being able to exist positively as a subject and being sent back to total insignificance.
>
> (Castel 2002: 319)

Whereas insurance against the work accident sought to propose a solution to class struggle, catastrophe risk operates with the subject qua owner. Insurance against catastrophic events makes clear that the modern subject was constituted not just through labour but through property. Thus, where insurance against the work accident modified the agonistic relation between capital and the working class, where the 'shameful opposition between the owners of capital and those who, living only by their labour, remain[ed] enslaved to them at the same time as they [were] proclaimed politically sovereign' (Donzelot 1988: 396), insurance against catastrophic events undermined social solidarity. As Rozario has noted in the context of emergency management in the US, not *all* victims of disasters received the same kind of help and not everybody profited from disaster relief to the same degree. In the US, under the 1950 Disaster Relief Act, businesses and shop-owners were more readily awarded loans and grants, as they were considered vital for economic recovery. As a result, disaster relief promoted the transfer of public money to those with property.

Furthermore, property insurance against catastrophe and disaster helped launch a capitalist economy, as fire insurance enabled investments and speculation in real estate and building grounds:

> Overall, the diffusion of insurance engendered a sense of security in the face of nature's recurrent harms, by spreading the costs of calamities from individual victims to communities. As a result, it most likely encouraged the sort of risk-taking behavior on which capitalism depends ... enabling and encouraging risk and providing a measure of protection against the severest consequences of failure.
>
> (Rozario 2007: 83)

For example, a central objective of fire insurance offered in Copenhagen was not just to protect people from harm but also to guarantee and secure new investments and loans in property which would not have taken place without such guarantees against losses (Feldbæk *et al.* 2007: 107). Fire insurance was therefore instrumental in securing the economy and the release of credit. After the Great Fire of London, property speculators were among those who started offering fire insurance (McKellar 1999: 68). Fire insurance protected credit investments in property, generated income through annual premiums and, by reducing investment risk, drove up prices of property. In New York (1839) and San Francisco (1906), property prices rose drastically after buildings were destroyed by fires, with bare lots being sold off at a higher price than finished buildings before the crisis.

Insurance contributed to the release and recycling of investment money, which enabled new development and investment opportunities – a process that Rozario (2007: 86) has aptly described as 'destructive creation', i.e. the regeneration, renewal and expansion of capitalist economy through a process of destruction that also provided a moment of opportunity.[10] Through the promise of indemnity insurance contributed to the creation and circulation of money in the economy. As Swiss Re, a prominent reinsurer, sums up:

> [F]ire insurers have always played an important role in business by protecting credit secured by real property. Even advances in technology – with major investment required for many projects – would not be feasible without fire insurance. Finally, and in its modern extended form which includes natural perils, it has an essential macroeconomic part to play in the management of natural catastrophes which goes far beyond providing compensation for claims.
>
> (Swiss Re 2009: 14)

In the twentieth century, when the risk of fire could be managed through probabilistic reasoning, insurance against other catastrophes such as war and natural disasters has served a similar objective. Insurance knowledge and practice were closely entwined with the capitalist economy:

> [D]iscussions about the restitution of disaster victims had long been absorbed into larger debates about the proper distribution of risk in a modern capitalist society. By the twentieth century it seemed both unfair and uneconomical to require individuals and private businesses to bear the full costs of 'unforeseen' natural calamities. The advantage of insurance was that it spread risk without involving the government. It encouraged capital investment and innovation; it was the safety net that made industrial capitalism work.
>
> (Rozario 2007: 160)

Moreover, insurance schemes against catastrophes were often directly modelled on the basis of fire insurance. For instance, fire insurers in the US played an instrumental role during World War II by safeguarding the war effort through the provision of fire insurance. 'Every Fire is Sabotage Today' was the heading under which insurers drew attention to their products during

World War II. Without fire insurance, they argued, production would be delayed bringing the war effort in jeopardy. To be a patriot, then, meant to be insured. Fire insurers also played a central part in the implementation of the War Damage Corporation, which was a programme set up by Congress in 1942 to insure loss or damage to property as a result of an enemy attack (Goldin 1943: 75).[11]

After World War II, Herman Kahn suggested a similar insurance scheme against damage caused by a nuclear war in the RAND Civil Defense Study. Explicitly locating civil defence in the history of war-damage insurance and fire insurance, the report recommends that the government should provide property insurance against nuclear war through the establishment of a so-called War Damage Equalization Corporation (WDEC):

> Our proposal is to find some way to induce people and corporations to pay something toward this insurance *before* the attack, the money to be spent on long-range civil-defense measures that would enhance the ability of the economy to recuperate after the attack ... In general, the WDEC would raise money from general taxes or sell some type of insurance, on a compulsory or voluntary basis, to firms and individuals. In return, it would be giving them at least some minimum of economic security in the postattack period ... On the basis of Senate hearings on public demand for war-damage insurance, current sales of fire insurance, and the war-damage-insurance experience of World War II, we think that a voluntary insurance scheme might raise upwards of $2 billion a year; a compulsory scheme would raise even more.
>
> (Kahn 1958: 9, 10)

This kind of thinking was partly rooted in the post-war mentality of social welfare: it was a means to provide people with some sort of compensation and means for recovery. At the same time, however, the objective was to stimulate capital investment. Kahn not only thought that insurance would be able to pay for civil defence measures more broadly, he also believed that guaranteed compensation would boost investments in property.[12] The argument for insurance was also supported by several economists, who pointed at the profitability of such schemes. Hirshleifer, a RAND economist, stated that war-damage insurance in World War II had returned a profit to government of $210,000,000 and claimed that nuclear insurance too would foster 'a tremendous amount of new and replacement investment every year' (Hirshleifer 1955: 193). Finally, insurance was supposed to guarantee social stability after an attack by making sure that social and economic life would continue largely unchanged, allowing people to go on with their everyday life. As Kahn argues, insurance would make post-nuclear life possible and, as such, 'it would inspire people to take both a more realistic and a more constructive attitude toward the postwar world' (Kahn 1958: 10).

Insurance implies that risks need to be *profitable*. Through the classification of events to be insured and losses to be compensated, insurance has been a key factor in the reorientation of individuals and corporations around a capitalist order in ways that best suit business interests. Contrary to fire insurance, which still sought to ameliorate the consequences of property-less existence, terrorism risk takes the division between propertied and property-less subjects for granted and reinforces the distinction by providing services for the former, while keeping the latter in a state of social and political insignificance.

Assurantial knowledge

Insurance, then, is one of the technologies mobilized in the *dispositif* to govern terrorism and the future of potentially catastrophic risks. Terrorism is potentially catastrophic and the insurance industry tells us they can ensure the continuity of social and economic life by underwriting this catastrophe risk. For instance, Chicago-based AON Corporation, a global leader in risk management, insurance and reinsurance broking, argues that '[t]errorism could devastate your organisation. An attack on, or near, your facilities could result in loss of life, property damage, denial of access and business interruption. In an increasingly litigious society, liability is also becoming a major concern' (AON 2005). The insurance industry needs to define terrorism, create a 'calculable' rendering of terrorism and constitute the subject who is to be insured; it simultaneously defines profiles for the 'terrorists' and reproduces a 'we' that is to be insured against terrorism. The insurance industry has offered remarkably consistent definitions of terrorism. According to Pool Re, which was set up in the UK in 1993 by the insurance industry in cooperation with the government to offer terrorism insurance, terrorism refers to

> … acts of persons acting on behalf of, or in connection with, any organisation which carries out activities directed towards the overthrowing or influencing, by force or violence, of Her Majesty's government in the United Kingdom or any other government de jure or de facto.
>
> (Pool Re 2010)

Pool Re had been set up in the context of the IRA and London bombings in the early 1990s, particularly the Bishopsgate terrorist incident in April 1993. At the time, losses covered by Pool Re and the insurance industry only involved fire and explosion. After 2001, Pool Re revised the definition of losses from terrorist incidents to include an 'all risks' approach and remove exclusions relating to chemical, biological, radiological or nuclear (CBRN) attack. In the US, TRIA defines terrorism in very similar terms as:

> Acts committed by individual(s) acting on behalf of any foreign person or interest to coerce the civilian population of the U.S. or to influence the policy or affect the conduct of the U.S. government by coercion.
>
> (Marsh 2009: 2)

Recognizing the difficulties in offering an uncontested definition of terrorism, the OECD devised a non-binding 'checklist' to be used by the insurance industry for compensation purposes. The OECD task force on the definition of terrorism singled out two criteria: (1) means and effects and (2) intention:

Criterion 1 – Means and effects

A terrorist act is:

- an act, including but not limited to the use of force or violence, causing serious harm to human life, or to tangible or intangible property;
- or a threat thereof entailing serious harm.

Criterion 2 – Intention

A terrorist act is committed or threatened:

- with the intent to influence or destabilize any government or public entity and/or to provoke fear and insecurity in all or part of the population;
- in support of a political, religious, ethnic, ideological or similar goal.[13]

(OECD Council 2004)

All these definitions focus on the intent of terrorist acts as destabilizing or threatening governments. This allows for the extension of terrorism to cover not just a continuum of threats but also different forms of political action. For instance, Wendy Brown (2003) and Naomi Klein (2007) have both described the 'war on terror' as a means for securing market conditions at both a domestic and a global level. Along similar lines, the Slovenian philosopher Slavoj Žižek has pointed out that what is missing from Rumsfeld's pairing of knowns and unknowns are the so called 'unknown knowns', the obscene practices we pretend not to know about: 'What if the war on terror is not so much an answer to the terrorist attacks themselves as an answer to the rise of the anti-globalization movement, a way to contain it and distract attention to it?' (Žižek 2004: 61). Finally, Gordon Lafer has pointed out that the 'war on terror' aims at 'undoing workers' power in the workplace; pushing back against labor's growing political clout; and breaking apart the labor-community coalitions that threatened to exercise too much democratic control over capital' (Lafer 2005: 334). From forbidding the right of unionization to airport security personnel to branding as unpatriotic those workers who refused to accept wage and benefit cuts, the 'war on terror', shows Lafer, has served to constantly undermine the power of the labour force and any attempt at rolling back corporate capital.

In practice, the definition of terrorism offered by the insurance industry undergoes a further modification. Terrorism is defined not only for the purposes of compensation but also, most importantly, for quantifying risk. Insurers have increasingly had recourse to modelling to calculate losses that may result if a particular event were to occur. According to Gordon Woo, architect of the RMS terrorism risk model:

> Modeling a specific scenario is essentially a complex engineering problem, not dissimilar, in principle, to the scenario analysis conducted for natural perils such as windstorms and earthquakes. Given the dynamics of the energy source and the geometry of energy dissipation, the vulnerability of engineering construction of different types may be evaluated.
>
> (Woo 2002a)

Modelling makes assumptions not only about intent, but also about the structure of terrorist organizations, intelligence and social interaction. It entrenches an idea of 'new' terrorism as different from earlier forms of violence, which is religious-based and advocates mass casualties. It also models terrorism through analogy with other risks, be those natural disaster risks or war risks:

> [W]hile large-scale terrorism risk resembles war risk, it is more complex. When a country is at war, there is an identifiable opponent and a well-specified geographical area for combat. With respect to terrorism, the enemy is comprised of networked groups throughout the world who can attack anywhere and at any time.
>
> (Kunreuther and Michel-Kerjan 2004: 9)

Defining and classifying terrorist acts entails the classification of kinds of people. In a paper published one year after 9/11, Swiss Re described the challenges it faced in the following terms:

> The totally inconceivable lack of human respect on the part of the planners and the terrorists who carried out the attack; The unimaginable cold-bloodedness of the attack using innocent airline passengers – men, women and children – as human bombs; The concerted action carried out uncompromisingly and with totally devastating precision by kamikaze pilots; The intention of achieving maximum media impact.
>
> (Swiss Re 2002: 20)

Besides explaining why 9/11 took the majority of the insurance industry by surprise, statements such as these capture how insurance creates danger through abnormality. The abnormality that insurance represents cannot be radically different from normality, as abnormality refers to a specific understanding of the normal as statistical average that yields possibilities for calculation. All abnormal characteristics are to be defined in relation to a normal thing; they can only be derived and computed in relation to the normal.[14] If normality is average, then abnormality is a degree of deviation which can be modelled and understood from the standpoint of the normal.

For insurance experts such as Woo, the terrorist is only a variation of and deviation from 'normal' rationality:

> Omar Saeed Sheikh, the convicted killer of the Wall Street Journalist Daniel Pearl, was a London school chess champion, and a student of mathematics at the London School of Economics, before he switched from economic to war games. A mathematician might play a war game like chess: cold-blooded enough to dispose mercilessly of opponents; and hard-headed enough to sacrifice one's own forces if this was the optimal move ... Those who are skeptical that terrorism risk can be understood and modeled underestimate the intelligence and rationality of al-Qaeda.
> (Woo 2002b)

For insurance practices, however, the average normal also functions as the right normal, which means that the normal blurs the 'is' and the 'ought', the descriptive average and the normative state towards which one should strive. This approach to normality and abnormality that blurs the descriptive average and the normative reinforces the imaginary of continuity between present and future. In its attempt to neutralize or even prevent the possibility of catastrophic irruptions in the future, insurance does not just colonize the future by depicting the possibility of a 'next attack'. Insurance is also restorative, in as much as it attempts to bring people back within the circuits of social order (Lobo-Guerrero 2007). By blurring the tension between 'is' and 'ought', practices of insurance sustain the normal and the present in its existing configuration.

Defined as a deviation from the average, the actuarial definitions of terrorism can be infinitely expanded to encompass more and more possibilities that are seen as deviations from the 'ought/is' of the present. Unsurprisingly, therefore, the insurance coverage of terrorism has also been extended to other events – strikes, popular unrest, dissent – considered disruptive of the existing property regimes. As such, terrorism insurance smoothes out contradictions at the heart of the normal and creates a continuum of threats by connecting these to terrorism risk. For example, AON annually publishes a 'Global Terrorism Risk Map' that ranks the threat of terrorism in relation to foreign investment potential. The risks included are not just those of terrorism but include widely diverging issues such as extreme right-wing violence, nationalism, separatism, single-interest groups, Marxist-inspired violence, religious extremism and narcotics trade (AON 2010). Bundled under the label of terrorism, these acts have little in common other than the fact that they are social disorders that can lead to destabilization. Consider for instance the following claim scenario by Philadelphia-based ACE USA, which provides stand-alone insurance against 'non-certified' acts of terrorism:

Claim # 1 – A Domestic Terrorist Act
Location: Manufacturing plant in the United States

Situation: A truck allegedly delivering supplies drives through the security gates of a plant. Once inside the gate, the truck veers toward the main manufacturing section. The truck explodes as it hits the building.

As the police investigate the crime, they determine that the driver was actually part of a conspiracy to destroy the company because the company's products polluted the environment.

Claim: Damages from the destruction total $15 million of property damage and $30 million of business interruption losses. The claim adjustor determines that the event is an act of terrorism. The insured has purchased TRIA coverage from the all risk carrier; however, the act is never "certified," since the conspirators were not foreign, nor were they working for a foreign entity. The claim is denied since the all risk coverage included coverage only for "certified" terrorist acts.

Coverage could be afforded under a non-certified stand alone policy purchased from ACE USA. Coverage could also be afforded under a combined coverage stand alone policy purchased from ACE USA.

(ACE 2006)

As the scenario shows, terrorism insurance has also become available against 'non-certified acts of terrorism', i.e. acts that do not follow the definition of terrorism as provided in TRIA. Although with the extension of TRIA in 2007, domestic terrorism has been included as a 'certified act of terrorism', the above example nonetheless helps to illustrate the point that insurance companies provide terrorism insurance against criminal or politically motivated acts that do not fit the federal definition of a terrorist attack.[15] The only commonality of these risks seems to reside in their potentially disrupting effects upon businesses, which leads to a blurring of terrorism, crime and forms of political violence and resistance.

This chapter has taken issue with the inattention to insurance in security studies. Often considered to be the 'other' of national security, insurance and its formulation as social security have been relegated to the margins of academic interest. Analyses of neoliberalism have further reinforced this inattention by exposing the disappearance of traditional practices of insurance towards the privatization of risk management and forms of risk embracing. Assurantial practices as defined by Éwald acquired an almost nostalgic aura of lost solidarity in the face of risks. Drawing inspiration from the role of insurance in catastrophic events such as large fires, natural disasters and war, this chapter relocated insurance as a practice of security. Moreover, it showed that insurance has not simply passed from an imaginary of social solidarity to one of an individualized, neo-liberal subject: preserving the capitalist way of life has always figured predominantly in the *dispositif* of insurance. It has been sustained by an imaginary of a capitalist subject whose life and property need to be protected against dangerous occurrences in the future.

Insurance reminds us how 'life' is intrinsically connected to issues of property. Practices of security are not simply securing liberal regimes but are also securing existing property regimes and propertied citizens not only against terrorism but against many other forms of disruption. As a result, the future that insurance imagines is an endless and unmodified replica of the present, the normal is what should always be, thus suspending possibilities of symbolizing conflicts and processing different relations to the other. As two risk management experts have argued in an article on insurance and terrorism, the insurance industry contributes to 'the social and economic continuity of the country' (Kunreuther and Michel-Kerjan 2005: 51). Upon signing TRIA, which was designed to bail out the insurance industry in case of catastrophic losses resulting from acts of terrorism, former US President George Bush remarked:

> My administration is determined to make America safer, to make our economy stronger ... Yesterday I signed into law the new Department of Homeland Security, to organize our government for the long-term challenge of protecting America. Today, with terrorism insurance, we're defending America by making our economy more secure. Both these achievements show the unity of our nation in a time of testing, and our resolve to lead America to a better day.
>
> (Bush 2002)

Insurance, here, is directly related to the protection of the American homeland understood as the indefinite survival of its economy. The state is required to step in, not to protect the population, but to buttress insurance mechanisms. What underwriting practices restore are actually social and economic processes disrupted by terrorism rather than simply individuals. The compensation system is thought to help the economy rebound after an attack, thereby reducing the vulnerability to terrorism. It can also reduce the 'amount of social fragmentation caused by the attacks' (OECD 2005: 65). As Thierry van Santen, President of the Federation of European Risk Management Associations (FERMA), argues: 'Day after day we see that terrorism has no frontier, and that one of the terrorists' objectives is to destabilize the economies of developed countries' (AON 2005: 15). The 'we' to be secured is not the cultural or democratic 'we', but the propertied 'we'. The security of social relations is imagined in terms of possible destabilization of economic processes.

Life is valued only in as much as it can resume its role within social and economic processes. The construction of property-less people, who do not own anything or do not have self-ownership, is one of the processes that prepare certain categories for elimination by institutionally marking them as potential future victims (Balibar 2005: 32). A note accompanying the

Project ARGUS exercises in the UK – 'Even if you are insured, behave as if you were uninsured' – appears in a different, more sinister light. 'Behave as if non-insured' is not just indicative of the need to be prepared but also of the possibility of victimhood. Mark Duffield (2008) has aptly noted that the distinction between insured and non-insured life, between populations supported by regimes of social protection as opposed to those expected to be self-reliant, is a key distinction between the developed and underdeveloped worlds. Without insurance, which helps restore subjects to social life, subjects in developing states are left on their own and exposed to other forms of regulation. Insurance reproduces the life-chance divide between the developed and underdeveloped worlds by valorizing propertied life, the life that defines its worth through ownership or can be translated into property and ownership for others.

The actuarial knowledge deployed to assess terrorism has recourse to classification of what terrorism is, and taxonomies of who is involved in terrorism. The effects we have unpacked show that underwriting terrorism has fostered the imaginary of the indefinite continuity of the present, capitalist social and economic processes, the propertied subject, and normality as the blurring of 'is' and 'ought'. The definition of terrorism instantiates forms of continuity between all actions deemed destabilizing for social and economic processes. Insurance also enacts a society stabilized in the present, whatever its inequalities and injustices. If forms of underwriting have shown their resilience and adaptation in governing terrorism, the following chapters will consider imagination and aesthetics as two new technologies for 'knowing' the unknown of a catastrophic future.

5   Imagining catastrophe

Can you imagine?

In 2009, the ABC TV channel in the US produced a television show entitled *Earth 2100*, which takes viewers on a journey through what the next century may bring. In the show, the future is portrayed through a range of worst case scenarios or what the programme announces as the catastrophic scenario of a 'perfect storm' made up of uncontrolled population growth, dwindling resources and climate change: 'The scenarios in Earth 2001 are not a prediction of what will happen but rather a warning about what might happen. They are based on the work of some of the world's top scientists and experts, as well as peer-reviewed articles from publications around the world ... This program was developed to show the worst-case for human civilization.'[1] *Earth 2100*, unlike fictional accounts of worst case scenarios and catastrophes to come, brings together fiction and science, news reporting and entertainment. The news anchor Bob Woodruff introduces a fictional character from the future called Lucy (born in 2009), whose voice is added to those of news reporters, and there are interviews with academics like Thomas Homer Dixon, Jared Diamond and Peter Gleick, all known for predicting catastrophic scenarios of social and ecological transformation.

Earth 2100 nicely illustrates the new injunction to infuse imagination into security knowledge. When the understanding of the future in preventive and predictive models is perceived as insufficient, imagination is mobilized in response to the problematization of the unknown. For instance, the 9/11 Commission concluded that the failure of imagination was the most important failure leading to 9/11 (National Commission of Terrorist Attacks upon United States 2004). A similar failure of imagination is taken to be cause of public inaction concerning climate change, as 'people just can't seem to fathom how catastrophic climate change will be' (Becker 19 December 2009).

The recourse to imagination appears as a solution to the incapacity of human understanding to encompass the futurity and magnitude of a potential catastrophe. Not surprisingly, perhaps, 9/11 has triggered an increasing recourse to imagination in both film and fiction, which mediate both popular and expert understandings of the next catastrophic event. Richard Ericson and Aaron Doyle have argued that tackling uncertainties is 'overlain with non-probabilistic reasoning that is aesthetic, emotional and experiential' (Ericson and Doyle 2004b: 4–5). Éwald has also pointed out that the possibility of catastrophe 'invites one to anticipate what one does not yet know … one must be wide open to speculation, to the craziest imagined views' (Éwald 2002: 288–289). Finally, noting the affinities between the form of terrorist attacks and the representation of disasters in Hollywood movies, Lee Clarke has argued that imagination, rather than calculation, underpins our understanding of terrorism: 'Some say that September 11 changed everything. That's not true. But it did imprint upon our imaginations scenes of horror that until then had been the province of novels and movies. We now imagine ourselves in those images' (Clarke 2005: x).

Hollywood films like *Armageddon, Independence Day* or *The Matrix* are now seen as premonitions of metropolitan landscapes as sites of apocalyptic destruction, while Don DeLillo, Paul Auster, Chuck Palahniuk or Bret Easton Ellis are deemed to have offered fictional forecasts of what happened on 9/11 (Petersen 2005). Homeland security experts have drawn not just on the imaginations of Hollywood directors, but also on those of sci-fi writers. For instance, 'Science Fiction in the Service of National Security' is a group of sci-fi writers who have joined the Homeland Security Department in its 'war on terror'. According to one of the group's members, Greg Bear, sci-fi writers 'offer powerful imaginations that can conjure up not only possible methods of attack, but also ideas about how governments and individuals will respond and what kinds of high-tech tools could prevent attacks' (Hall 2007).

Security experts themselves have also sought to become more imaginative, as organizations and bureaucracies are now required to expect the unexpected and replace the improbable with the mere possible and imaginable. Catastrophes are thus both the stuff of Hollywood films and the product of expert imagination. The reports by the National Intelligence Council, already mentioned in this book's introduction, are a prime example of imagining the worst about the future in the intelligence community.[2] Even in the rather mundane settings of scenario-based imaginative enactments (Collier and Lakoff 2008) of preparedness exercises, imagination is one of the main ingredients for taking on the unknown future. However, rather than assuming that imagination is 'unreason', 'crazy' and 'wild', this chapter argues that imagination is indispensable to the pursuit of knowledge and the problematization of the unknown. Imagination is not the opposite of knowledge, but a vital element in all cognition. Nor is it something external, a 'skill' that security professionals can learn from fiction writers.

As we have argued in the previous chapters, potentially catastrophic disruptions have not done away with knowledge; rather, different modes of knowledge have been reassembled and recalibrated in a *dispositif* at the limit which is largely conjectural, even as it mobilizes other styles of reasoning. Imagination underpins these modes of knowledge in their attempt to dispel secrecy and ignorance, compute risk and uncertainty, and prepare for surprise and novelty. Through imagination, a range of apparently disparate details, perceptions, ideas and assumptions can be brought together in a seemingly coherent whole. Placing imagination within processes of cognition allows us to explore the changing role of imagination in relation to knowledge and understanding.

In what sense has imagination become the panacea of security knowledge of the future catastrophe? What is the relationship between imagination and the unknown? To unpack the relationship between imagination and knowledge, we start with a brief discussion of the concept of imagination. Although many different meanings have been ascribed to the concept, this chapter revisits Immanuel Kant's understanding of imagination as a faculty involved in all cognition. For Kant, imagination entails a temporal play between the past and the present: the absent past becomes present in the imagination. As imagination deals with absences and non-actuality, imagination also seems the most adaptable faculty to tackle the uncertainty of an unknown future.

In particular, we seek to draw attention to Kant's distinction between reproductive and creative imagination to consider the various ways in which imagination has entered into security knowledge. It is argued that, at first sight, scenarios seem to work within the reproductive paradigm of imagination, where imagination is subsumed to the reproductive knowledge of security professionals. Given the historical distrust of imagination in security knowledge, this is perhaps no surprise. Nonetheless, productive or creative imagination is not effaced. For example, during the Cold War, the reproductive imagination of security professionals was interrupted by anti-nuclear campaigns, which deployed imaginative scenarios to counter the ordering implied by Cold War security knowledge. The imagination of catastrophe today, we argue, reconfigures these elements into a different *dispositif*. The radical imagination of catastrophe is incorporated within security knowledge. Yet, these syntheses are not simply ordered representations of the world which are communicable to others, but can also lead to a breakdown of common sense. By bringing out the role of imagination as an epistemic category, this chapter reveals the uneasy and unstable relationship between imagination and knowledge on the one hand and that between reproductive and creative imagination on the other.

Imagination beyond image and fantasy

In *The World of the Imagination*, Eva Brann explains that imagination has been 'the pivotal power in which are centered those mediating, elevating, transforming functions that are so indispensable to the cognitive process that philosophers are reluctant to press them very closely' (Brann 1991: 32). This is not just true for philosophers. Despite increasing references to the role of imagination in security governance (Dupuy 2002a, De Goede 2008b, Salter 2008b, Grusin 2010), security scholars have yet to consider the particular role of imagination for knowledge. Imagination is often discussed simply as representation through image and therefore mainly analysed in the realm of the visual.[3] Since Aristotle wrote that the soul never thinks without an image, the imagination-image connection has been tightly knit in Western thought. Associated with the construction of images, imagination has usually been connected with fiction, literature and popular culture.[4] When considered in relation to cognition, it has been generally rendered in negative terms, as that which needs to be surpassed, limited or constrained by reason. Lorraine Daston (2005: 16) has termed this 'the fear and loathing of imagination in science' that emerged through the gradual separation of the artist and scientist and the association of imagination with art. While subjectivity and objectivity became increasingly connected with art and science respectively, the history of imagination as essential (although not without dangers) to philosophy and science was effaced: 'Pure facts, severed from theory and sheltered from the imagination, were the last, best hope for permanence in scientific achievement' (Daston 2005: 30).

As security knowledge has been generated in a field which legitimates itself through an appeal to rationality and scientificity, it appears as if imagination would have no place within the world of security professionals. However, as Foucault reminds us, the distinction between science and imagination has been less clear-cut in the past. Particular understandings of imagination have also sparked the development of scientific knowledge. For instance, Foucault shows how the development of medical knowledge in the sixteenth century is not the result of the emergence of the pathological, but of the appearance of powers of the body and of imagination (Foucault 1973). Drawing on Foucault's analysis in *Madness and Civilization*, which argued that imagination 'succeeded in creating knowledge of the anticipation of madness that linked images, speculative hypothesis and association', Philip Bougen and Patrick O'Malley (2009) have expanded the point to the uncertainties of security. The insertion of random events into the governance of the future has led to 'associations' of images and data which draw on the epistemology of 'correlation' in complexity theory.[5] Imagination, hence, appears to be linked with the aspiration to conjectural epistemology that Ginzburg opposed to Galilean science (see Chapter 3) and plays a crucial role in the assemblage of data.[6] Rather than opposed to knowledge, imagination is rendered as essential to knowledge about the future.

At the same time, this implies that it is possible to divide between 'good' and 'bad' imagination. John Sallis has pointed out that 'imagination has a double effect, a double directionality, bringing about illumination and elevation, on the one hand, and deception and corruption, on the other, bringing them about perhaps even in such utter proximity that neither can, with complete assurance, be decisively separated from the other' (Sallis 2000: 46). This double rendering as promise and danger often appears as a hierarchy of imagination and fantasy. Imagination refers to the faculty which is related to understanding and judgement, while fantasy is imagination liberated of any such constraints. Kant is critical of fantasy (*Phantasie*), which is akin to madness, and privileges imagination (*Einbildungskraft*) as a faculty which contributes to our understanding of reality and ability to act in the world.[7] Fantasy is most often connected with desire and prohibition. Thus, Susan Sontag could remark about disaster movies that 'one job that fantasy can do is to lift us out of the unbearably humdrum and to distract us from terrors, real or anticipated by an escape into exotic dangerous situations which have last-minute happy endings' (Sontag 2004: 42). For Kant, imagination does not replace reality as in a 'flight of fancy', but is intimately entwined with the need to connect concepts and appearances or perceptions.

Yet, the distinction between fantasy and imagination is an unstable one. In its initial use by Herman Kahn, scenarios referred to utopian or apocalyptic fantasies of the future rather than the deployment of imagination as part of cognition. However, as imagination-cum-fantasy was largely associated with the Romantics and art (and in that sense far removed from the scientific discourse of strategic thought), scenarios also needed to tame imagination, prevent it from running wild, and subsume it to conceptual understanding. As described in manuals of scenario planning, a scenario 'identifies some significant events, the main actors and their motivations, and it conveys how the world functions. Building and using scenarios can help people explore what the future might look like and the likely challenges of living in it' (Shell 2003: 8). At the same time, imagination can also orientate judgement through feelings of pleasure and pain. Imagination is thus not a substitute to or negation of reality, as Éwald's 'wild speculation' seems to suggest. Related to questions of knowledge and cognition, imagination entails a particular ordering of the social world.

Two paradigms are often considered to have dominated this understanding of imagination.[8] The first one is mimetic and goes back to Aristotle for whom imagination is a 'sort of movement' that does not occur apart from perception (Engmann 1976). It refers to imagination as the reproduction of sensible perceptions in the mind.[9] For him, imagination is a 'second degree of absence. In sensing, the object itself is present to the senses, though only its form is received, whereas in imagining the object itself is also absent' (Brann 1991: 42). Aristotle firmly established the triad sensation-imagination-intelligence in the history of philosophy.

The second paradigm is that of 'creative', 'inventive' or 'productive' imagination, which is often thought to have emerged with Kant. Imagination for Kant is the mediator between our sensorial perception of the world and the concepts used to make sense of the world. Imagination has a role in '*constituting the real as the real*' (Hengehold 2007: 18 emphasis in original). In the *Critique of Pure Reason* (1781), Kant distinguished imagination from other mental functions. Imagination is the faculty that realizes the synthesis of sensation and understanding, a particular human faculty that mediates the sensory knowledge of the world. Yet, this is not simply identifiable with sense perception as David Hume initially intimated. Contra Hume, Kant argued that imagination cannot refer to simple associations of already existing impressions and ideas. Imagination is the faculty of representing an object even '*without its presence* in the intuition' (emphasis in original) (Kant 1999 [1781]: 256). Imagination is linked to the absent and the non-real, non-actual. It provides a sort of unstable middle ground between the faculties of understanding and intuition. At the same time, imagination becomes centrally responsible for knowledge as a meeting ground of the understanding and sensibility (Brann 1991: 90).[10]

Cornelius Castoriadis (1997) and others have castigated Kant for subsuming imagination to 'true knowledge' and thus rendering it only capable of reproducing the 'same'.[11] Other philosophers, by contrast, have found in Kant's theorization the potential for a concept that surpasses the limits of reason, a 'radical imagination' characterized by invention and the possibility of positing new worlds (Makkreel 1984, Warnock 1994, Stevenson 2003). As Linda Zerilli has formulated Hannah Arendt's reading of imagination in Kant, '[i]magination, when it is considered in its freedom – nothing compels us to consider it as such – is not bound to the law of causality, but is productive and spontaneous, not merely reproductive of what is already known, but generative of new forms and figures' (Zerilli 2005: 163).[12] The kind of understanding made possible by exercising imagination concerns our ability to see objects and events outside the economy of use and the causal nexus (Zerilli 2005: 177).

Ultimately, however, a distrust of imagination lingers in Kant's *oeuvre*. Although imagination, alongside sensations and concepts, plays a role in cognition, it is ultimately trumped by the powers of reason in the encounter with the sublime.[13] If Kant liberated the constraints of the imagination, he reintroduced them through the sublime, which is an 'outrage on imagination' (Kant 2006 [1798]: 137). In the encounter with the sublime, the role of imagination is changed. For Kant, the sublime is a 'state of mind represented by the representation of boundedlessness or the infinite' (Makkreel 1984: 303). Kant distinguishes between two forms of sublime: the mathematical sublime and the dynamic sublime. The mathematically sublime is the 'absolutely large' in comparison with which everything else is small (Kant 1951 [1790]: 86–89). It cannot be grasped by means of our senses only and leads to the acknowledgement that 'the mind has a power surpassing any standard of sense' (Kant 1951 [1790]: 89). If the mathematical sublime concerns magnitude, the dynamic sublime is brought about by unbounded power. Kant refers particularly to the power of nature expressed in catastrophic events such as storms, erupting volcanoes or hurricanes. Imagination fails in both cases and reason is relied upon: reason 'produces the idea of infinity to soothe the pain of the mathematical sublime, and answers the dynamic sublime by reminding itself of the irreducible dignity of the human calling to live as free moral agents who legislate to themselves the law of their own reason' (Ray 2004: 9). When the poles of sensibility and cognition need to be mediated through imagination, there is always the danger that this mediation may go awry, giving way to a 'lesser' form of imagination: fantasy.

Unbinding imagination

The 9/11 Commission Report criticized bureaucracies for lack of imagination, for failing to notice signs that were indicators of the attacks. However, imagination as a 'technology of futurity' has a longer history and needs to be understood in the continuity of Cold War problematizations of nuclear war through military simulations, war games and (anti-)nuclear scenarios.[14] Often associated with the war games of the Cold War, scenarios have never completely disappeared from security practices. Emergency planning knowledge holds that plans need to be tested in order to assess their adequacy, locate any gaps and correct mistakes. Moreover, scenarios have also been used effectively in designing strategies for mitigating other types of hazards and for establishing property insurance premiums in the cases of earthquakes and floods.

As we noted in Chapter 2, nuclear strategists were very much concerned with risk management in an uncertain, complex environment.[15] Strategists problematized nuclear war within a field of knowledge that granted them a certain authority vis-à-vis the military. Systems analysis, developed by RAND-analyst Albert Wohlstetter (1958) in his influential study of American vulnerability to a surprise attack, provided the raw data and clues for scenarios. Put simply, systems analysis calls for a holistic view on strategy that includes all relevant factors. By computing a large range of empirical parameters (e.g. range of missiles, missile targets, funding allocation and the location of bases) that could impact upon the decision-making process, strategists could begin to imagine the material consequences of hostile interaction between nuclear powers. Alongside systems analysis which provided the data-input, game theory, introduced to the RAND Corporation by John von Neumann, further facilitated in setting up scenarios of risk escalation. Besides rigorous and parsimonious analytical frameworks, these forms of knowledge relied heavily upon intuition and imagination as indispensable elements to knowledge creation.

The intuitions gained by playing these games and scenarios, referred to as 'synthetic history' or 'future history', were seen as superseding history and formed the basis for operational strategy (Digby *et al.* 1988, Kahn 1960, Goldhamer and Speier 1959). For Kant, sense is the faculty of intuition in the presence of an object while imagination is intuition in its absence. The intuitions arising out of simulations and laboratory experiences create particular sensorial regimes which imagination can synthesize and work upon. As Kahn argued: 'Thermonuclear wars are not only unpleasant events they are, fortunately, unexperienced events, and the crises which threaten such wars are almost equally unexperienced. Few are able to force themselves to persist in looking for novel possibilities in this area without aids to their imagination' (Kahn 1962: 143). The creation of 'new' sensory contexts which imagination could synthesize was indispensable to the creation of security knowledge about the future.

Despite their high level of sophistication, scenarios and simulations could not be taken to explain or predict social behaviour in the real world. Kahn warned that although scenarios 'dramatize and illustrate possibilities that might otherwise be overlooked ... one must remember that the scenario is not used as a predictive device. The analyst is often dealing with the unknown and unknowable future' (Kahn 1962: 144, 145). Scenarios act out unpredictable futures. In acting-out, they create a sensorial regime of visibility and promote particular concepts that render this regime understandable.[16] Cognitive understanding based on logics followed from the work of imagination, the cultivation of which was at the heart of strategic thought. Imagination was able not only to synthesize sensory data, but it provided the much needed link between sensory perceptions and conceptual understanding. Scenarios and simulations are not simply events which frame a potential catastrophic situation in order to locate faults in the existing preparedness strategies. They are spectacles, theatrical arrangements, played by decision-makers as well as by ordinary people. Scenarios are 'exercises in imagination' to be 'scripted and acted out' (Thackrah 2003) and create a sensorial environment in which perceptions are created. Imagination would assemble and synthesize those perceptions and reformulate the future for the purposes of decision-making. Scenarios work on the human sensorium, and draw on the senses and imagination to palliate the limitations of rationality: 'In order to be useful tools, however, a scenario must be a cohesive story – just like a novel or short story – with believable characters, and a good plot that follows a plausible chain of events. Most importantly, the scenario must challenge the reader's assumptions and ardently test their current thinking and strategies.'[17] Strategic imagination, then, viewed nuclear war as 'part of one great "play", both in the sense of theatrical spectacle and in the sense of a game to be played' (Zins 1991: 129).

In setting out plausible stories that linked sensations to understanding, strategic imagination also made use of analogies and metaphors. Kahn (1965) in particular was careful to choose metaphorical expressions: he recommended the use of the metaphor of 'rungs on the escalation ladder' instead of 'strike', for example. Similar to the metaphor of the 'escalation ladder' was that of 'an elevator stopping at various floors' (Kahn 1965, see also Schiappa 1989). Kahn's metaphors and analogies between a nuclear strike and everyday life domesticate the future through the invocation of a different imagination, that of everyday, familiar objects.[18] They also domesticate the collective imagination of the nation by representing it as a 'crowd to be calmed' (Schiappa 1989: 260).

Imagination thus became a governmental technology of futurity which could project undesirable unexpected events and help find ways to tame them. During the Cold War, rational choice models colonized the uncertain future and turned nuclear war into something calculable and manageable by reducing sensations to input into a scenario or simulation. Imagination was therefore subsumed to the rational calculation of survival – the criticism that Castoriadis addressed to Kant could be equally valid of the use that civil strategists made of imagination during the Cold War. Nonetheless, another use of imagination emerged in these debates about the uncertainty of a nuclear escalation, as the anti-nuclear camp sought to reclaim imagination from its expert use.

The nuclear imagination supported by the rationality of game theory and systems analysis and by the sensory context of scenarios and simulations had made it possible for analysts to navigate through the future of nuclear conflict and plan post-attack survival. For the anti-nuclear movement, however, the challenge was to counter the rational knowledge produced by experts endowed with the professional capacity to control and manage the future. They pointed out that knowledge gained through scenario planning was severely limited by the structure of the game. In scenarios, for example, events that were not under the control of any government ('nature') were kept under control by the game referees, while any move out of tune with the material strength of a country was not allowed (Goldhamer and Speier 1959).

The anti-nuclear movement argued that strategic imaginations of the unthinkable actually brought the world closer to the unthinkable, increasing the probability that something unforeseen would happen. Strategic studies, Jonathan Schell notes, 'ignores that the very outbreak of a nuclear war already assumes the breakdown of reason and rationality' (Schell 1982: 32). Contra Kahn, who called planning a prudential exercise, the anti-nuclear movement argued that deterrence was a self-fulfilling prophecy filled with contradictions: it insisted on planning for nuclear war in order to prevent it and called for the production of nuclear weapons in order to minimize their impact. Understanding nuclear war as a game to be played, defence intellectuals brought the world closer to catastrophe than it otherwise would have been. The unforeseeable, unpredictable and unknowable were kept largely outside the scenarios. Imagination merely played an ordering role by domesticating the senses and allying them with concepts. What was needed, instead, was to unbind imagination from rational knowledge and show its creative power. In particular, Schell's influential *The Fate of the Earth* stands out as an important counterpoint to Kahn's *Thinking about the Unthinkable* and other futurological work.[19] Claiming that thinking about nuclear war necessarily involves 'approximations, probabilities, even guesses' (Schell 1982: 24), he deploys imagination in a different sense than intimated by Kahn:

> [U]sually, people wait for things to occur before trying to describe them. (Futurology has never been a very respectable field of inquiry). But since we cannot afford under any circumstances to let a holocaust occur, we are forced in this one case to become the historians of the future – to chronicle and commit to memory an event that we have never experienced and must never experience.
>
> (Schell 1982: 21)

The anti-nuclear movement proposed to deploy imagination not as a way of managing the unthinkable of nuclear war, but as a worst case scenario. It insisted that the mere *possibility* of catastrophe should be treated as *certainty*, because 'our uncertainty is forced on us not so much by the limitations of our intellectual ability as by the irreducible fact that we have no platform for observation except our mortal frames' (Schell 1982: 77). The aim is not to guarantee the survival of pre-attack societal values in the post-attack world. Rather, worst case imaginations of catastrophic futures serve as the limit which prompts us to invent different, less destructive futures. Schell argued that 'it may be only by descending into this hell in imagination that we can hope to escape descending in it in reality at some later time' (Schell 1982: 5).

The productive imagination embraced by the anti-nuclear campaigns could not be subsumed to the concepts of strategic studies. According to Wessel, it is merely a version of 'the hoary appeal to unreason, tied to a strong contempt for scientific method' (1962: 14). In his view, productive imagination was to be subsumed to scientific reason. In an analysis of the peace movement for the RAND Corporation, A. E. Wessel summarizes the actions of the peace movement as largely anti-scientific:

> In fact, it is held that although some knowledge of the results of nuclear war or an arms race can be obtained using scientific technique, a description of the future (or even specific consequences) based solely on scientifically generated information and methodology is at best a misleadingly partial picture and at worst, totally wrong and insane as a source for national decision.
>
> (Wessel 1962: 13)

For the anti-nuclear movement, however, creative imagination could open the possibility of a radically different future, as suggested, in different ways, by Arendt and Castoriadis. This was achieved by unbinding the imagination from the limitations of reason. As Robert Lifton, another influential academic writing against nuclearism, put it, the 'concept of nuclear winter enhances our imaginative task' and 'prods our imaginations in the direction of nothingness – a direction we must explore to grasp our predicament' (Lifton 1986: 86, 93). However, the encounter with the sublime also, ironically, led to a 'failure of the imagination', as the imagination is overwhelmed by the experience of a vastness or power. As Kant remarked, imagination is not 'exactly *creative*, for it is not capable of producing a sense representation that was *never* given to our faculty of sense' (emphasis in original) (Kant 2006 [1798]: 61). Through representations of catastrophe, the anti-nuclear campaigns create a sensorial regime that can become material for the power of imagination. Imagination is thus unbridled, its inventions bringing about a different possible world. It is not longer harmonized with sensorial perceptions and concepts of the understanding. The encounter with the sublime as the radical negation from which to think alternative futures is doomed to fail, as it would require a newly found relationship between the subject's mental faculties. The nuclear sublime, therefore, provides a temporary delusion only – as in Schell's and Lifton's work for example – where 'the effort to think the nuclear sublime in terms of its absoluteness dwindles from the effort to imagine total annihilation to something very much like calculations of exactly how horrible daily life would be after a significant explosion' (Ferguson 1984: 7).

The sublime catastrophe

After 9/11, counter-terrorism security knowledge has brought together the reproductive and creative use of imagination. On the one hand, imagination attempts to create a harmonious alliance between the faculties of the human mind. It aligns the concept of catastrophe, the techniques of emergency planning and the knowledge of prevention, precaution and preparedness with a sensorial regime of catastrophic events set out in scenarios and exercises. On the other hand, imagination is made to take hold of rational limitations in speaking of CBRN terrorism. Even though a future terrorist attack is mired in uncertainty, security experts repeatedly tell us that 'it will happen': 'we don't know where or when exactly, but it will happen'.[20] Nuclear and biological terrorism is now taken for granted as a possibility of the future. Disasters, crises, traumas, vulnerabilities, catastrophic and unpredictable risks are the terms that increasingly render the shape of the future. The message of Graham Allison's book on nuclear terrorism – 'We are courting colossal disaster, and we need to take action now' – has become the mantra of the professionals in charge of anticipating future catastrophes (Allison 2005). *Expecting the Unexpected* is the title of a report by the UK National Counter-Terrorism Security Office (NaCTSO), which condenses the relation to the future post-9/11 as 'business continuity'. This could just as well be a motto for the overarching relationship that security professionals have with the unexpected and potentially catastrophic future. Indeed, the phrase is not a NaCTSO invention, but appears in numerous reports that stress our changing relationship with the future. We are told to expect the unexpected of radiological disasters (Stern and Buglova 2007), to expect the unexpected of workplace emergencies (Oregon OSHA, n.d.) and to expect the unexpected of diseases and pandemics (International Risk and Disaster Conference 2008).

Although imagining the unexpected has long been part of managerial studies of business and organizational behaviour (Weick and Sutcliffe 2001), its problematization post-9/11 has led to an explicit concern with integrating imagination within expert knowledge. The Cold War civil defence experts, in imagining games and scenarios for a nuclear attack, relied on the few minutes' notice that the Soviet Union was supposed to give them. Today's counter-terrorist professionals stress the difference between an 'earlier' IRA-era type of terrorism, in which notice and expectation of an explosion was taken for granted, and the unexpected nature of post-9/11 bomb explosions.[21] 'Expecting the unexpected' formulates the paradox of the relation to the future: the desire to 'tame' the future and calculate possible and probable occurrences of danger while recognizing that the future is characterized by uncertainty, the unknown, and the unexpected.

The double role of imagination as both harmonious and unbridled is apparent in counter-terrorism exercises. For example, Project ARGUS, which was set up by NaCTSO, is a multimedia simulation, which takes place in real time and asks players to make decisions in the event of a terrorist attack. The project does not address the public at large, but particularly those in charge of crowded places, business representatives and safety managers.[22] The project is focused on bolstering preparedness measures for business communities and professionals. The videos used during the exercises repeat similar scenarios of bombs and secondary devices exploding in a shopping centre, a club, outside a restaurant or in a hotel.[23] While the staging of the simulation requires participants to both imagine the future attack and subsume it to the expertise conveyed to them by counter-terrorism experts and emergency planners, imagination is summoned both to subsume sensations to general conceptual frameworks provided by the experts and to evade the limits of conceptual frameworks. The video simulation offers the perceptual material which subjects need to recombine and synthesize for the purposes of action.

While creating sensory contexts about an explosive device, a secondary explosive device and international terrorism, which need to be combined with the subjects' previous perceptions, the session also indicates that synthesizing perceptions is not enough. The subjects are told that they will need to perform 'dynamic risk assessment' in the case of an incident. Dynamic risk assessment means assessing the type of incident and feeding the resulting judgement to the police. What this situation of both pre-given conceptual frameworks and dynamic risk assessment shows is that imagination needs to mediate both sensations and concepts. However, in these exercise scenarios, the use of imagination plays a reproductive function. It limits scenarios to a set of ideas – 'secondary device', 'invacuation', 'safe spaces' – and reinforces repetition and automatism through the use of mnemonics. When contacting the emergency services, the mnemonic CHALET contains all the indications for the information needed: C (casualties), H (hazards in the areas), A (access to the location), L (location of the incident), E (emergency services required), T (type of explosion). In the event of a Mumbai-type shooting, four Cs encapsulate the exemplary behaviours required: C(over), C(onfirm), C(ontact) and C(ontrol).[24]

After the 2008 Mumbai attacks, the ARGUS exercises have a Mumbai-type scenario: mass shooting in the same crowded places.[25] Instead of being visual, this scenario is read out by the counter-terrorism experts. Whereas in the case of preparedness against terrorist attacks the use of a 'limited reach' scenario and the exclusion of CBRN attacks from the discussion focuses imagination upon a series of actions to be taken, the second scenario undermines the use of imagination as a spontaneous, synthesizing force leading to judgement. A Mumbai-type scenario can be seen as a sublime event, in which imagination is in regress when confronted with an abundance of power. Ultimately, within the second type of scenario, it is difficult to imagine surviving random shooting. Hence, when a counter-terrorism expert hinted that in a Mumbai-type of attack one can condense action under 'four Cs' (cover, confirm, communicate and control), one of the participants quipped 'cry' or 'client – hide behind a guest'.[26] The exercise participants expressed confusion and anxiety. When confronted with overwhelming power, the relation between imagination and reason becomes a lot messier and imagination cannot be easily domesticated. Imagination also produces unexpected effects in moments when the perception-imagination-understanding continuum is destabilized. For instance, in another ARGUS session, the CTSAs had problems starting the DVD and then making use of the replacement DVD player brought in to replace the non-functional one. An exercise participant had to repeatedly come to the front of the room and help start the right section of the DVD. The situation gave rise to jokes among the players.[27]

Therefore, counter-terrorism preparedness is not the simple and direct action it is represented to be in scenarios and simulations. 'Unexpected events' can be disruptive for the very enactment of exercises and actions that attempt to govern them. Counter-terrorism scenarios assume that the less we know about the enemy and the threat, the more we need to use our imagination. Introducing a theory of imagination within the generation and creation of security knowledge allows us to see that imagination is not the panacea of a 'new' security *dispositif* in the war on terror. Civil strategists during the Cold War attempted to limit the use of imagination by reducing the scope of perceptions and providing particular rational concepts which imagination was to mediate. For the anti-nuclear campaigners, productive imagination could be unleashed in the encounter with the potential catastrophe.

Confronted with the possibility of catastrophic unexpected events, counter-terrorist experts combine, we argue, the two roles of imagination. Extricating the different roles of imagination allows us to understand what exclusions are necessary, what processes are elided and what 'messiness' is ordered in the acquisition of security knowledge. Imagination is constitutive of security knowledge, while not being necessarily subordinated to rational frameworks. However, the 'failure of imagination' cannot be answered by the 'routinization of imagination'. The faculty of imagination is indispensable to knowledge production and understanding. In that sense, imagination is already 'routinized' in its reproductive function. The failure of imagination needs to be understood in relation to past and present sensations as well as existing conceptual frameworks; it also needs to be understood in its productive capacity that is not impeded by the sense-imagination-understanding continuum or by the shock of the sublime.

Collective imagination

Imagination, in its Kantian understanding, is a subject-centred process. Yet, imagination is also social and collective (Appadurai 2000: 6). Security experts share in a collective imagination that is not only cognitive in a subjective sense but also social. Imagination is not only a subject-centred and mentalist concept (Chakrabarty 2000: 178); it is also important for *common sense*, the sense that fits us in a community with others.[28] According to Robert Mitchell, the shift from a subjective to a collective sense of imagination took place in the eighteenth century:

> [T]he emergence of a collectivist concept of imagination within early eighteenth-century financial discourse often recontextualized older conceptions of this faculty, enabling satirists, for example, to map the dynamics of the imagination – its capacities for inversion and amplification – onto social relations.
>
> (Mitchell 2008: 119)

Imagination creates particular modes of sociality. This can become explicit in the role of leaders and leadership; leaders' imagination can imply the creation of enthusiasm in the masses that follow them. The collective imagination can also underpin other social formations: the nation as an 'imagined community' (Anderson 1991) is one such form of sociality.[29]

The collective imagination of security experts – particularly through the intervention of emergency planning and disaster management – mediates knowledge of both terrorism and dangerous subjects. In cases of unexpected and potentially catastrophic events, this subject is not only the terrorist, but also paradoxically the 'crowd' as a collective subject. The scenario for a preparedness exercise in the UK called 'Stage Fright', which took place in 2000, before the 9/11 attacks, offers an overwhelming range of detailed pre- and post-eventual information which points to a collective imagination of the crowd:

> It is Friday 24th March 2000, and you are in attendance at a Pop Concert at The National Stadium, Hampden Park.
>
> The act which is headlining is 'Tiny Murmur' who are currently one of the biggest bands in the charts. They are supported by the 'Bacon Boys' who recently shot to No. 1 with their debut single, and who are quickly attracting their own following.
>
> The concert is a sell out with a total of 54,500 fans in attendance. 17,000 fans are seated in the main stand, with 22,000 fans standing on the pitch area. The remaining 15,500 fans are seated on the east and west stands. Both the fans standing on the pitch area, and the fans seated in the East and West stands are allow unrestricted access to each other's area in a free flow arrangement. In effect, this allows fans to stand or sit as they wish.

Both acts appeal to a wide range of audiences. 'Tiny Murmur' have been in the business for over 15 years, and have a loyal following of older and younger fans. 'The Bacon Boys' are in the 'Boy Band' mould, and their following are predominantly although not exclusively teenagers and below. The make up of the crowd is predominantly female, and the younger fans are accompanied by their parents or other adults. [...]

There have been a number of arrests prior to the concert for drugs and alcohol offences. On the whole the crowd's spirits are high, and there is a general feeling of excited anticipation.

The concert begins at 19:00 hours.[30]

The detailed set out of the scenario in Stage Fright is not exceptional. Most scenarios consider such meticulous detail as the necessary paraphernalia to create a realistic impression. Scenarios, experts emphasize, need to appear as realistic and credible as possible while at the same time offering novel imaginations of the future disaster or catastrophe.

Yet, the abundance of details is not simply used with the purpose of achieving realism. Details also create a 'forensic' rather than 'foresight' imaginary typical of the conjectural style of reasoning. The details provide clues for the disaster to come and the responses to be undertaken. They offer material for the conjectural style of reasoning discussed in Chapter 3. For example, the distribution of exits and communication between the east and west stands in the stadium contains the anticipatory forensics of a chaotic and panicked crowd. The crowd is also gendered, scripted as overwhelmingly female, which creates increased resonances of panic and a need for protection. The explicit scenario is thus underpinned by an almost subterranean scenario, which contains clues, assumptions, ideas and perceptions. The crowd is already in a state of 'excited anticipation', while the previous arrests and offences function as premonitory signs of worse to come. This collective imagination of the crowd – reshuffled in many preparedness exercises – mediates experiences and representations of crowd panic and theories about crowd behaviour in crowd psychology, psychiatry and modelling.

In fact, in many of the post-9/11 scenarios, the crowd typifies the collective imagination of the subject of catastrophe. The 'crowd' has become entrenched as a subject through the constitution of 'crowded places' as objects of terrorist attacks. As the UK government has put it in a consultation document, *Working Together to Protect Crowded Places*, 'the trend is for terrorists to attack crowded public places, which represent targets with little or no protective security' (Home Office 2009a: 10). If crowded places are 'attractive targets for terrorists', then the 'crowd' is the subject to be managed and controlled in a catastrophic event (see Communities and Local Government and Home Office 2010). Former UK Home Secretary Jacqui Smith described the government's CONTEST (2009) counter-terrorism strategy as putting greater emphasis on tackling terrorism through 'civil challenge' in 2009. As the *Guardian* reported:

Smith said that 30,000 workers had been trained to help respond to a terror attack as part of the strategy, and said that programme would be extended to a further 30,000 people. The home secretary denied it amounted to 'snooping'. She said: 'If terrorists want to target crowded places, the places where we live, work and play, I think it's right that we put in place, as we have done, a programme of training for the people that manage our shopping centres, pubs, restaurants, clubs and hotels. That's what we're doing to help people be vigilant of the threat from terrorism and to deal with a terrorist attack were it to happen.'[31]

ARGUS exercises also play out the domestication of the collective imagination of crowds. The problem of terrorist attacks is that of public spaces and mobile crowds: 'In airports and stadiums you can monitor access, they are contained. Public spaces are not contained.'[32] Secure Futures, a UK-based company focusing on technological innovation to respond to national security challenges, formulates its crowded places programme in terms of panic and traditional crowd psychology:

> Crowds and public places are very difficult to protect and if tragedy or danger strikes, it can often mean mass casualties, major damage as well as widespread panic and fear. There is a loss of control, communication and containment.
>
> (Secure Futures 2010)

Containment of spaces resonates with the containment of crowds, which are depicted as affective gatherings, easily panicked and in need of leadership. Therefore, ARGUS exercises emphasize the importance of leaders who channel the energy of crowds and make decisions whether to 'evacuate' or 'invacuate'. The participants in the exercises learn about strategies to reassure and calm down crowds.

   The collective imagination of crowds in security knowledge is still redolent with the nineteenth-century psychology of crowds as formulated by Gustave le Bon.[33] For le Bon, crowds are destructive of liberal autonomy and individualism. Crowds are emotional and driven to extremes, he argues. Moreover, the behaviour of crowds relates directly to their imagination: 'How is the imagination of the crowds to be impressed?' (le Bon 1995: 62). The collective imagination of crowds works through contagion and suggestibility, rendering the crowd 'almost blind to truth'. The collective imagination of crowds is also opposed to the imagination of 'nations', 'peoples' or that of 'the public'.[34] Productive or creative imagination is thus rendered negative and transferred upon a panicked crowd. In the next chapter, we examine how this concern with the crowd has prompted a regime of practices through which the bodily senses of individual citizens are disciplined in staged encounters with unexpected and catastrophic futures in an attempt to literally deconstruct 'crowds' through individualization.

This chapter has argued that that imagination is constitutive of security knowledge. The injunction to make use of imagination to render the next terrorist attack or catastrophic weather event intelligible is not only about image and representation. Imagination creates the future as a new epistemic 'reality' by mediating between the senses and understanding. However, the faculty of imagination as a subjective faculty is not only reproductive; it can be productive of new concepts and even sensations. This productive capacity – often dented in the encounter with the sublime – is paradoxically reframed as an injunction to 'routinize' it.

The acquisition of security knowledge in the Cold War as well as the 'war on terror' has relied on the use of imagination, even if important changes have taken place. We have unpacked different ways in which imagination can be mobilized and linked to strategies of risk management. For strategic theorists, game theory was the preferred tool for imagining nuclear war and for making the unthinkable thinkable. Imagination served a governmental purpose within the rationality of risk management, as the knowledge produced as 'future history' contributed to making an uncertain future controllable and amenable. For the anti-nuclear war movement, however, imagination was to be unbounded. They urged individuals to think of the unthinkable in all its radical alterity. In the war on terror, both strategies have been reconciled by security experts. On the one hand, imagination mediates sensations and concepts that are presented through scenarios and simulations while, on the other, it is 'in regress', given the overwhelming of the senses by the sublime. Nonetheless, as Kant was well aware, imagination cannot function outside experience and perception. Ultimately, the creation of security knowledge about the future depends upon the triad imagination-sensations-concepts rather than on imagination alone.

6   Aesthetics of catastrophe

Sensing the unexpected

In the previous chapter, we have shown that imagination acquires epistemic primacy in relation to the unknown and the unexpected. Given the injunction to imagine the catastrophe to come and to anticipate the unexpected, it is important to consider the transformation of processes of cognition and understanding. Although imagination – as both a subjective and collective process – works in relation to sensorial perceptions and understanding, the radical uncertainty associated with thinking unexpected and potentially catastrophic events appeared to set imagination as the dominant term in this triangulation. Either through synthesis or through separation, the 'disorderly' potential of imagination is kept at bay, even if it is invoked through the sublime catastrophe. Nonetheless, as we have shown, the emphasis on imagination as a sort of panacea to the security problems professionals are confronted with does not do away with the function of the senses in the constitution of security knowledge. Imagination draws on the resources of sensorial stimuli.

In this chapter, we explore the ways in which a sensorial regime of anticipation is created, deployed and managed as a particular mode of knowledge in itself. To this purpose, we draw upon an understanding of *aesthetics* as action upon the senses to explore the ways in which aesthetic technologies are constitutive of anticipatory knowledge of the catastrophe to come. Unknown unknowns and the unexpected depend upon a sensorium of anticipation which needs to be created. Subjects are invited to inhabit the future catastrophe and make use of sensorial knowledge. Just as the unknown modified the epistemic status of imagination, the unexpected challenges the epistemic role of the human sensorium. The sensorial regime of anticipation is increasingly disconnected, we argue, from thought. Moreover, by working upon the senses, this anticipatory regime interpellates subjects not just through fear but through seduction and pleasure. Preparedness exercises can be, for instance, theatrical sites rather than sites of fear and anxiety.

This chapter begins by considering how an aesthetic regime of the senses is mobilized in the field of knowledge to foster perceptions of the catastrophe to come. The human senses are not simply one element in the process of knowledge production – sensorial perceptions can transform the rules of other styles of reasoning without contradicting them. The chapter then goes on to argue that risk models, preparedness and citizen vigilance take place in an aesthetic modality which works upon the human senses and creates a sensorium attuned to catastrophe. The aesthetics of catastrophe entails modalities of tactilizing the senses in order to render the future palpable and foster subjects who can inhabit the future not just through fear and anxiety but also through desire. Insurance, preparedness and vigilance are three strategies in which the senses are made actionable. Similarly to imagination, sensorial perceptions are fostered in order to fill the imagined space of the future. Finally, we consider how this emerging aesthetic regime is integrated within particular forms of cognition through an epistemology of conjecture and forms of conjectural mapping, which, we argue, needs to be understood in relation and in opposition to Fredric Jameson's 'cognitive mapping' (Jameson 1988).

Aesthetics as sensorial regime

In style with the fashion in international relations theory to speak of theoretical and empirical orientations in terms of turns, Roland Bleiker (2009, 2001) has recently identified an aesthetic turn in international political theory. Although this claim has been contested by others for whom aesthetics 'remains a minority interest, routinely ghettoized' (Danchev and Lisle 2009: 778), the past decade has witnessed the appearance of a growing number of articles and journals on world politics that draw on aesthetic resources such as poetry, visual culture, popular culture, literature, photography and notions of the sublime.[1] Generally, these contributions consider the ways in which art intervenes in social and political problems, and resists or reinforces domination (Jabri 2006).

The questions of catastrophe, the unexpected and the unknown appear to tilt the aesthetics of catastrophe towards the sublime, which Jean-François Lyotard (1994) has called the unrepresentable. For him, art should relate to catastrophe through a particular form of negativity, which provides art's only escape from being hijacked for ideological and totalitarian purposes. After all, the 'aestheticization of politics' under fascism and the 'politicization of aesthetics' in the Soviet Union made art complicit in both the concentration camp and Gulag. Instead of defining utopia, art should bear witness to the catastrophe of ideological meta-narratives by bringing to light the irreconcilable gap separating art from reality. Art can help prevent the catastrophe from happening only by preserving the memory of the unbridgeable separation between life and art. As Bleiker argues: 'Aesthetic approaches embark on a direct political encounter, for they engage the gap that inevitably opens up between a form of representation and the object it seeks to represent' (Bleiker 2009: 21). The sublime appears as an ambivalent moment of both opening and closure as subjects are 'encouraged to *overcome* these difficult feelings through the use of reason, the enjoyment of catharsis and the promise of transcendence' (emphasis in original) (Lisle 2006: 843). What Debbie Lisle notes about exhibitions on war and violence is also valid for other disasters and catastrophes. Aric Mayer (2008), for instance, has argued that the aesthetics of catastrophe either relies on the documentary realism style to create empathy or on the landscape style to depict the breadth of the event.

Catastrophic futures – from the next terrorist attack to the next pandemic or climate change – appear to mirror the problem of the unrepresentable. Yet, in as much as the unknown is not the opposite of knowledge, the unrepresentable is not necessarily the limit of representation. Rather, both instantiate a boundary, a form of partition of the sensible in which modalities of knowledge are renegotiated. Against the current tendency to conflate the meaning of aesthetics with art, it may therefore be useful to recall that the Greek word *aistheta* referred more broadly to that which could be perceived by the senses (Leslie 2000: 34). For Alexander Baumgarden in the eighteenth century, aesthetics was a science of the 'lower cognitive power' (sense perceptions). Aesthetic experience is different from rational, cognitive experience as it opposes intuition and feeling to logic and reason. The basis for aesthetic judgement is subjective: 'Aesthetic value might be measured by the ability of a thing perceived to engender vivid experience in the viewer' (Leslie 2000: 35).

According to Terry Eagleton, German aesthetics was born as a supplement to pure reason (Eagleton 1990), while English empiricists reduced all cognition to aesthetics. For Kant, however, the two are neither entirely separated nor collapsed onto each other. Aesthetics becomes a particular moment and instantiation of cognition that does not judge things according to their purpose, but merely according to their form. The Kantian-inspired understanding of aesthetics as a priori forms of sensibility comprises everything that 'takes root in the gaze and the guts and all that arises from our most banal, biological insertion in the world' (Eagleton 1990: 13). Although Kant's distinction between taste as the 'proper' realm of aesthetic judgement and the lesser interest in the agreeable and disagreeable is thought to be the start of a modern understanding of aesthetics as a theory of art (Bowie 2003, Adorno 2004), we take aesthetics to comprise the whole human sensorium rather than just contemplative judgements of taste. Aesthetics applies to sensible experience that takes not art but the body as its object: 'Aesthetics is born as a discourse of the body'.

As it works on the body, aesthetics is not just about subjective judgement but also pertains to the social as the senses can be mobilized for governmental purposes. Eagleton has argued that the increased relevance of aesthetics in bourgeois societies was a reaction to the need of organizing social life in the wake of the demise of feudal institutions:

> The ultimate binding force of the bourgeois social order, in contrast to the coercive apparatus of absolutism, will be habits, pieties, sentiments and affections. And this is equivalent to saying that power in such an

> order has become aestheticized. It is at one with the body's spontane-
> ous impulses, entwined with sensibility and the affections, lived out in
> unreflective custom. Power is now inscribed in the minutiae of subjec-
> tive experience, and the fissure between abstract duty and pleasurable
> inclination is accordingly healed.
>
> (Eagleton 1990: 13)

In the eighteenth century, aesthetics held the promise of a 'non-polemical, consensual framing of the common world' (Rancière 2004a: 18) and carried the possibility of 'a community of subjects now linked by sensuous impulse and fellow-feeling rather than by heteronomous law, each safeguarded in its unique particularity while bound at the same time into social harmony' (Eagleton 1990: 28). Aesthetics creates a community of senses in the absence of law, or of knowledge and predictability. As capitalism isolated individuals whose relations were mediated only through abstract rights, aesthetic prac- tices focused on bodily habits had to 'cohere an otherwise abstract, atomized social order' (Eagleton 1990: 231).

The senses also provide a reservoir for power to exploit and a territory to take hold of. Aesthetics, therefore, 'signifie[d] a creative turn to the sen- suous body, as well as an inscribing of that body with a subtly oppressive law' (Eagleton 1990: 9). In that sense, aesthetics is somewhat parallel to the Foucauldian analysis of the creation of 'docile bodies' through systems of surveillance, although the former does not break up the body into daily patterns but focuses on sensations and perceptions as a source of knowing. Jacques Rancière has reformulated this understanding of aesthetics in the contemporary context through reference to aesthetics as the entire 'distri- bution of the sensible' (*le partage du sensible*) (Rancière 2004b, 2005). The sensible needs to be understood not as reason or reasonableness, but as both perception and what is perceived and perceivable. By framing perceptions and self-perceptions, aesthetics establishes a particular relation between the senses, the individual and the community. Aesthetics is intrinsically linked to the configuration and reconfiguration of space and time through which certain forms of speech and visibility are rendered perceptible. According to Rancière, aesthetic practices 'suspend the ordinary coordinates of sens- ory experience and reframe the network of relationships between spaces and times, subjects and objects, as well as the common and the singular' (Rancière 2009: 25).[2]

In this reading, aesthetics is related primarily to the human sensorium and historically and socially constituted sensorial experience. It is about pleasure and pain, about feelings that emerge in relation to sensations. Art of course partakes in the distribution of the sensible and the configuration of community through configuring our perception of speech and visibility.[3] It is hardly surprising, therefore, that bureaucracies have found inspiration in (popular) art to develop an aesthetics of the unexpected. The unexpec- ted is not only that which is not expected, waited or hoped for, but also that which is not seen (from Latin *spectare*). The expected and unexpected are etymologically entwined with seeing and the senses. As the senses mediate the relation to the unexpected, we can speak of an aesthetic regime of anticipation. The aestheticization of catastrophe in popular culture and art has relevance beyond beauty or the sublime; it is a way of being that mobilizes affections of the body in response to sense information and invites subjects to inhabit catastrophic futures. Aesthetics works on the senses, while imagination links perceptions achieved through the senses with forms of understanding. Aesthetics is therefore an indispensable element of all modes of knowledge and styles of reasoning. The experimental style of reasoning has its own sensorial experiences; so do computer simulations. However, when the unknown and the unexpected are problematized as the limits of knowledge, the experience of the future needs to be sensorially created. The sensorial regime, we contend, becomes increasingly disconnected from particular styles of reasoning and even acquires a life of its own.

A blog by an environmental journalist entitled 'Artists desperately needed to inspire change' sets out the privileged position that art has for creating 'feelings' of the future: 'Knowledge does not often inspire action. Feelings like compassion and anger do. Good art generates passion. The point is that the artists' view is invaluable precisely because they are not experts and do not have the authority granted by science. They are only as persuasive as their images' (Leahy 2008). At the limits of knowledge and predictability, art is called upon to confirm and repair the social bonds of an order threatened by a catastrophic future.

Al Gore's documentary *An Inconvenient Truth* successfully exploits graphs, PowerPoint, images and movement to convey an image of imminent catastrophe. The sense of impending catastrophe is felt through well-orchestrated movements such as Gore going up a ladder to reach the end of a graph which has itself gone through the roof! The Hollywood blockbuster *The Day after Tomorrow* is thought to have shaped the public's understanding of the impact of climate change, despite its inaccurate scientific depictions. Enacting the catastrophe to come fictionally can create more 'realistic' and 'plausible' situations than scientific data.[4] For similar reasons, the Ken Sprague Fund started the International Political Cartoon Competition:

> Cartoons can reach parts that other arguments can't. We have been inundated with doom-laden predictions and scientific facts on the inevitability of global warming, but here we can exorcise our fears. Powerful, uncompromising and uncomfortable images bring home to us what it will really mean – not a Costa del Sol on the Welsh coast and palm trees in the garden, but desertification, hunger and poverty.[5]
>
> (Adam 2008)

As Rancière (2004) has noted about art in general, artistic renderings of catastrophe become a form of social mediation or 'public service'. For instance, the former Danish Climate Minister, Connie Hedegaard, sponsored a collection of poems on global warming in an attempt to raise awareness about climate change (Grotrian *et al.* 2008). Lloyds of London has commissioned a book of poems on the subject of climate change as part of their 360 Risk Insight project. The rationale for the project has been that '[e]veryone is waking up to the dangers of global warming and environmental damage, and it is only right that poets and poetry should be contributing in an active way to communicating this crucial message both within and beyond the financial community' (Lloyds 2008). A 2008 exhibition at Tate Modern imagined London under unrelenting rain and used Tate Modern as a shelter for people and artworks (Morgan 2008). The aesthetic mobilization of the senses does not work solely through climate change-related art. TV productions such as *24* or *The Agency* are thought to have played an important role in the public's understanding of terrorism (Zizek 2006, Erickson 2007, Hoskins 2006, Grusin 2010). In 2006, a comic book adaptation of the 9/11 Commission Report was published and sold on Amazon (Jacobson and Colon 2006).

Aesthetics, then, refers neither to the gap between representation and its object (Bleiker 2009), nor to the abstraction of art practice (Sylvester 2001). These cultural forms, from sci-fi movies to computer games, function beyond the confines of art as an aesthetics of catastrophe. Even though we see art emerging as a core element in governing catastrophic futures, it is necessary to situate these productions in the larger perspective of an aesthetics that governs the full sensorium of subjects: taste, feeling, touch, nerves, and emotions. They need to be understood in a broader sense as technologies that govern the perceptible and the sensible. Alongside art, computer simulations or visualizations are also mobilized in the sensorial regime.

Risk sensorium: modelling catastrophe

At first sight, calculations of risk and aesthetics seem to belong to two different realms. Risk management is generally considered as the art of the rational, objective and the calculable, while aesthetics refers to the domain of perceptions and the senses. Technologies of risk management address a rational, calculable subject that prudently assesses and minimizes the risks that could happen to her. The senses and desires of the body have been relegated to the realm of moral hazards in insurance practices. Sensuous reactions are to be suppressed as much as possible, as they are thought to stand in the way of an objective assessment, evaluation and management of risks (Sunstein 2002). Swiss Re, a leading reinsurance company, deplores that 'the public debate about risks of the future is often dominated by equally irresponsible scaremongering and trivializing reassurance, both of which hamper any attempt at rational risk management' (Swiss Re 2004: 6). The World Economic Forum (WEF) 2009 report on global risks similarly observes that '[w]hen faced with risks, humans often respond in ways that are deeply rooted in their physiological and neurological make-up. Fear, doubt, fight or flight are all emotions and responses that limit our capacity for rational decision-making' (World Economic Forum 2009: 12).

Rendering the unknown of catastrophe actionable as a risk is, we have argued, a modality of making it knowable through particular styles of reasoning. Just as imagination is an intrinsic part of knowledge production, aesthetics also underpins all forms of knowledge. However, the recourse to aesthetics in anticipation of catastrophic futures becomes legitimate, even where risk management has long denied any role for aesthetics.[6] For some, this is rooted in the acknowledgement that in the confrontation with a fundamentally unknowable future, subjects can no longer ground their decisions and choices in knowledge. The ideal of a prudent citizen, presupposed by risk managers, who rationally calculates the costs and benefits of her actions unravels at the horizon of an unknown and unexpected future. As Slavoj Žižek observes: 'There is a priori no proper measure between the "excess" of scaremongering and the indecisive procrastination of "Don't let's panic, we don't yet have conclusive results"' (Žižek 1999: 336). Engin Isin has also pointed out the emergence of the neurotic citizen who 'is incited to make social and cultural investments to eliminate various dangers by calibrating its conduct on the basis of its anxieties and insecurities rather than rationalities'. Contrary to the Foucault-inspired understanding of subjects as bionic citizens, as disciplined and docile bodies, the neurotic citizen 'is also invited to consider itself as part of a neurological species and understand itself as an affect structure' (Isin 2004: 223, see also Walklate and Mythen 2010). According to Žižek and Isin, these shifts in subjectivity have not been fully appreciated by the risk literature, where the self-reflexivity associated with catastrophic and de-bounded risks in the world risk society is seen as pre-eminently a cognitive rational strategy independent of the material and sensorial frames that underpin knowledge and subjective relations to social practices (see Elliott 1995).

Isin identifies the shift towards a neurotic citizen as a move beyond risk. Although governing subjects through neurosis certainly has become more outspoken in a range of realms, it is important to stress that these elements have always been part of risk management. The bionic citizen and the neurotic citizen are not of two completely different orders, but are folded upon each other in risk management. Rather than the neurotic subject versus the bionic subject, one could perhaps speak of the aesthetic subject, who is governed through the senses as much as through knowledge. Cognition itself does not function in the absence of the senses and imagination. Cognition is about the 'desire to grasp what is given to the senses' (Arendt 1978: 57). Even though risk managers continue to oppose rational calculability to aesthetics and the catastrophe sensorium, the divide between statistical and probable knowledge on the one hand and sensorial enactments on the other is not sustainable. Perceptual data is continually hooked up to statistical tools that enable the taming of future. For risk managers, therefore, the aesthetics of catastrophe appears as both necessary and problematic. On the one hand, perceptions and feelings are disavowed; on the other, risk managers tap into sense perceptions to increase rational decision-making:

> [R]ecent research shows the importance of reframing the probability dimension so that people pay attention to the consequences of an event. Rather than specifying that the chance of a disaster occurring next year is greater than 1 in 100, experts could indicate that the chances of a disaster occurring in the next 25 years exceeds 1 in 5 ... Empirical studies have shown that people are much more likely to overcome their risk misperception and to consider undertaking protective measures when they focus on a probability of greater than 1 in 5 over 25 years rather than 1 in 100 next year because the longer time horizon is above their threshold level of concern.
>
> (World Economic Forum 2009: 12)

Although the probabilities are exactly the same, the objective data is nevertheless perceived differently when the time frame is altered. Hence, the appeal to rational, objective reasoning relies upon the manipulation of perceptions.

Risk management requires an aesthetic sensibility in the sense that Kant gave to this term. Risk models of catastrophes perpetuate statistical knowledge with the addendum of aesthetic enactment, as is clear for instance from Swiss Re's *Global Risk Landscape* report. Although the report argues that '[f]or the purposes of risk management, prophecies of doom ... are of little practical use; they describe developments – although conceivable in detail with a great deal of imagination – we do not yet know whether they may become reality' (Swiss Re 2004: 10), it is peppered with full-page images, mainly from sci-fi novels and films.

Once statistical and probabilistic knowledge faces the limit of the unexpected and the unknown, aesthetics becomes a technology that can give free rein to the human sensorium for the governance of catastrophic events. In creating a parallel flow of aesthetic perceptions to calculations of risk, the Swiss Re report establishes aesthetics as a parallel mode of knowledge based on conjectural reasoning. It is apparently set at a distance from the risk calculations – however, the images of a different 'world' work in conjunction with risk calculations. Interestingly, these pictures become increasingly dystopian through the report. If the front picture is optimistically titled 'the sky is the limit' and the two following images still symbolize future progress captured by man's colonization of the moon, the final picture presents a rather bleaker image of the future.[7] Under the heading 'preparing for the future', there is an image of a NASA vessel leaving Earth, suggesting perhaps that at some point in the future it may well be necessary to leave Earth as a result of global catastrophes. As such, it reinforces the report's claim that today's world is characterized by fewer accidents (the manageable by-products of industrial progress) and more catastrophes (Swiss Re 2004: 13).

Figure 6.1 An image from Swiss Re's 2004 *Global Risk Landscape* report depicting the eponymous hero of Jonathan Swift's *Gulliver's Travels* looking up at the floating city of Laputa. © akg-images

At the same time, the aesthetics of anticipation does not simply run parallel to other modes of knowledge. Knowledge cannot be separated from an aesthetic element. Risk models and probability calculations have an aesthetic quality themselves. Aesthetics is not just a supplement to rational risk models, but is also the very form in which these risk models appear. There is beauty and pleasure in illustrations and abstract graphs that structure our risk perceptions. Catastrophe risk models do not just discipline the sensuous apprehension of the world or subsume it to rational calculability, they become sensorial data that constitute the material of anticipatory cognition among security professionals as well as ordinary citizens. Insurance companies, for instance, increasingly rely on modelling the impact of worst case scenarios such as the impact of a dirty bomb detonating in a major American city. RMS has incorporated 3D modelling of the effects of bomb explosions on American soil into its probabilistic calculations of catastrophic risk exposure.

The register of the senses is exploited in the management of risk as an attempt to render the unknown future material and palpable. As risk management heavily relies upon a sensuous apprehension of the unexpected,

Figure 6.2 Risk Management Solutions incorporates 3D modelling of the effects of bomb explosions on American soil into its probabilistic calculations of catastrophic risk exposure. © 2010 Risk Management Solutions

the modes of relating to the future become increasingly aestheticized. When the future cannot be known, let alone predicted, expecting the unexpected falls back on the senses as the dominant way of relating to the future.

Preparedness as aesthetic enactment

The aesthetics of catastrophe is not restricted to catastrophe risk modelling. Increasingly, security professionals, high-level officials, civil servants, emergency responders as well as ordinary citizens are required by law to take part in exercises and simulations or become the eyes and ears of security experts. As such, we suggest, they are increasingly regimented within the sensorial regime of future catastrophic events. Although this may take place at different sites – from public spaces and artistic expressions to preparedness exercises – surprise and novelty require subjects to inhabit the future. As we shall see, the mobilization of the senses is both pleasurable (it is fun to take part in exercises or read cartoons) and disciplining. Instead of subjects being coerced into being vigilant and prepared, they are mobilized in a more playful sense that arrives at the conjunction of power and aesthetics. Nonetheless, they contribute to what Louise Amoore (2007) has referred to as a watchful politics acted out through vigilant visualities. Seeing the future is primarily about foresight and the anticipation of the unknown event. However, sight is not the only sense activated by exercises: rather, a vigilant synaesthetics is at work. By making the unexpected visible and perceivable, preparedness exercises stage an encounter with the future in which subjects are not just spectators but active participants.

Aesthetics coexists, alongside imagination, as part of a governmental regime in which the governance of future events needs to be continually improved through re-imagination and re-enactment. How do rehearsals of the future become particular ways of acting upon the senses and creating a catastrophe sensorium? How do they turn specific ways of seeing and perceiving into tools to prevent terrorism? If imagination helps to make present that which is absent, preparedness exercises offer the opportunity to inhabit the imagined future sensuously. Preparedness has been defined as both a state of anticipation and the ability to effectively respond to an attack (Purpura 2007). As Chapter 3 has shown, preparedness knowledge is produced through exercises and simulations. However, imagination does not exhaust how we relate to the unknown future. Although Edward Borodzicz has defined *mental modelling* as sufficient to identify an appropriate strategy to tackle the impact and consequences of an emergency (Borodzicz 2005: 79), exercises also entail a form of practical knowledge that emerges out of action alongside imagination: they transform anticipation into action (Godet and Roubelat 1996: 164).

Driven by NATO and US initiatives, exercises have become widespread across the world and are targeted at various professional levels. From the series of TOPOFF exercises in the US, which involved high-level professionals and up to 10,000 participants representing more than 200 international, federal, state, local, tribal and private agencies and organizations, to the KRISØV exercises in Denmark, which bring together over 300 persons from 40 different authorities with the purpose of preventing, managing and recovering from a catastrophe, to Project ARGUS in the UK, which targeted businesses and comprised about 20 to 50 participants per session, the form and remit of exercises and scenarios vary enormously. What these exercises have in common is that they seek to test emergency plans to locate gaps in emergency management: '*Exercise* is the generic term for a range of activities that test emergency response readiness, evaluate an emergency response plan, and assess the success of training and development programs' (emphasis in original) (New York Consortium for Emergency Planning Continuing Education 2007). Exercises allow for corrections, lessons to be learned, and the training of staff in an attempt for continual improvement for the encounter with the 'real' catastrophe. According to the Civil Contingencies Secretariat in the UK: 'Planning for emergencies cannot be considered reliable until it is exercised and has proved to be workable, especially since false confidence may be placed in the integrity of a written plan' (Civil Contingencies Secretariat 2009). Thus, Aragon exercise in the UK, a preparedness exercise for civil nuclear installations, formulated its objectives as 'tests': testing the operation of the Local Emergency Centre; testing the operation of the Central Emergency Support Centre; testing arrangements for the provision of information to the media; and testing the strategic decision-making process at the Local Emergency Centre (British Nuclear Group 2007).

The move away from the archival-statistical knowledge involved in risk prevention to an enactment knowledge produced by acting out future threats (Collier 2008: 225) depends on exercises to create new sensorial perceptions of the world. This is illustrated nicely by Project ARGUS (introduced in Chapter 5), set up by the National Counter-Terrorist Security Office (NaCTSO). ARGUS is a combination of multimedia simulation and tabletop (i.e. role-play, realism) exercises where participants explore a scenario in groups and in conversation with an expert panel. The exercises are led by Counter-Terrorism Security Advisers (CTSAs) in collaboration with the Fire and Rescue Service, Health Emergency Services and Local Authority Emergency Planners. The emphasis is on discussing a specific set of problems that the scenario raises and possible ways to respond to them. As the same time, the exercises also depict a scenario, through audio and/or audiovisual media, which takes place in real time, and asks players to make decisions in the event of a terrorist attack, which means that elements of tabletop and live exercises are incorporated.

Project ARGUS combines a series of video and audio materials to develop a credible terrorist attack scenario to which participants are expected to respond (NaCTSO 2008). The project does not address the public at large, but focuses on those in charge of crowded places such as business representatives and safety managers. By July 2008, an estimate of 460 ARGUS exercises had been held across the UK for primarily retail businesses in crowded places (House of Lords 2008). A section of the project, ARGUS Professional, focuses on the role of architects and designers in building design. Here, the professional skills of participants are emphasized as counter-terrorism tools. Participants are informed that their specific knowledge and skills make them responsible for endeavouring to prevent terrorist attacks at the planning and design stages of any development. There are two other primary packages, one aimed at workers in the retail industry and one aimed at those involved in the night-time economy, as well as bespoke or adapted events for hotel workers and so on. Similarly to ARGUS Professional, the Retail and Night Time Economy (NTE) ARGUS packages seek responses from assembled members of the business community to the question of what their response would be in the event of an attack, and what plans they already have in place, or could develop, to deal with the effects of the scenario on their own business. Much like the Professional package, the expertise of participants as a counter-terrorism tool is emphasized: people who guard nightclub doors become surveillance features, the management skills of shop workers make them the people most likely to cope with taking control and restoring order in a situation characterized by panic and chaos, and so on.

The exercises are a feed-forward mechanism for further scenario planning and training as a result of the gaps identified in preparedness through the enactment of a scenario. In that sense, they function as rehearsals rather than performances (Davis 2007). The appropriation of the disastrous future through exercises is largely sensuous. A key assumption of Project ARGUS is that preparedness requires members of business communities and professional groups to 'expect the unexpected', to govern themselves through reference to a future wrought with uncertainty to be certain that they can respond. In the absence of knowledge, aesthetics can reframe space and time by regimenting our senses in such a way that the unexpected can be sensed and synthesized in intuition. Faced with the unknowns of surprise and novelty, preparedness exercises focus cognition on the sensorial input.

At the same time, preparedness is an exercise in normalizing reactions to the unexpected. Preparations in the present – from gathering plans for buildings, lists of employees and clear delimitations of roles according to existing work hierarchies – mean that the future is normalized on the model of the present. This does not necessarily imply that the future is simply an extended present, as Helga Nowotny (1985) has suggested. The unexpected raises the problem of creating sensorial mappings of the future in the present. Thus, Project ARGUS in the UK advises attention to behaviours that are 'out of place' or 'out of normal pace': activity inconsistent with the nature of the building or location and normal activity that is repeated abnormally often. Spatial and temporal inadequacy are the two elements that define suspicious behaviour and which are to be located through the mediation of the senses. Hence, the Metropolitan Police Service (UK) narrates suspicious behaviours as follows:

Terrorists have to live somewhere. They store their equipment and materials somewhere. They need vehicles. They have people who help them – and these people might come and go at strange times of the day and night. They may make unusual financial transactions or use false documents to hide their real identities. They may be behaving differently to how you've known them to behave in the past.

(Metropolitan Police 2006)

Sensorial perceptions are not just induced through exercises. Art, serving as an instrument of public service, also plays a role in the mobilization of the senses with the objective to be ready for the next catastrophe. FEMA, for example, has created a website dedicated to preparing children for disasters and catastrophes. The website is replete with cartoon images. Claiming that 'Being a Disaster Action Kid is Fun!' and that 'Disaster Action Kids are prepared!', the site is illustrative of the conjunction between pleasure and discipline in aesthetic forms of power.

Injunctions of vigilance entail a politics of distrust. The 'If you suspect it, report it' campaign in the UK raises distrust to the level of everyday sensorial experience. Integrated both within the ARGUS simulations and publicized in the form of posters, suspicion becomes tactilized as sensorial experience.

You can become a FEMA Disaster Action Kid and get a certificate! Disaster Action Kids also get to be part of a special E-mail group, and will receive exciting news and information directly from FEMA on a regular basis.

a Disaster Action Kid is Fun! Disaster Action Kids are prepared! They know what items are needed in a disaster supply kit. They know how to protect their pets during a disaster. They also know what to do during each type of disaster. Being a Disaster Action Kid isn't easy, but it's worth it! Get your friends involved, too. All you need to do is read about disasters on this site, do the activities and test your knowledge.

When your checklist is complete, fill in this form to get a certificate with your name on it. Then just print it out!

FEMA.gov | DHS.gov | Kids.gov | Important Notices | Site Help

Figure 6.3 In the US, FEMA has created a website dedicated to preparing children for disasters and catastrophes (http://www.fema.gov/kids). © 2010 FEMA

The fostering of vigilant visualities has been defined as undermining trust in society – shopping, commuting, going out are all reframed as risky activities, where even one's neighbours can be potential sources of danger. Although suspicious behaviours are left open to whatever is not normal, out of place, unexpected (Project ARGUS), counter-terrorist experts have increasingly drawn out lists of behaviours and places to be watched. The US project 'IWatch' lists the following behaviours and activities to report:

- People drawing or measuring important buildings.
- Strangers asking questions about security or building security procedures.
- Briefcase, suitcase, backpack, or package left behind.
- Cars or trucks left in No Parking zones in front of important buildings.
- Intruders in secure areas where they are not supposed to be.
- Chemical smells or fumes that worry you.
- People asking questions about sensitive information such as building blueprints, security plans, or VIP travel schedules without a right or need to know.
- Purchasing supplies or equipment that can be used to make bombs or weapons or purchasing uniforms without having the proper credentials.[8]

The rationale for the need to see, watch, touch and smell abnormal behaviours – a US advertisement literally asks 'Can you smell a terrorist'? – is explained by dry reconnaissance. Suspected terrorists need to 'undertake rehearsal trips as a practice exercise to areas they plan to attack in an attempt to ensure their plans can be carried out to the letter' (Norfolk Constabulary 2008). As Ann Larabee has remarked:

> Watches, knapsacks, cassette players, contact lens cases, and suitcases have become the new 'lethal technologies' remaking the ordinary world into a place of apocalyptic violence. Thus, uncertainties about the potential dangers inherent in technological systems have shifted to external, pathological agents who invade, disrupt, and destroy passive structures .
> (Larabee 1999: 148)

Social relations are mediated through the senses, which have come to play a pivotal role in the knowledge of catastrophic events. Everyday and unexceptional artefacts such as watches, shoes, suitcases become the perceivable signs of a dangerous future. In the ACPO-Metropolitan Police campaign in 2006, vigilance was said to render the world transparent, visible and representable. Particular types of behaviour appear suspicious, from taking photographs in public spaces to the unmistakeable white van, which has been one of the fixtures of counter-terrorist simulations from the IRA era to that of Al-Qaeda. A BBC Council DVD on how to prepare for terrorist attacks in shopping areas from 1999 features the white van which is found outside the shopping

Figures 6.4 and 6.5 Posters from the Metropolitan Police's 'If you suspect it, report it' campaign. © 2006 Metropolitan Police and Association of Chief Police Officers, UK

centre in the wake of the attack (British Council 1999). After 9/11, the white van still precedes the attack in simulations. Visual fixtures frame the social space. Yet, this topology of the human sensorium is inadequate as a topology of the social. Understanding sociality entails a particular relation between knowledge and the senses. Moreover, it requires an understanding of the senses as socially located and historically constructed.

In preparedness exercises and vigilance campaigns, the senses become directly linked with action. Post-9/11 counter-terrorism exercises and simulations such as ARGUS do not attempt to understand what happens and relate sensuous impressions to a conceptual understanding. To the contrary, the emphasis is on response and preparedness. The circumstances of a crisis, the situation from which it appears, are basically of no interest to the exercise. For example, the situation explored in ARGUS is that of normal everyday life – the pre-evental circumstances of the bomb explosion are not explored. While the Retail package situates its event in a paradigm of Islamic terrorism through the audible cry of a bomber who shouts 'Allah Akbar' before the explosion, the emphasis remains on response. Suicide bombers are not political actors but become literally objectified through the labelling of 'person-borne' devices for participants to either detect and prevent from exploding, or from which to calculate a likely damage level that such a device would cause so that participants can factor that into their responses. The CTSAs refer to these pre-evental circumstances as simply international terrorism. Even though it is somewhat taken for granted in ARGUS sessions that Al-Qaeda is the driving force behind international terrorism, the term is both vague and flexible enough to fit different types of emergencies.

The question is not what happened but how to act – the unexpected does not leave time for cognition, but relates action directly to sensorial input. The emphasis is on response and preparedness, not on understanding the meaning of the attack. Subjects are not supposed to think themselves but are meant to act on the basis of sensorial stimulations. Preparedness reduces cognition to the possibility of sensing the unexpected. Even when citizens are asked to convey information to the police, this exchange remains at the sensorial level – for example, 'What do you see?', 'What type of gun is it?' – rather than providing cognitive information about a situation. Sensations are no longer materials for the purposes of cognition. Sensations are fostered as cognition itself, cognition which is overtaken by imagination. Being in touch with reality becomes simply collecting and reporting stimuli. This is evident from the ways in which everyday activities become the subject of counter-terrorist action over and against common sense. As such, the aesthetics of catastrophe offers an uneasy reminder about the illusion that the abstract and 'cold' rationality of statistical and probabilistic knowledge could be counter-acted by the concrete knowledge of embodiment and the senses: Project ARGUS and a growing number of campaigns to locate and report suspicious behaviours have resulted in photographers increasingly becoming the target of police action. The acting subject is the sensorial subject. The simulation links sensations and perceptions directly to action.

Conjectural mapping

The aesthetics of catastrophe entails reliance upon the senses to locate the 'clue' in the present behaviour or traces from the past that could be indicative of a future event. However, clues do not emerge only through the mediation of the human sensorium. They are also activated through specific technologies of 'mapping'. Mapping does not refer only to social network theories and their conceptualization of ties, clusters and reach of particular organizational forms. Mapping is understood here as a cartographic capacity of representing the real world. Unlike geographers imagining maps so detailed that they are able to capture the totality of territories, mapping the catastrophe to come is a technology focused on the clue, on representing conjectural relations that may reveal the 'secret' of the 'hidden reality'.

The sensorial regime of anticipation is taken up at different sites where it interacts with other modes of knowledge: models of risk are integrated within insurance calculations, simulations and exercises become part of emergency planning, and sensorial data submitted by citizens is input into databases. The form of knowledge that emerges in these different sites is a mapping of increasing connectivities of digital data. Sensorial input is entwined with the proliferation of data under a digitally managed system of knowledge. In a sense, these systems can be seen as attempts to recapture a pre-Kantian empiricist form of knowledge which is exclusively mediated through the senses by eliminating doubt or shifting to a higher authority (that of the intelligence expert and the database). The data that is gathered from citizens is entered into police databases and processed. Nonetheless, as the 9/11 Commission Report reminded us, dots or clouds of data are insufficient – it is necessary to connect the dots. Connecting the dots is pursued through correlations and patterns that algorithms might throw out rather than through the old-fashioned model of scientific knowledge: hypothesis, testing and modelling (Anderson 2008). The WEF's Risk Interconnection Map is a good case in point. Bringing together a wide variety of geopolitical, economic, environmental, social and technological risks, its objective is to map the interconnectivity of these risks. However, the lines between the different risks represent not directions of causal relations between these risks but conjectural correlations.

Nonetheless, mapping has become an important technology of data gathering. The sensorial regime of anticipation is a digital regime, which amasses vast quantities of data:

> At the petabyte scale, information is not a matter of simple three- and four-dimensional taxonomy and order but of dimensionally agnostic statistics. It calls for an entirely different approach, one that requires us to lose the tether of data as something that can be visualized in its totality. It forces us to view data mathematically first and establish a context for it later.
>
> (Anderson 2008)

For the purposes of databases, knowledge is understood as a 'pattern that is interesting (according to a user-imposed interest measure) and certain enough (again according to the user's criteria)' (Frawley *et al.* 1992: 58). As is shown by the AIR landmark database of potential terrorist targets, such maps tactilize a sensorial regime of seeing and sensing the unexpected catastrophe.

We propose to call these technologies conjectural mapping in contradistinction to Jameson's cognitive mapping. The notion of cognitive mapping comes from a 1988 text by Jameson and is inspired by American urban planner Kevin Lynch's book, *The Image of the City* published in 1960. Jameson writes that

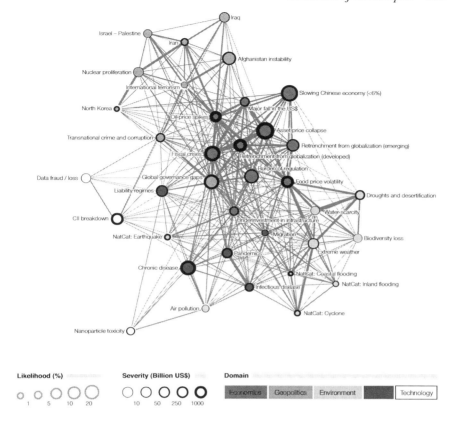

Figure 6.6 The World Economic Forum's Risk Interconnection Map. © 2010 World
   Economic Forum

> Lynch taught us that the alienated city is above all a space in which
> people are unable to map (in their minds) either their own positions
> or the urban totality in which they find themselves ... Disalienation in
> the traditional city, then, involves the practical reconquest of a sense of
> place and the construction or reconstruction of an articulated ensemble
> which can be retained in memory, and which the individual subject can
> map and remap along the moments of mobile, alternative trajectories.[9]
>   (Jameson 1991: 51, see also Jameson 1988)

Conjectural mapping does not amount to cognition – the more relations and
links are added to the map, the more incomprehensible it becomes. That is,
the more data, connections and people feature as input into these maps, the
less it can be given meaning in Jameson's sense of cognitive mapping. Art
works engaging the interconnectedness of the social system probably capture
most explicitly what is at stake in the new rationality of connecting the dots of

vast quantities of data. Art has also engaged in forms of mapping, often map-pings that are unseen and unsensed in the sensorial regime of catastrophe preparedness and prevention. For instance, Mark Lombardi's conceptual artwork maps conspiracies that underpin US foreign policy.[10] After 9/11, an FBI agent called the Whitney Museum of Modern Art to see a drawing by Mark Lombardi on exhibit there. The drawing shows the links between finance and international terrorism. An article in the *New York Times* called Lombardi's work 'The Sinister Beauty of Global Conspiracies' (Heartney 26 October 2003). All the correlations do not amount to cognition but appear to overwhelm the senses.

Heath Bunting's work is set in the same tradition of conceptual art and uses mapping to render the intricacies of data connections. His *Status Works* project plots on a map the information required to make a purchase over the internet in relation to new legislation defined in the UK government's 2006 Terrorism Act. Just as Lombardi's 'celestial maps' are cartographies of the circulation of wealth in a well-rounded system and Bunting's works are cartographies of the circulation of data, catastrophe models and simulations are cartographies of the circulation of risk and vulnerability. Although the maps trace connections and links on the basis of theoretical and empirical considerations rather than through the emergence of 'clues', they do not amount to cognitive mapping. What they share with conjectural maps is the 'urge to know', but they do not necessarily entail cognitive mapping as mean-ingful understanding. Moreover, they are ultimately closed systems. Once the relations are mapped out, there is little possibility to change them. In that sense, they remain more akin to what Deleuze and Guattari have called the tracing of traditional cartography rather than the map:

> What distinguishes the map from the tracing is that it is entirely oriented toward an experimentation in contact with the real. The map does not reproduce an unconscious closed in upon itself; it constructs the uncon-scious. It fosters connection between fields. [...] The map is open and connectable in all of its dimensions; it is detachable, reversible, suscep-tible to constant modification. It can be torn, reversed, adapted to any kind of mounting, reworked by an individual, group, or social formation.
> (Deleuze and Guattari 1987: 12)

The unexpected emerges through sensorial renderings of what is out of joint. Sensorial stimuli become data that are connected and produce maps of the catastrophe to come. This reliance of knowledge production on an aesthetic regime of anticipation, which eludes the historically and socially constructed nature of the senses, impedes the understanding of catastrophic events. As sensorial data is fed into expert knowledge, exercises do not distinguish between different events, their background and causes but focus on immedi-ate and urgent action. Preparedness in that sense is itself conjectural, based on connections of clues, details and signs – which are often experienced

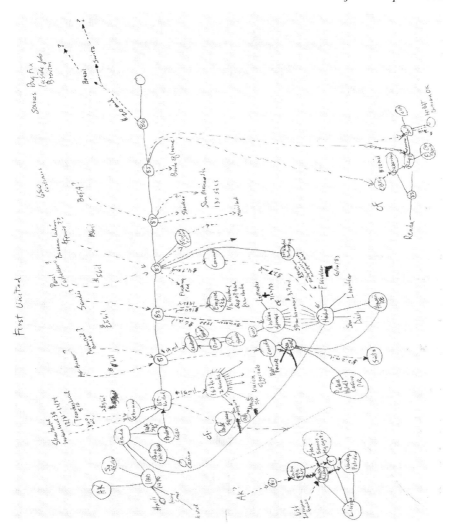

Figure 6.7 'First United' by Mark Lombardi. Digital image: © 2006 The Museum of
Modern Art, NY; photo: © 2010 SCALA Archives, Florence

through the situated and embodied knowledge of each subject. Connecting
sensorial data in maps also amounts to what we have called conjectural mapping, which takes the everyday as it clue but does not seek to understand
and relate these inputs to a larger social structure. Rather, this chapter has
argued that the regime of knowledge deployed to govern catastrophic futures
increasingly works through the senses in an attempt to constitute subjects as
prepared and vigilant. Whether it is through rehearsal of futures in exercises
or through public campaigns and art works, the human body is disciplined

to be watchful, aware, attentive and suspicious, and to attune the senses to the unexpected.

The disciplinary nature of these injunctions, however, should be clearly distinguished from the disciplinary practices Foucault identified in relation to the prison, the barracks and the asylum. Whereas the latter worked through the division and distribution of bodies, exercises, by contrast, are embodied practices through which bodies are encouraged to act out a role and be creative. The investments subjects make in performing these roles are intended to be pleasurable and exciting rather than dull and repetitive. For example, at a large police exercise at a football stadium in Groningen, the Netherlands, some 1,500 participants were asked to act as hooligans performing a riot. One participant claimed that they were not told how far they could go but should improvise. When the 'hooligans' ran out of tennis balls to throw at the police, they began throwing stones and started to push over police vehicles. Jan-Peter Alberts, exercise leader, called off the exercise but refused to call it a failure. He stressed instead the 'lessons learned' for preparing against the unexpected.[11]

Preparedness exercises discipline the body by offering a fun and exciting experience. As one report about a TOPOFF exercise points out:

> Even though the attack was simulated, the chaos at the scene was overwhelming at first, Plummer [Portsmouth Fire Chief] says. "There was an unbelievable amount of things going on at once", he explains. Additionally, the victims … were made up convincingly by professional make-up artists. "It was very real", he notes. "They had arms missing, that kind of stuff, they played it out as if it had really happened."
>
> (Erickson and Barratt 2004: 5)

If the idea of the neurotic citizen that sees and governs herself as an affect structure was a useful complement to the prudent, calculating subject produced through the disciplinary gaze at various institutional sites, the concern over unknown and unexpected futures produces aesthetic citizens where power is inscribed in subjective experience and at the same time experienced as pleasurable thrill.

What is the meaning of a catastrophic event? Understanding catastrophe is not equivalent to the knowledge of catastrophe as an object. Understanding catastrophe entails problematizing the political investment involved in naming an event as 'catastrophic' and in the desire to know and 'tame' the unexpected. The next chapter turns to these political investments by placing catastrophe in a continuum of events and exceptions.

7 Catastrophe, exception, event

> Something must happen in order for there to be something new.
> Alain Badiou (1998: 124)

Politics at the limit

As the previous chapters have argued, catastrophe is a figure of the limit, the limit of knowledge as well as the limit of governmental practice. Catastrophe is often placed in a continuum – or used interchangeably – with a series of other terms: disaster, crisis, emergency and contingency, on the one hand, and risk, uncertainty and hazard on the other. Yet, as we have noted earlier in this book, catastrophe is also often differentiated from all these, most clearly through the inability to function as an attribute of management. Catastrophe is also opposed to the other main governmental word used in relation to undesirable irruptions in the future: planning. 'Unknown unknowns', 'expecting the unexpected', 'imagining the unimaginable' – these all speak to the idea that while future catastrophic events need to be made actionable, they cannot be planned for. Here, underlining the difference that catastrophes introduce, insurance experts tend to speak of '*catastrophic* events' and, in the United Kingdom, security experts and others often use the terminology of '*extreme* events' and of '*catastrophic* emergency'. As the limit of knowing and governing, catastrophes name an excess or an exception. They cannot be confined to what is taken for granted, but rather require the wholesale reassessment of what is to be done. At the same time, catastrophes are also moments of disruption, of an opening in the way things are, as suggested by its theatrical etymology. They are events in the sense of signalling the new, the unpredictable upturn of the state of things. Catastrophes speak of a limit that cannot be tamed, yet they do not challenge the obviousness of security knowledge and the conjectural style of reasoning that appears as self-evident: *of course* we need particular modes of preventing and preparing for the catastrophe, and *of course* we need to imagine, insure against and build resilience against catastrophes. However, all this is not a matter of course, but the result of struggles over power and knowledge.

This chapter therefore asks what the politics of catastrophe entails. What alternative forms of diagnosis can be employed to make sense of the limit of knowledge, the predictable and the continuous? How can we engage politically with this limit? How is it possible to challenge security practices that depend on conjectural forms of knowing? To answer these questions, this chapter seeks to de-naturalize the forms of knowledge through which catastrophic events have been placed in a series that includes risk, disaster, crisis and emergency. Thus far, international relations scholars have mainly drawn on theories of the exception in order to think about the limit. This chapter therefore revisits catastrophe as an event that can be defined as potentially exceptional. Diagnoses of exceptionalism, it will be argued, guard us from embracing too easily the conjectural regime of power/knowledge, but do not exhaust the notion of catastrophe as something surprising and unexpected. The second line pursued in the chapter is the rendition of catastrophes through causal knowledge about structures and sociality. Rather than tackling the limit as an exception, the limit of catastrophe is rendered as a critical juncture. Although this challenges the taken-for-granted knowledge of prevention and preparedness, this diagnostic does not fully appreciate the rupturing character of catastrophes either. Finally, drawing on the rather unexpected alliance of the work of Michel Foucault and Alain Badiou, this chapter argues for the particular role and singularity of catastrophe as an event that is neither causally determined nor completely divorced from the power relations in which it emerges.

Constituting exceptions

After 9/11, catastrophic events have been often discussed through the vocabulary and theories of exceptionalism. Carl Schmitt defines the state of exception as the intense political moment where people are grouped according to the friend/enemy division: 'Every religious, moral, economic, ethical, or other antithesis transforms into a political one if it is sufficiently strong to group human beings effectively according to friend and enemy' (Schmitt 1996: 37). For Schmitt, exceptionalism is defined not only by the capacity to override the law, but also by the capacity to call the legal order into being: 'Order must be established for juridical order to make sense. A regular situation must be created, and sovereign is he who definitely decides if this situation is actually effective' (Schmitt 1996). The state of exception integrates political communities according to friend/enemy lines and creates homogeneous identities that need to be defended.

The sovereign decision on the exception is defined as the precondition and possibility for the functioning of the law. Law and social order depend upon a founding crime or upon an act of war. This is the paradox of modern liberal political communities which define themselves as governed by the rule of law: the law needs a founding crime, a moment of violence or injustice –

the exception – in order to function (Burke 2002, Derrida 2005). As former Vice-President Dick Cheney argued:

> Homeland security is not a temporary measure just to meet one crisis. Many of the steps we have now been forced to take will become permanent in American life. They represent an understanding of the world as it is, and dangers we must guard against perhaps for decades to come. I think of it as the new normalcy.
>
> (Cheney 2001)

The diagnosis of the catastrophic event through exceptionalism has led to analyses of the new normality that has been institutionalized through the 'war on terror' and an exploration of the unfounded decisions at its core. Security practices do not simply concern the identification of threats or risks; they are politically constitutive acts that assert the unity of a political community (Huysmans 2006: 49). Scrutinizing this new normality, the diagnosis of exceptionalism has revealed the continuities of illiberal practices within liberal states that stem from the exceptional governance of risks and dangers (Aradau and van Munster 2007, 2008b, Bigo and Tsoukala 2006, De Goede 2008a, Jabri 2007, Neocleous 2008). The Iraq War (Diken and Laustsen 2005, van Munster 2004), refugee camps and airport holding zones (Noll 2003, Salter 2008a), humanitarian intervention (Edkins *et al.* 2004, Dauphinée and Masters 2007), detention centres of terrorist suspects (Neal 2006), and the shoot-to-kill policies of the London police (Vaughan-Williams 2007) have all been recognized as exceptional practices or sites where the new normality is founded through a sovereign decision. They exemplify 'an array of illiberal policies and practices that are legitimated through claims about necessary exceptions to the norm' (Neal 2006: 31). For instance, Guantánamo Bay has been described as the realm of 'normless ... decision making in which the executive powers possess fully discretionary authority' (Scheuerman 2006: 118).

However, debates about exceptionalism are not just about the strengthening of executive government, sovereign decisions and the possibility of modern liberal states to collapse into authoritarian regimes (Walker 2006). Perhaps even more fundamentally, exceptional policies change the principles around which our societies are organized and governed. As Huysmans observes, exceptionalism is

> not simply about civil liberties, the legality of going to war, and the constitutional limits to strengthening executive-centred government. Since these political, legal and social contests strongly reiterate fear of the enemy they directly bear upon the extent to which one is structuring and possibly institutionalizing fear of the enemy as the organizing principle of politics in both national and international society. The question then becomes to what extent security responses that claim to aim at protecting freedom and equality are actually displacing freedom and

equality with fear of the enemy as the central principle around which politics is organized.

(Huysmans 2004: 338)

Giorgio Agamben's work makes explicit the political implications of a politics of fear. Agamben's reformulation of the enemy as *homo sacer* or bare life places the decision on the enemy at the heart of the sovereign decision on the value of life as political on the one hand and disqualified, abject or bare life on the other. According to him, the decision on the exception suspends the legal order and creates a space of indistinction between norm and exception. In this zone of indistinction, the central figure one encounters is that of *homo sacer*, bare life stripped of all its value in the sense that violence against him/her remains unpunished. The Hobbesian social contract that brings the sovereign into being masks the fact that sovereignty essentially operates through a ban: 'The originary relation of law to life is not application but abandonment' (Agamben 1998: 29). The creation of bare life as the originary gesture of sovereignty most explicitly renders the inseparability of sovereignty and the subject, i.e. the ways in which sovereignty is constitutive of abjection.

Based on his writings on international relations, Schmitt would probably disavow this ahistorical reading. In *The Nomos of the Earth*, Schmitt (2003) explicitly argued for upholding the plurality of states as found in the nineteenth-century *Jus Publicum Europaeum* against what he saw as dehumanizing tendencies in liberalism. For him, the construction of enemies within the European system of state remained a relation between equals, while liberal universalism pushed enemies beyond the boundaries of humanity. The enemy of liberalism, according to Schmitt, becomes equated with inhumanity and evil. Yet, Schmitt's conservative support for a traditional inter-state rendition of the international was made possible only by another exception that functioned at the limits of this international system. In other words, the self-restrained enmity among European sovereigns depended on the representation of the colonial world as an empty space where European states could fights wars without restraint.[1]

The exception, then, was a space carved within the colonial global space. The loss of these territorial boundaries in the process of decolonization, the subsequent universalization of space and the emergence of humanity as a global subject have reinforced Schmitt's belief that boundary drawing, the division of space or territory is the fundamental act of constituting a stable order. Exceptions were made possible by the global colonial relations of power as the disavowed basis of modern international law (Anghie 2004, Hussain 2003). Just like domestic law, international law thus depends upon an exception. As Judith Butler has formulated it,

[law] leaves open the possibility of its own retraction, and, in the case of the Geneva Convention, extends 'universal' rights only to those

imprisoned combatants who belong to 'recognizable' nation-states, but not to all people … The Geneva Convention is, in part, a *civilizational discourse*.

(Butler 2004, emphasis added).

Universal legal provisions do not necessarily provide a guarantee against exceptional politics enabled by colonial relations of power. In the international sphere, the limits of law and life are superposed over the limits of modernity and civilization. So-called functional states are opposed to failed or weak states. 'Failed states', argued the US Director of National Intelligence, are 'terrorist safe havens and ungoverned regions that endanger the international community and its citizens' (McConnell 2007). Indeed, the United States now regards failed and fragile states as larger threats to national and international security than great power struggles and balance-of-power politics.

Although the radical uncertainty associated with terrorism at first sight appears to confirm the Agambenian adage that the exception has become the norm in as far as conjectural technologies of surveillance indiscriminately target the whole population (stop-and-search policies, biometric identifiers or the introduction of identity cards), practices that appear to go beyond racial and cultural characteristics do in fact re-inscribe these categories upon the population. Thus even though the official Home Office report on the 7/7 London bombings pointed out that nothing marked out the four men involved in the attacks, that they were all 'unexceptional' (Home Office 2006), conjectures based on the 'objective' data of actual behaviour (travel records, internet searches, financial habits, etc.) often have a decidedly cultural, religious and racial bias (Amoore 2007). These measures allow for increased flexibility in targeting various categories of the population – some on grounds of generalized surveillance and others on grounds of statistical evidence and risk profiling or plausible correlations.

Although diagnoses based on Schmittian and Agambenian notions of the exception have rendered the arbitrary discrimination at the heart of a politics of fear after 9/11 more visible, such diagnoses may well overestimate the power of the sovereign decision both domestically and internationally. Jan Werner Müller (2006) has remarked, for instance, that Schmitt overestimated the capacity even of hegemonic powers to reshape law and perceptions to suit their interests. Susan Buck-Morss (2007: 171) has rightly castigated Agamben for his a-historical proposition of sovereignty and bare life, which leads to a 'timeless ontology of power'. Construed as bare life, the subject of sovereign power always appears as deprived of any agency and dissolves the view of society as mediated and shaped through social relations (e.g. property, class, legal, technological, gender) that have conditioned modern democratic politics (Huysmans 2008). As we discussed above, the state of exception is inscribed differently upon various sectors of society and experienced differently by particular categories of populations (see also Jabri 2007).

Moreover, camps and other exceptional sites such as Guantánamo Bay are imbued with knowledge and technologies of governance: from ration cards and hygiene education to psychological therapy (Johns 2005). Rather than empty spaces of bare life, camps and other exceptional spaces are governed through bureaucratic technologies and regulations, often reminiscent of colonial and political histories. Although theories of exception provide a view of power that draws attention to sovereign practices of violence at work in liberal states, they are largely indifferent to that which happens. As the political and analytical emphasis is placed on the decision, the naming of the exceptional moment and the enemy, more routinized forms of power and exclusion are somewhat ignored. Or, as Mitchell Dean argues, 'if the governmentality perspective misses the sovereign decision imbricated within regimes of practices, Schmitt misses the normalizing practices that surround the exception' (Dean 2007: 163). Didier Bigo (2002), who has focused on the security experts that manage 'unease' within society on a daily basis, has pointed out that exceptional security practices can be understood in the context of ongoing processes of bureaucratic and market-driven routinization. Bonnie Honig (2009: xv) has also suggested we should 'de-exceptionalize the exception' and look at the 'ordinary' politics of how decisions are taken in these situations.

The vocabulary of catastrophe provides a promising route of de-exceptionalizing the exception.[2] On the one hand, it draws attention to the knowledge involved in the way in which the future is made amenable to governance. As such, it distances us from the exclusively legal realm of decision by reinserting questions about the deployment of sovereign power into a politics of knowledge. Rather than focusing on the exceptional moment, the politics of catastrophe draws attention to the epistemic regime of conjectural reasoning and imagination through which the future is rendered actionable. On the other hand, the politics of catastrophe does not efface the insight that exceptional moments can turn fear of the enemy into a constitutive principle of social and political order. To the contrary, it provides a diagnosis of what governing through worst case scenarios entails. Worst case scenarios of nuclear terrorism, for instance, imbricate expertise and decision at the limit of knowledge, war and strategies of surveillance, injunctions to integration, and sensorial awareness to abnormal behaviour. However, rather than simply speaking of an a-historical sovereign decision, it situates these decisions within a regime of knowledge that makes possible correlations and connections about catastrophic events.

Metapolitics of causality

Unlike theories of exception, catastrophes have been analysed from a completely different perspective in, among others, anthropology and geography. The aim of this perspective is not to draw attention to the politics of fear and the sovereign forms of power at the heart of conjectural regimes of power/

knowledge but to make catastrophes visible as events that can be subjected to different forms of knowledge. Even if the focus of many scholars has been on natural disasters, their diagnostic analysis focuses on causes and is very different from the analysis of exceptionalism. Doug Henry has put in a nutshell the approach to disaster in anthropological literature: 'In its approach to studying disasters, this has meant calling attention to how risks and disasters both influence and are products of human systems, rather than representing simply isolated, spontaneous, or unpredictable events' (Henry 2005: 1). Catastrophes and disasters in this view are not unknown or unexpected. To the contrary, for this literature the unknown and the unexpected appear as 'ideological' categories that hinder any critical inquiry into their causes. The objective, then, is to make the unknown known and show that what may seem unexpected in reality is an expectable outcome of causal processes.

As we discussed to some extent in Chapter 4, Rousseau's response to the Lisbon Earthquake was formulated exactly along these lines. He lamented those, such as Voltaire, who wondered what reasons God could have had to punish the inhabitants of Lisbon as opposed to those in any other major European city. Instead, Rousseau shifted the terrain of the question by arguing that what turned the earthquake into a disaster was not God or the tremor as such but the fact that it took place in one of the world's largest and most densely populated cities. As he wrote in a letter to Voltaire: 'Without departing from your subject of Lisbon, admit, for example, that nature did not construct twenty thousand houses of six to seven stories there, and that if the inhabitants of this great city had been more equally spread out and more lightly lodged, the damage would have been much less and perhaps of no account' (Rousseau 1992 [1756]: 110).

However, according to Rousseau, the tremor should not be interpreted as an exogenous event to be managed through planning; it should rather encourage a more endogenous perspective addressing the social structures of society that allowed the tremor to take on catastrophic proportions. For Rousseau the question of catastrophe was not answered by reducing society's vulnerability, while leaving its institutions intact. The reduction of vulnerability was not a matter of restoring normality but involved an inquiry into the social institutions or the social evils (such as property and inequality) that made the disaster possible: 'What crimes, wars, murders, what miseries and horrors would the human Race have been spared by someone who, uprooting the stakes or filling the ditch, had shouted to his fellows: Beware of listening to this impostor; you are lost if you forget that that the fruits belong to all and the Earth to no one!' (Rousseau, 1992b [1755]: 43).

Some two centuries later, the German writer, philosopher and peace activist Günther Anders made a similar point in relation to the catastrophe of Hiroshima, which for him signalled the human incapacity to link their subjective experiences and action to broader social structures and their outcomes. Speaking in this context of a subject without a world (*Mensch ohne Welt*) he claimed that it is '[u]nnecessary to stress that the talk about "natural catastrophe", which should erase our moral responsibility, is just talk. Our crime rests exactly in the fact that we let our crimes take the form of natural catastrophes' (Anders 1981, our translation). Anders is particularly interested in the catastrophe that is to come – the self-destruction of humanity resulting from the possession of nuclear weapons. In that sense, his diagnosis has proven appealing in the renewed anticipation of the potential self-destruction of humanity through environmental catastrophe. Jean Pierre Dupuy in particular has read Anders's work in this light. For Dupuy (2005) – and to some extent Anders himself – it is not ignorance, not knowing or the limit of knowledge that is a limit to our capacity for action, but rather our capacity to imagine the catastrophe to come. Yet, Anders does not oppose imagination to knowledge as strongly as Dupuy does. For Anders, the limits of imagination are rooted in the limits of the constitution of the modern subjects. Consequently, the nuclear era is merely the finalization of a process that began with the Industrial Revolution, when the division of labour created a fragmented subject, attached to its specialized tasks and unaware of social totality. Under conditions of capitalism, Anders maintained, work is increasingly detached from acting. Acting requires that the subject can oversee the consequences of her act. Yet, much of today's production is undertaken by machines and computers, where human labour is reduced to the abstract and distant activity of operating these systems (Anders 1981: 100–101). For Anders, Hiroshima merely represents the most extreme condition of this development – hence his provocative statement that Hiroshima is everywhere:

> The actor's alienation from his act is perfect, and has been so for 15 years, since 1945, because also the Hiroshima pilots could no longer recognise their deeds as 'deeds' or, in any case, not as 'their' deeds … This Hiroshima-trap is, however, a trap for all of us. Because we are all, as workers, condemned not to know what we do.
>
> (Anders 1981: 191 our translation)

Human beings, then, have been turned into peripheral actors that no longer act but only act along as cogs in the wheel of a largely technology-driven production process (Anders 1956). Interestingly, Jonathan Crary's research on the changing regime of perception in early modernity locates a similar change in the production of subjects by focusing on the shift from classical regimes of perception to attention: 'At the moment when the dynamic logic of capital began to dramatically undermine any stable or enduring structure of perception, this logic simultaneously attempted to impose a disciplinary regime of attentiveness' (Crary 2001: 13). Attention became a problem of government given the inattention that was caused by the sensorial surplus of industrial capitalism. Hence, '[i]t was through the new imperatives of attentiveness that the perceiving body was deployed and made productive and orderly, whether as student, worker or consumer' (Crary 2001: 22–23). New constructions of attentiveness occurred through reconfigurations of subjectivity in the nineteenth century. Attention meant both the narrowing of perceptions, as well as the screening out of some perceptions. The incapacity to imagine the future catastrophe is the result of the impairment of 'cognitive mapping' and the concurrent reconfiguration of sensation and understanding.

More recently, the geographers Michael Watts and Mike Davis have shown how natural disasters emerge out of particular socio-economic conditions and in turn trigger changes in these systems. Famines and scarcity crises, for example, are the results of changes in market conditions. Changes in production in developing countries have been influenced by practices of circulation and the integration of the 'Third World' in global systems of trade. In the case of Northern Nigeria, the reproduction of the peasant family became dependent upon the production of export commodities (Watts 1983), while the 'imaginary of the Third World' as a depleted place of starvation was created by Victorian imperialism and the restructuring of production and circulation (Davis 2001). In India, for example, grains and rice were transported by road or canal from non-famine areas to areas of shortage. The colonial introduction of railways led to the movement and storage of grains for export, while the telegraph transferred price information so that market prices were maintained in India. The colonial authorities also reorganized the production system to increase taxation. The political ecology literature has pointed out a shift in analyses of food security from the 1970s focus on food supplies and trade to analyses which emphasize the political economy of production and access to food supplies. It is worth quoting Mahmood Mamdani's cautionary statement about the analysis of disasters:

> True, disasters are not natural but social catastrophes. [It is] also true that they are the result of social conditions: deforestation, soil erosion, desertification. Lack of rain does not cause a famine, it is simply the occasion for it. It triggers off the famine. But, why do people cut down forests? Why do they overgraze? Why do they work the same old tired land without resting it? Is it out of malice? Or sheer ignorance? Not really. My basic point is that, so long as they look for individual solutions to what are in fact social problems, they have very little choice given the social relations they are trapped in. What are these relations? How and when were they created? Can they be changed? These are some of the questions I intend to discuss today.
>
> (Mamdani 1985: 93)

Mamdani takes the case of peasant exploitation in Uganda. Given the forms of direct and indirect exploitation in which the peasants are caught, their individual solutions can only be contradictory.

In a similar vein, others have questioned the focus on preparedness and exceptional policies in the case of Hurricane Katrina in the US. As Karin Fierke asks: 'Would it have been so difficult to pay a bit more attention, in message and action, to those in new Orleans who were on the verge of dying, and somewhat less to a shoot to kill policy directed at the looters, who in many cases were trying to provide food for the starving?' (Fierke 2007: 201). Andrew Lakoff has called for the investigation of Katrina's long-term social determinants and conditions of possibility:

> [W]hile preparedness may emphasize saving the lives of 'victims' in moments of duress, it does not consider the living conditions of human beings as members of a social collectivity. To consider Katrina a problem of preparedness rather than one of population security is to focus political questions about the failure around a fairly circumscribed set of issues. For the purposes of disaster planning, whose key question is 'are we prepared?' the poverty rate or the percentage of people without health insurance are not salient indicators of readiness or of the efficacy of response. Rather, preparedness emphasizes questions such as hospital surge capacity, the coherence of evacuation plans, the condition of the electrical grid, or ways of detecting the presence of *e coli* in the water supply. From the vantage of preparedness, the conditions of existence of members of the population are not a political problem.
>
> (Lakoff 2006)

Other literatures are particularly concerned with the socio-economic effects of disasters and post-disaster reconstruction. Mark Pelling and Kathleen Dill (2010) have recently categorized these approaches as analyses of either 'accelerated status quo', where change is limited to a speeding up of pre-disaster trajectories, or 'critical juncture', where change refers to an irreversible change. As disasters hit hardest those in vulnerable situations – inequalities of gender, class and race being particularly important – the post-disaster situation can exacerbate these vulnerabilities and inequalities. Such has been the much-discussed case of reconstruction after the Katrina disaster in the US or the 2004 tsunami in South-East Asia. Against this background, disasters 'demonstrate a manifest failure in the social contract and open space for renegotiation in the values and structures of society' (Pelling and Dill 2010). Pelling and Dill are particularly interested in the redistribution of rights and responsibilities following a disaster. Anthony Oliver-Smith also formulates the anthropologists' interest in power and politics in similar terms: they seek to 'examine how disasters shape, maintain, destabilize, or destroy both political organizations and relations' (Oliver-Smith 1996: 309).

This research on disasters appears counter-posed to the diagnostic of exceptionalism that has been attached to the 'war on terror' and other catastrophes. The 'un-ness' of catastrophe – unexpected, unpredictable, unknowable – is replaced by a careful analysis of the conditions of emergence of catastrophe. Yet, to a certain extent, these analyses leave little space for the politics of knowledge too. Rather, knowledge underpins a form of metapolitics where knowledge is split according to social positions. There are no epistemological uncertainties in the materialist structural edifice. Causes are known and solutions can be found. Even though Mamdani for instance argues that any solution to disaster must be based on forms of organization that are both popular and developed around concrete issues (Mamdani 1985), he also suggests that these forms of organization depend upon the 'education' of the people, thereby entrenching an unequal relation between those who (already) know and the ignorant peasants. In that sense, the surprise and novelty associated with catastrophe challenge hierarchies of knowledge. If risk and uncertainty remain in the realm of expert knowledge – i.e. only some have access to this knowledge – while ignorance and secrecy presuppose the unequal distribution of a general knowledge, then knowledge is available but only some 'see' it. This raises the problem of the inequality of knowledge between social groups. Not only are certain forms of knowledge legitimated as superior to others, but knowledge is differentiated between what people know about a situation and the scientific knowledge of that situation. Moreover, much of the research that emphasizes the structural causes of disasters leaves little room for the unexpected. Although scholars stress that disaster research should become more attuned to the struggles that redefine political, economic and social relations after a disaster, their research is generally focused on the present and its causes and potential 'path dependencies' rather than the anticipated event.

If this literature is structurally overdetermined, evacuating novelty and surprise from structure, the surprise and novelty associated with the notion of catastrophe may challenge hierarchies of knowledge. The very possibility of not knowing the event that comes already shatters regimes of expert knowledge, even when these attempt to re-establish themselves by reshaping and reformulating existing modes of knowledge. The politics of catastrophe today is also anticipatory and deployed largely pre-event. It reshapes social, political and economic relations and fosters subject in the absence of the event itself. Knowing catastrophes to come creates regimes of knowledge that mobilize different styles of reasoning and their particular ways of creating truthful statements. A conjectural style of reasoning adds a regime of plausibility and ways of creating and validating veridical statements and evidence.

At the same time, the limit of knowledge becomes problematized in ways that challenge ideas of expert control. Knowledge production about catastrophes to come rehearses particular versions of catastrophe and silences others; at the same time it places itself on less stable bases and it is continuously haunted by the question of unknowability it has opened.

The politics of events

Ideas of exceptionalism and causation shift diagnoses of catastrophe either to the pole of predictability or to that of unpredictability and surprise. Theories of the state of exception help map a conjectural regime of knowledge that imbricates sovereign power with more mundane forms of power in its attempt to govern future catastrophic events. However, as we have seen, it does not allow us to think of catastrophe as the invention of something new or a radical break. The politics of exceptionalism is entwined with the temporality of repetition, of cancelled futures. The aporia of the linearity of progress and the repetitiveness of the ever-same has continually undermined the possibility of the radical new and of a subject that resists. Causal explanations of catastrophes also problematize a complete identification with current responses to catastrophe by bringing out alternative trajectories of catastrophe as socially and economically embedded. Their appropriation of the vocabulary of catastrophe can be seen as a strategic move to reverse a relationship of forces and lift catastrophic events out of the security knowledge. The price for doing so, however, has been to reduce the catastrophic event to a structural element. As such, they leave intact the question of what constitutes an unexpected irruption and ultimately the question of what is new. As Žižek puts it,

> one should maintain the crucial distinction between a mere 'performative reconfiguration', a subversive displacement which remains within the hegemonic field and, as it were, conducts an internal guerrilla war of turning the terms of the hegemonic field against itself, and the much more radical act of a thorough reconfiguration of the entire field which redefines the very conditions of socially sustained performativity.
>
> (Žižek 1999: 264)

How, then, does one understand the novelty of the event or the 'upturn' of catastrophe? Badiou's work, we contend, brings to light political investments that are not exhausted by either the politics of exception or the politics of causality. For Badiou, politics is about searching within a situation for 'a possibility *that the dominant state of things does not allow to be seen*' (Badiou 2004a: 82, emphasis in original). Badiou summarizes his concern with the conceptualization of disruptive events in relation to the emergence of the 'new' as follows:

> My unique philosophical question, I would say, is the following: can we think that there is something new in the situation, not outside the situation nor the new somewhere else, but can we really think through novelty and treat it in the situation? The system of philosophical answers that I elaborate, whatever its complexity may be, is subordinated to that question and to no other.[3]
>
> (Badiou and Bosteels 2005: 252)

An event always emerges out of a particular situation. Events do not come out of nowhere. Badiou tries to sustain the novelty of the event without collapsing it under utter unpredictability or the 'miracle'. The event is something new that interrupts what Badiou calls the 'encyclopedia of knowledge'. As an event, the catastrophe lays bare the limits of knowledge, but does not erase them. The event qualifies as an immanent break: it proceeds in the situation but also surpasses it. It appears as unpredictable, not simply as premeditated by historical causes that can be known. The event is a disjuncture between past and future that dismisses any idea of continuity between the two. Rather, the event interrupts time 'as the possibility of another time', as 'a vanishing mediator, an intemporal instant which renders injunct the previous state of an object (the site) and the state that follows' (Badiou 2007: 39). As Colin Wright (2008) has put it, nothing in the structural conditions of the event guarantees the occurrence of the event. The event, a radical break between past and future, is best seen as an absolute beginning. For example, the French Revolution – one of Badiou's favourite examples – needs to be both situated in the circumstances of French society in the eighteenth century and seen as supplementary to them. No matter how much knowledge we have of French society and power relations, the 1789 Revolution was not thinkable from within the structure of the *ancien régime*.

Badiou thus reserves the term 'events' to political actions that upturn 'what is', i.e. disrupt the order of things and ensure that the world will never be the same. The 'new' emerges in a situation through the work and organization of singular elements as an event. In this sense, Badiou's language on these issues is strikingly similar to Foucault's language of eventalization understood as the uncovering of the 'polyhedron of intelligibility':[4]

> What do I mean by this term? First of all, a breach of self-evidence. It means making visible a singularity at places where there is a temptation to invoke a historical constant, an immediate anthropological trait or an obviousness that imposes itself uniformly on all. To show that things weren't 'necessary as all that'; it wasn't as a matter of course that mad people came to be regarded as mentally ill; it wasn't self-evident that the only thing to be done with a criminal was to lock them up; it wasn't self-evident that the causes of illness were to be sought through individual examination of bodies; and so on. A breach of self-evidence, of those self-evidences on which our knowledges, acquiescences and practices rest: this is the first theoretico-political function of 'eventalization'.
>
> (Foucault 1991: 76)

Here, Foucault deploys the notion of event to question that which is universal, constant and necessary to reveal the singular and the contingent as products of arbitrary constraints (Foucault 1984: 45, 47). Although the notion of event has been associated mainly with other thinkers such as Heidegger, Whitehead, Deleuze or Badiou, most of Foucault's books start with descriptions of events: the torture of Damiens in *Discipline and Punish*, the grand internment of lepers and the Ship of Fools in *Madness and Civilization*, the publication of Pinel's *Traité medico-philosophique* in the lectures on psychiatric power, or that of Kant's text *What is Enlightenment?* in the series on *Governing Self and Others*. These are not unknown events. Many have garnered extensive analytical attention. Foucault, however, offers a different decipherment, a different perspective. He does not invent, discover or emphasize new events or reinterpret them in order to discover hidden and somehow neglected meaning. The events work on the surface and Foucault attempts to counter-actualize the event, to return, in one form or another, to the event in order to re-problematize it (Colwell 1997).

How can this understanding of the event inform a politics of catastrophe? Security knowledge assumes that the 'unknown unknowns' of catastrophic events come from nowhere at the same time as being somehow exhausted through attention to details, signs and clues that are built into the conjectural regime of power/knowledge. Unlike this regime of knowledge, thinking the event also brings to the fore the disrupting dimensions of catastrophe. An event is also an interruption of the 'encyclopedia of knowledge'. In *Logiques des mondes*, Badiou introduces a temporality of the anticipation of the future, when a truth, although incomplete, 'authorizes anticipations of knowledge concerning not what is but *what will have been if truth attains completion*' (Badiou 2004b: 130, emphasis in original). As opposed to Foucault, Badiou does not see 'truth' as the effect of power but as the ways in which an event renders existing forms of knowledge ineffective. Truth disrupts power and is taken for granted. Even more explicitly, Badiou argues elsewhere that truth operates 'through the retroaction of an almost nothing and the anticipation of an almost everything' (Badiou 2004b: 130). Yet, he also declares that 'it is quite impossible to anticipate or represent a truth' (Badiou 2006: 399). However, this does not mean that nothing can be known about a truth-event in the present. Although the event is not oriented towards a future, Badiou's vacillation between anticipation and its rejection in favour of the present moment is indicative of the challenges that the event raises for the politics of knowledge.

As we have seen, this interruption would need to contend with both the conditions of possibility and conditions of validity of knowledge. Ultimately, Badiou leaves little room for the politics of knowledge itself. Knowledge is instead subsumed to the politics of events. The 'truth' of the event takes over and radically restructures existing knowledge. Yet, we have shown that it is difficult to oppose truth to the conjectural regime of knowledge in as much as the latter is indifferent to truth. It works with signs and clues that do not establish the 'truth' but a regime of plausibility that validates evidence and veridical statements in a different way from modern conceptions of truth.

Even if conceptualizing the event does not account for the epistemic regimes and changes in modes of knowledge and styles of reasoning, it allows us to include these various dimensions of a catastrophe. Catastrophes are an unanticipated upturn, an opening which is unknown and unexpected, while at the same time being situated. The politics of catastrophe emerges in the disputes between what can be known and what cannot and how the unexpected lays bare structure and dispositions and challenges them. Arguably, this approach has also informed political philosophical and historical writings on the social catastrophes of the twentieth century: total war, totalitarianism and the Holocaust (Katznelson 2003). These events were so shocking that they could not be understood in any causal sense. Hence, the titles of two of the most influential books published on these events – Hannah Arendt's (1973) *Origins of Totalitarianism* and Karl Polanyi's (1944) *The Great Transformation. The Political and Economic Origins of Our Time* – explicitly speak of origins in the plural. The authors did not seek to explain these events as the outcome of causes. On the contrary, Arendt was well aware that these events could not be grasped through notions of causality: 'Within the framework of reconceived categories, the crudest of which is causality, events in the sense of something new can never happen' (quoted in Katznelson 2003: 102). As Ira Katznelson notes in his superb study of political knowledge in the twentieth century:

> What was required, both believed, was not just the study of the period of emergency, implying a possible return to normalcy, but a deeper and more fundamental consideration of origins, a search by the means of historical social science for the sources and elements of a catastrophe so far reaching that, as they believed, the world had begun anew.
>
> (Katznelson 2003: 64)

Catastrophes have a peculiar temporality that situate them outside the linear progression of past, present and future. They do not arise out of a past which prepares and causes it; they are rather treated as eruptions in the present with the aim of producing an upheaval in the order of things. Like Arendt, Theodor Adorno did not consider Auschwitz a 'marginal situation' (Tiedemann 2003: xix), but a catastrophe deeply embedded within the structures of society. He argued that 'Hitler imposed on men in the state of subjection a new categorical imperative: to organize thought and action as to make the repetition of Auschwitz, or any other similar occurrence, impossible' (Adorno 1973 [1966]: 358). The relentless injunction of 'never again', the ethical imperative to avoid a repetition of Auschwitz, entails an engagement with the conditions of modernity and democracy. In a sense, Adorno's 'never again' picks up on Rousseau's critique of society in the wake of Lisbon. As Adorno notes in *Education after Auschwitz*, the imperative for the 'never possible' is needed because 'the fundamental structure of society and its members, which brought it on, are today the same' (Adorno 2005). The fact that Auschwitz happened, stresses Adorno, is the 'expression of an extremely powerful societal tendency' (Adorno 2005: 20). Against those who saw Auschwitz as unspeakable, unthinkable, and inconceivable, Adorno argued that it needs to be placed within the context of modernity, particularly the Enlightenment drive towards the extinction of non-identical thinking. The conditions of possibility for this realization are more or less traceable to the deep structures and logics of European modernity and the capitalism from which it is inseparable (Ray 2004: 2).

These catastrophic events had to be understood but could not be explained through causal reasoning (which somehow would place them in a story of continuity between past and future). Neither could they be seen as exceptions, as normality was explicitly implicated in the production of these events. Total war, totalitarianism and the Holocaust rather 'identified the break between past and present as entailing a breach so fundamental that even the best contemporary work written in terms of crisis was underestimating the novelty of the situation' (Katznelson 2003: 79). This understanding of catastrophe qua event has important political consequences. Catastrophic events function as an upturn, the moment of discontinuity and of potential novelty. At the same time, they don't emerge out of nowhere any more than they can be exhausted by structural causes. The disruption brought about by an event is catastrophic in the sense of an 'overturn' that reconfigures the present and replaces the existing socio-politico-economic relations by radically different ones.

Thinking the politics of catastrophe in relation to exceptions and events does not mean that we erase the singularity of particular catastrophes or that we aim to collapse 'natural' and social and political disasters. As Anders argued and many have pointed out since, the separation between nature and society, what is necessity and what is politics, has always been itself a political act.

Although Badiou does not directly engage with the 'politics of catastrophe', it is important to consider the relation between his conception of the new and the radically novel disruption of catastrophic events. While the current biopolitics of catastrophe appears to share similarities with an event of epistemic change there is also a deeper unease with the novelty that catastrophic events can bring about. Thinking about the politics of catastrophe in terms of the event will always raise the question of whether the cuts and discontinuities produced through the process of eventalizaton are justified. Obviously, other events could be singled out, which would bring out different periodizations and which would create the intelligibility of the present in different ways. Nevertheless, understanding the politics of catastrophe through the political category of events tells us that thinking the future needs to be done in relation to the present. Anticipating future catastrophic events from the standpoint of a present which is cognitively rather than conjecturally mapped would make – we would hope – questions of catastrophe political in the sense of both a disruption in epistemic regimes and practices of subjectivation.

8 Conclusion

> What has to be understood is that our responses to peril are fundamentally
> driven by the need to make sense of our very humanity. They are not just about
> solving the next crisis but about who we are as a people and persons.
>
> Robert Wuthnow (2010: 2)

This book has argued that catastrophe as a signifier of the future appears
as a figure of the limit. It suggested that the current preoccupation with the
next catastrophe has advanced a problematization of the future as something
unknowable and unexpected. Although the governance of catastrophe shares
some features with, for instance, risk, disaster and emergency, it draws upon
different styles of reasoning that amount to a particular regime of knowledge
to render these unexpected events actionable and governable. The politics
of catastrophe raises questions about governing in time, the limits of knowledge and the very possibility of cognition. But how new is the governance
of catastrophe? On a general level, visions about the end of times have been
with us since the beginning of times. Biblical notions of the apocalypse and
various versions of millennialism have been a constant in human history. In
the much more limited sphere of security experts, the concern with unknown,
catastrophic futures cannot be easily dated either. Did it begin with the Cold
War, at the end of the Cold War, Chernobyl, 9/11 or with the advent of a
global risk society?

In a somewhat simplified fashion, the answers given by scholars in the
field of security studies can be divided into two opposite camps. One has
emphasized the novelty of modes of knowledge (possibility, enactment, anticipatory or speculative security knowledge) and practices (Guantánamo Bay,
exceptional sovereign practices, quasi-ubiquitous surveillance, changes in
war practices, technology, limitations of freedom, retrenchment of equality under the hegemony of neo-liberalism). Another group of scholars, by
contrast, has focused on the continuities of knowledge – from civil defence
to intelligence – and has situated these in ongoing bureaucratic routines,
struggles and forms of power. Obviously, the story is neither one of complete continuity or absolute discontinuity. Rather, different authors stress and

accentuate other elements. Yet, the question of novelty and periodization continues to constitute a problem for security scholars. From risk to disasters and from humanitarian interventions to insurance, many have been inspired by a biopolitical reading of security practices (Dillon and Reid 2001, Lobo-Guerrero 2010) by drawing on Michel Foucault's lectures at the Collège de France (2004b, 2007). However, the biopolitics of security as theorized by Foucault is an eighteenth-century development. Although several authors have recently attempted to bring together sovereignty and biopolitics, either by considering life as the proper domain of sovereignty or by supplementing biopolitics with necropolitics, these periodizations make it difficult to understand the reiteration of the shift from sovereignty to biopolitics in current contexts (Agamben 1998).

Foucault's discussions of the security *dispositif* and associated biopolitical governance pointed out its emergence around the problematization of the aleatory, the contingent and the event and also located the emergence of words like 'risk', 'danger' and 'crisis' in the eighteenth century and the transformation of rationalities of governing. Unlike discipline, which attempted to control everything, the *dispositif* of security allowed for events to cancel themselves. As Foucault has put it, what was at stake for the new *dispositif* was not the 'nullification of phenomena in the form of the prohibition, "you will not do this", nor even, "this will not happen", but in the form of a progressive self-cancellation of phenomena by the phenomena themselves' (Foucault 2007: 66). At exactly the same time at which Foucault places the emergence of this rationality of governance, questions of how to govern were opened anew in the wake of a major event: the Lisbon Earthquake of 1755. In a sense, the governance of unexceptional events – such as food shortages or epidemics – is inter-linked with the governance of catastrophic events such as the Lisbon Earthquake. The eighteenth century also sees the question of epidemics posed in catastrophic terms. The new rationality of political economy that Foucault ascribed to the Physiocrats – Turgot or Quesnay for example – emerged in the context of debates generated by the catastrophic Lisbon Earthquake. On the one hand, the Physiocrats had been influenced by the Leibnizian doctrine of optimism, which found itself on trial after the Lisbon Earthquake. As Werner Stark remarks, Leibniz's theories provided the 'historical background and intellectual bases for the theories of the French Physiocrats and Scottish philosophers' (Stark 2003 [1947]: 6). On the other hand, the Marquis de Pombal's reconstruction of Lisbon followed Physiocratic theories and principles of mercantilism and enlightened despotism.

The Lisbon Earthquake is widely held to have been central to the development of European thought. From the ruins of Lisbon, it has been argued, emerged a different order, based on Enlightenment values and capitalist modernity. As Walter Benjamin (1999) said in a radio play for children, the Lisbon Earthquake stimulated scientific research, measurement and prediction and, as such, carried the promise of overcoming evil through technological inventions. In fact, the very concept of catastrophe as a particular type of event and as a social and political stake about the future was an eighteenth-century invention (Mercier-Faivre and Thomas 2008). What counts for the problematization of catastrophe is not so much the destruction it causes but the ways in which it transforms representations of and knowledge about the world. As we have shown, insurantial practices also emerged in the context of catastrophic events that appeared at the time of the Lisbon Earthquake. The catastrophic event was both entwined with the existing politics of knowledge and was among the conditions of possibility for the emergence of new modes of knowledge.

We have explored how the knowledge of catastrophe becomes self-authenticating and gains objectivity. Rather than focusing on political and institutional struggles – how knowledge, to quote Ian Hacking (1992: 131) again, is 'pushed and shaped by social vectors of every sort' – we have tried to show how the styles of reasoning about catastrophes build an unquestioned regime of truth. Or, perhaps more appropriately to the knowledge of catastrophes to come, how they amount to an unquestioned regime of plausibility and possibility. By looking more closely at the governance of the 'next terrorist attack', we have analysed the challenge of the unknown future through a genealogical method that interrogates problematizations of security as being embedded not just in professional struggles but also in the formulation and redeployment of styles of reasoning that regulate and decide on the acceptability of discursive statements and technological knowledges. Styles of reasoning, an idea we have borrowed from Hacking, are 'put in place in a network of people, answering to the needs, interests, ideology, or curiosity of some of its members, defended by bluster or insidious patience' (Hacking 1992: 131). Yet, besides these conditions of possibility, styles of reasoning also raise the question of conditions of validity. They give rise to particular forms of objectivity and entrench ways of knowing.

Although various styles of reasoning have been mobilized for securing catastrophic futures, we have suggested that conjectural reasoning increasingly needs to be considered as a particular style of reasoning itself. Conjectural reasoning looks for clues and insignificant details and draws links based on criteria of plausibility rather than truthfulness. However, the conjectural reasoning discussed here undergoes several strategic modifications in comparison to Ginzburg's analysis. It is not focused on the individual case, but is automated and sped up by computing technologies. The knowledge of catastrophes to come works with assumptions of two worlds: first, the world of appearances and, secondly, the 'hidden' world where clues can be gleaned and processed. The question of the limit leads to the isolation of imagination and the aesthetics of particular ways of accessing the 'hidden' world. Imagination and aesthetics were discussed as offering privileged access to this hidden world and hence indispensable to knowledge production and acquisition. Moreover, both imagination and aesthetics are not only individualized, mental faculties but also socially and historically constructed. Imagination needs to be understood as both subjective and collective. Similarly, sensorial perception does not only define individual experience, but also collective constructions of seeing, hearing, smelling, touching and so on.

The imagination and sensorial perceptions of clues, signs and details – through scenarios, exercises, conjectural mapping and vigilance – entrench the idea of two worlds by attempting to directly access the 'hidden' world. For instance, preparedness is often justified on the basis of conjectures. Any element in the biography of a suspected terrorist (be those suspected only for terrorism-related matters) is correlated with a potential terrorist attack in a different place. If suspected terrorists were travelling between London and Luton, then one can assume that a terrorist attack may happen in Dunstable, which is 'down the road' from Luton.[1] Or, in a different context: if Glasgow was possible, why not Doncaster? Terrorist attacks do not just take place in London. There are many crowded places in South Yorkshire, we were told in an ARGUS session. Other correlations are also conjectural, such as the correlation between international and domestic events: the international becomes domestic, CTSAs point out during preparedness exercises. Hence preparedness against Mumbai-type attacks is rehearsed domestically in the UK

How can we challenge the objectivity acquired by conjectural reasoning and epistemologies of the hidden world versus the world of appearances? How do we think catastrophe as an upturn of normative systems and power relations without buying into its governmentality? First of all, it is important to recognize that the distinction between the world of hidden facts and the world of appearances is a highly unstable one. It is a particularly modern experience with roots in the experience of confession and access to deep meanings. Slavoj Žižek for instance has replaced the hidden character of 'unknown unknowns' with the depth of 'unknown knowns', transferring the analysis to things which are known but disavowed and oppressed. Similarly, the structural analyses of disaster and catastrophe proposed by the Marxist-inspired literature in human geography and anthropology made visible a different way of thinking the distinction between appearances and the hidden world by causally linking the manifestation of catastrophe to, as Marx put it, the hidden abode of production. For Foucault, genealogy is a methodology of the surface. The 'hidden' and the invisible is that which is silenced by particular configurations of power and knowledge – be they political struggles or antagonistic modes of knowledge. Approaching catastrophic events as particular epistemic objects has allowed us to distinguish particular modes of knowledge and practices deployed in the anticipation of catastrophe from the diagnosis of exceptionalism. September 11, Katrina or the Haiti Earthquake more recently have all been analysed as exceptional and the occasion for exceptional politics. Yet, theories of the exception are not epistemological – they are interested in jurisdiction rather than veridiction and the politics of knowledge in which catastrophic events are shrouded

Nevertheless, there is a danger that a Foucauldian analysis of events and eventalization is recaptured back into the structure. Foucault, of course, was well aware of this and the related danger that making visible alternative forms of knowledge also opens up for the possibility for these to be colonized, subjugated or annexed by existing, dominant forms of knowledge (Foucault 2003: 11). As we discussed in Chapter 7, it is problematic to reduce catastrophe to structural causes, as this erases novelty and surprise. Yet, catastrophic events also raise the fundamental question of what the political implications are of envisioning the future as a radical break with the present. The politics of catastrophe is both a politics of knowledge and a politics of events, of the unexpected, of that which happens and shatters what is.

Interestingly, in the eighteenth century, philosophers of science used the terminology of catastrophe indistinguishably from that of revolution. Tracing the mutations of these two concepts from the eighteenth century on, Catherine Larrère (2008) has located a shift in the mid-nineteenth century. Catastrophe, which started from the domain of theatre and of overturnings in the lives of individuals or collectives, started to become used in the domain of natural sciences to refer to transformations of the earth instead. By contrast, revolution, which referred to astronomic cycles, became inseparable from human history. Yet, the two have never been entirely separated and the distinction between the human, the social and the natural has been politicized time and again. As the term catastrophe and its associated regime of knowledge encompassed a continuum of events – from nuclear terrorism to extreme weather events and from pandemics to war – the connection and relation with the concept of revolution were obscured. The final chapter therefore placed catastrophe in a different continuum: catastrophe-exception-event.

Badiou's theory of events looks at the displacement of existing knowledge or what the calls the 'encyclopedia of knowledge' by the event. Badiou works within a paradigm of truth – the event brings about the truth of a situation and does not necessarily answer a regime of plausibility and conjectural reasoning. Badiou's theory of events challenges the model of two worlds: the event is not absorbed into structural conditions or conditions of possibility; at the same time it is not entirely foreign to the situation from which it emerges. The politics of catastrophe has been largely thought a politics of 'either … or': either predictability or unpredictability, either truth or plausibility, either knowns or unknowns. Thus, Jean-Pierre Dupuy could argue – against the formalization of the precautionary principle – that it is not scientific uncertainty which hampers efforts to tackle catastrophes to come, but the impossibility of believing that the worst would come (Dupuy 2008: 485). For him, the catastrophe is an event that comes out of nowhere and therefore only exists when it emerges as a possibility. A different reading of catastrophic events is possible when one thinks 'both … and' rather than 'either … or': both predictable and unpredictable, expected and unexpected, truthful and plausible, known and unknown, and necessary and improbable.

Notes

1 Introduction

1 For some of the most influential and recent discussions on the logic of security, see Dillon (1996), Buzan *et al.* (1998), Campbell (1998), Bigo (2004), Balzacq (2005), Hansen (2006), Huysmans (2006), Stritzel (2007), M. C. Williams (2007) and McDonald (2008). For an overview of these approaches, see Krause and Williams (1997) and the Case collective (2006).

2 The *Oxford English Dictionary* offers a 1943 usage that illuminates the professionalization of the use of 'incidents' in the UK context: 'Hunt & Pringle *Service Slang* There are no occasions, occurrences, or events in an airman's life. Anything that happens to him is an "incident" ... why, nobody knows.'

3 Similar courses and programmes have recently been developed at universities worldwide. Canada, Denmark, Israel, the Netherlands, South Africa and Sweden are just some of the countries where MA programmes in disaster and emergency management are offered to professionals. For a long list of higher education programmes on emergency management, homeland security and international disaster management in the United States, see the FEMA website: http://training. fema.gov/EMIweb/edu/collegelist/Alphabetical%20Listing%20of%20EM%20 HiEd%20Programs.doc (accessed 4 August 2010).

4 See, for example, the documentary film *Nuclear Tipping Point*, which focuses on conversations with four men intimately involved in American diplomacy and national security over the last four decades. These are former Secretary of State George Shultz, former Secretary of State Henry Kissinger, former Secretary of Defense Bill Perry and former Senator Sam Nunn.

5 The terminology of 'next catastrophe' has been used by Charles Perrow (2007). The qualitative differentiation of catastrophe from disaster and emergency is a relatively new development. Cold War manuals do not refer to catastrophe (e.g. Healy's *(1969) Disaster and Emergency Planning*), while most governmental and non-governmental actors use catastrophe as synonymous to disaster and crisis and therefore subsumable to existing managerial technologies.

6 Starting with a rail catastrophe in 1851, 'catastrophe' becomes a favoured term for technical accidents in *The Times*: railways, shipping, reservoirs and collieries become the sites of the new catastrophes.

7 Interview with Mathew Burrows, Danish Institute for International Studies, Copenhagen, 7 September 2009. In an article in *Foreign Policy*, Rozen (2009) referred to Mathew Burrows as '[t]he man reshaping how US intelligence views the future'.

8 Interview with Mathew Burrows, 7 September 2009.

9 See, for instance, Dean (1999), Rose (1999), Baker and Simon (2002), Ericson *et al.* (2003).

10 Osborne also points out that concepts such as 'revolution', 'crisis', 'Zeitgeist' or 'history' gained a specific historical meaning in this period.

11 We have suggested elsewhere that biopolitical technologies of risk management can be adjusted and transformed to answer the challenge of catastrophe (Aradau and van Munster 2007). The distinction between risk and uncertainty is one of the most frequently used to express the distinction between the calculability of statistics and supposed incalculability of the unexpected catastrophe. Nonetheless, rather than distinct categories, the two are continuously transformed (see e.g. O'Malley 2004).

12 Compared to Beck, Jean-Pierre Dupuy is more pessimistic about the possibilities of a radically different politics. Inspired by the 'failure of imagination' character-izing 9/11, he has argued, following Günther Anders, that 'we can no longer imagine the catastrophe' (Dupuy 2002a, 2005). Out of this predicament, Dupuy proposes a politics of enlightened catastrophism.

13 Jameson's definition of utopia is completely different from Koselleck's, for whom utopia is the real possibility of a society devoid of antagonism and hence equated with totalitarianism.

14 See for example the discussion of Foucault's work in Dreyfus and Rabinow (1983), Andersen (2003), Han (2002). Even if the periodization of Foucault's work often is made for heuristic or pedagogical reasons, it may nevertheless conceal impor-tant continuities in Foucault's scholarship as well as the ways in which Foucault returned to, reworked and redeployed his earlier findings.

15 See the Case collective (2006) on the terminology of schools in security studies.

16 See e.g. Ericson and Doyle (2004b), O'Malley (2004) and Bougen and O'Malley (2009).

17 See e.g. Ericson and Haggerty (1997), Huysmans (2006), Aradau (2008), Bigo and Tsoukala (2008) and van Munster (2009).

2 Securing catastrophic futures

1 A *dispositif* consists of 'discourses, institutions, architectural forms, regulatory decisions, laws, administrative measures, scientific statements, philosophical, moral and philanthropic propositions' (Foucault 1980: 194). Michel Foucault has emphasized the strategic function of the *dispositif* and its heterogeneous elements and its emergence at the intersection of power and knowledge. Gilles Deleuze has offered a more systematic reading of the *dispositif* through particular categories of lines of enunciation, visibility, subjectivation and force (Deleuze 1992).

2 The international relations (IR) theorists' periodization of risk society in terms of Cold War/post-Cold War is remarkably at odds with the periodization employed by the sociological approaches to risk upon which they claim to build. For instance, Ulrich Beck locates the 'risk society' well within the timeline of the Cold War and his distinction between a first and a second modernity implies a different periodization than the Cold War/post-Cold War one. The assumption that risk is characteristic of post-Cold War is also put in question by recent claims that 'the actual practice of how risks are handled in international affairs by the US has been in decline since the 1990s' (Bracken *et al.* 2008: 2). IR theorists often defend their periodization by claiming that military professionals only began to employ the vocabulary of risk after the Cold War. The language of risk was explicitly used in strategic studies – the discipline that informed many of the military practices of security during the Cold War – to think about how to secure the future against the contingency of a catastrophic nuclear war.

3 For a discussion of the role and significance of nuclear strategists in the formulation of American security policy, see Kaplan (1983), Trachtenberg (1991) and
Kuklick (2007).

4 For an exception, see the work of Lobo-Guerrero (2010). In their recent intellectual history of security studies, Buzan and Hansen (2009: 250) oddly hold on to
the view that risk is a somewhat marginal concept to security studies. Particularly
their claim that studies of risk have failed to engage debates in security studies is
peculiar. First, it ignores that risk is a specific way of problematizing security even
if the language of security is not explicitly used. Secondly, their statement that risk
is an oppositional concept to security and therefore of a different order overlooks
the fact that a wide range of scholars have developed their understandings of
risk through an explicit engagement with key theories in security studies. At a
minimum, therefore, an intellectual history of security studies should include a
serious inspection of the ways in which risk theorists have engaged with and contributed to core theoretical and empirical themes in security studies. By bringing
to light alternative ways of problematizing security than that offered by the logic
of securitization, risk actually offers some of the most profound contributions and
challenges to contemporary security studies. See e.g. Aradau and van Munster
(2007), de Goede (2008a), Petersen (2008) and the contributions to the 2008
special issue on 'Security, Technologies of Risk and the Political', *Security Dialogue*
39(2/3).

5 Foucault's genealogy of the European state had already revealed that domestic
and international security emerged together in the seventeenth century as part
of the twin rationalities of *police* and *raison d'état*, where a healthy and productive
population was considered a necessary precondition for a strong and powerful
state (Foucault 2007a). Similar points have been made by Mark Neocleous (2006)
and Kevin Rozario (2007) about the United States in the twentieth century.

6 See Aradau and van Munster (2007), de Goede (2008c), Muller (2008), Bougen
(2009), Anderson (2010b) and Grusin (2010).

7 The distinction between uncertainty and risk is based on the work of Frank Knight
(1946) and John Maynard Keynes (1964).

8 Jacqueline Best (2009: 359) has wrongly identified this view on uncertainty with
our work. However, our earlier writings on precautionary risk have been very
much concerned with the computation of the future in non-quantitative ways.
See e.g. Aradau and van Munster (2007) and the subsequent chapters (especially
Chapters 5 and 6) in this book.

9 IR scholars have wrongly attributed the origins of the language of risk to NATO's
post-Cold War strategy (Coker 2009, M. J. Williams 2008, Rasmussen 2004, 2006).

10 The idea of threshold is clearly present in the concept's meaning in ancient
Greece. 'Crisis' relates back to the verb *krinein*, meaning 'to separate', 'to divide',
'to discriminate' and 'to decide' (Ritter 1986, O'Connor 1987, Hay 1996).
Functioning as a central political, juridical and medical concept in antiquity,
the concept of crisis was not just related to division, both in the sense of separation and conflict, but also to *decision* in the sense of a final result or judgement. It
thus referred to critical (a term closely related to crisis) decisions made regarding
peace or war, life or death or right or wrong (Koselleck 1982: 617). According to
the *Oxford English Dictionary*, crisis implies a decisive moment or turning point in
which a change – for better or worse – is imminent.

11 This rendering of crisis marginalized Cuba's sovereignty and past US efforts to
depose Castro (Laffey and Weldes 2008). In offering a decolonizing reading of
the Cuban Missile Crisis, Mark Laffey and Jutta Weldes expose the processes that
render Cuba's agency and history invisible. However, the influence of the Cuban
Missile Crisis not just for security studies but also for organizational studies and
emergency management has remained largely unshaken.

12 See Chapter 6 for a discussion of how sensorial experience supplements the knowledge of catastrophic futures.

13 Herman Kahn especially was occupied by questions of civil defence and developed different scenarios outlining how long it would take for society to recuperate economically in the hypothetical event of twenty, forty, eighty million or even more deaths from nuclear war. He was optimistic that the war effort could continue: 'A properly prepared country is not "killed" by the destruction of even a major fraction of its wealth; it is more likely to be set back a given number of years in its economic growth. While recuperation times may range all the way from one to a hundred years, even the latter is far from the "end of history" … Despite a widespread belief to the contrary, objective studies indicate that even though the amount of human tragedy would be greatly increased in the postwar world, the increase would not preclude normal and happy lives for the majority of survivors and their descendants' (Kahn 1960: 21).

3 Conjectures of catastrophe

1 Arnold Davidson (2004) has discussed the work of Ginzburg alongside that of Foucault and Hacking, but does not explicitly draw attention to the idea of conjectural epistemology as a separate style of reasoning. Rather, his discussion of Ginzburg remains limited to the question of what constitutes a valid statement, not under what conditions a certain statement may become a candidate for truth or evidence (Davidson 2004: xii).

2 This is nicely captured by the title *The Encyclopaedia of Ignorance: Everything You Ever Wanted to Know about the Unknown*, a volume that brings together contributions from a range of well-known authors on physics and the life sciences (Duncan and Weston-Smith 1977).

3 Nancy Tuana (2004: 195) has called for attention to ignorance in feminist epistemologies of knowledge given 'the realization that ignorance should not be theorized as a simple omission or gap but is, in many cases, an active production'. She suggests that ignorance is linked to issues of cognitive authority, doubt, trust, silencing and uncertainty. The construction and reproduction of ignorance, of non-knowledge or lack of knowledge, requires heterogeneous techniques and alliances that are not separate from the construction and reproduction of knowledge but are an integral part of this process.

4 The role that secrecy holds in the problematization of terrorism is unique in relation to other catastrophic events. While the risk of climate change is also problematized as a man-made risk rather than an external accident (as risks to the social were problematized by insurance techniques), terrorism appears as an intentional risk which brings to the fore intersubjective relationships. As the sociologist Georg Simmel noted in his writings on truth, error and secrecy, '[n]o other object of knowledge can reveal or hide itself in the same way, because no other object modifies its behaviour in view of the fact that it is recognized' (Wolff 1950: 310).

5 See http://www.sdu.dk/Om_SDU/Fakulteterne/Teknik/Forskning/antiterror. aspx?sc_lang=en (accessed 12 May 2010).

6 Secrecy appears as a problem of knowledge not only in relation to the object of knowledge (terrorism) but also in relation to the subjects of knowledge (security and intelligence experts), as there is a 'fundamental tension between an increasingly networked world, which is ideal terrain for the new religious terrorism, and highly compartmentalized national intelligence-gathering' (Aldrich 2004: 734). In relation to police culture, Ericson remarked that secrecy is necessary for the capacity to act and maintain a competitive advantage, as well as a legal requirement (Ericson 1989). In his ethnographic study of the US intelligence community,

Johnston (2005) has however shown that intelligence generates knowledge in ways similar to other bureaucracies and suffers from the same pathologies that obstruct the generation, analysis and dispersal of knowledge in other organizations (e.g. bias, taboos, socialization, time constraints and rewards and incentives).

7   For a conceptual comparison of privacy and secrecy, see also Warren and Laslett (2010).

8   Carlo Ginzburg has pointed out that '[i]n a positivist perspective, the evidence is analyzed only in order to ascertain if, and when, it implies a distortion, either intentional or unintentional' (Ginzburg 1991: 121). Therefore the analysis of terrorism-related data is based on a few simplified possibilities: some behaviours are real and authentic, other behaviours are lies and still others appear as authentic when they are intentionally or unintentionally fake (or secretive). The evidence is seen as a 'transparent medium – as an open window that gives us direct access to reality', rather than as something that is part of an interpretive context.

9   On the assumptions underpinning the state politics of protection, see Young (2003).

10 As a noun, precaution means a particular measure taken in advance to avoid or minimize the effects of a danger, to maximize the likelihood of a good outcome, or to prevent something unpleasant or inconvenient from happening (*Oxford English Dictionary*). In this sense, precautions are part of the governance of terrorism as prudential conduct. 'Terrorism is a crime like any other, so follow the same precautions you normally take to avoid being the victim of a crime', notes a local authority website in the UK (East Riding of Yorkshire 2010). However, within the context of governing catastrophic events, we show that precaution takes on a wider and more specific meaning.

11 See http://www.londonfirst.co.uk/networks2/security–resilience/ (accessed 20 December 2010).

12 Genealogies of resilience trace its emergence to the disciplines of psychology and psychiatry in the 1940s and accredit it to Norman Garmezy, Emma Werner and Ruth Smith. A versatile concept, psychological resilience has developed in close connection with the concepts of vulnerability, trauma and criticality. The psychology of resilience emerged out of studies of children 'at risk' who did not develop psychological disorders. As psychological knowledge sought to sever direct linkages between antecedents and consequences in analyses of clinical risk and look at exceptions to the rule, it also found in resilience a way to 'keep hope alive in clinical practice: however much the dice are loaded against a good outcome, we know that many children escape their ill fate' (Wolff 1995: 565).

13 As medicine is faced with an great variety of phenomena, it cannot find a law for all of them. Indeed, as Foucault reminds us, the medicine of symptoms gave way in the eighteenth-century to pathological anatomy: 'The medicine of symptoms will gradually recede, until it finally disappears before the medicine of organs, sites, causes, before a clinic wholly ordered in accordance with pathological anatomy' (Foucault 1973: 150). For Ginzburg, it is thus no surprise that Sherlock Holmes's right hand is Doctor Watson.

14 For a discussion of the political implications of Ginzburg's analysis of conjectural knowledge as a form of knowledge that transcends history, see Palladino (2008).

4   Economies of catastrophe

1   For an exception in security studies, see Luis Lobo-Guerrero (2007, 2010). In an earlier article, we have also argued for the need to consider insurance in security studies (Aradau and van Munster 2008a).

2 The Act was extended in 2005 and then again for another seven years in 2007, and is known as the Terrorism Risk Insurance Program, Reauthorization Act (TRIPRA).
3 As the original Act stipulates, 'the United States Government should provide temporary financial compensation to insured parties, contributing to the stabilization of the United States economy in a time of national crisis, while the financial services industry develops the systems, mechanisms, products, and programs necessary to create a viable financial services market for private terrorism risk insurance' (US Congress 2002, Sec. 101[6]).
4 Another technology – the transfer of risks to the financial market in the form of CAT bonds – developed to govern other catastrophic risks such as floods and earthquakes (Bougen 2003), has been deemed immoral for terrorism. The Pentagon's attempt to create a futures market in terrorism, the so-called Policy Analysis Market (PAM), was therefore short-lived. For a discussion, see Looney (2004).
5 However, with the expansion of insurance beyond the wage system, solidarity is simultaneously undermined through the division of citizens in high-risk/low-risk groups. As insurance relies on the selection and classification of groups according to their riskiness, profiling entered the *dispositif* of insurance by using probabilistic and epidemiological knowledge to identify factors associated with risks of certain pathologies (Rose 2001: 8). Besides, insurance always operated with internal divisions based on the notion of moral hazard.
6 With the rise of neoliberalism, the focus of insurance has shifted from reparation to the prevention of loss occurrence, ultimately making insurance more a matter of individual responsibility and choice. In this sense, neo-liberalism has spelt the end of the solidaristic society in favour of a neo-prudentialism that tends to only insure the 'wise' against contingency. This, however, does not mean that insurance has disappeared as a way of governing the social, merely that it has been supplanted with new technologies and rationalities.
7 See, for example, Chester (2001), Alexander (2002), Neiman (2002), Dupuy (2005) and Dynes (2005).
8 However, the risk management approach should probably be attributed to the Marquis of Pombal, who was in charge of reconstructing the city and rebuilt the city in a way that would make it less vulnerable to future disasters (França 1988, Maxwell 1965).
9 For a history of fire insurance in Great Britain, see Pearson (2004). For a brief overview of the emergence of fire insurance in different national contexts, see the report on fire insurance by Swiss Re (2009).
10 In Lisbon, too, the 1755 catastrophe had positive economic impacts, as the city was rebuilt as a leading commercial centre for international trade (Pereira 2009). This is beautifully symbolized by the city centre, which is no longer structured around the king's domicile or the palace of Inquisition but around the newly designed square at the waterfront, with the telling name 'Commercial Square'.
11 The fire insurance industry was also called upon to participate in the war effort through a mapping of vulnerabilities and the development of protection standards (O'Connor 1943). Insurance thus played a significant role in the regimes of uncertainty that were constituted by the concepts of crisis and disaster (see Chapter 2). The exact role of insurance as a strategy of (nuclear) defence during the Cold War still needs to be unpacked in security studies.
12 A producer of concrete silos, who probably saw civil defence as a niche market, had offered to build a nuclear shelter on Kahn's property. When Kahn discovered that the entry of the shelter was too small for him to enter, he apparently ordered it to be turned into a swimming pool (Ghamari-Tabrizi 2005: 14).
13 The qualitative and quantitative definition of what constitutes serious harm is left to the discretion of different countries/insurers.

14 According to Hacking (1990: 166), it was Auguste Comte who made famous the continuity between the normal and the pathological, the pathological being only an extension of the variation of a normal organism. However, when Comte transferred the analysis of normality from medicine to the social sphere, he added an extra twist: the normal was not simply the ordinary healthy state, but the 'purified state towards which we should strive'. The in-built tension in the normal as the existing average and a figure of perfection to which we might progress is also present in representations of terrorists. They are often represented as either abnormal in the sense of evil or as a deviation from what the normal as the average can mean. They are either 'radicalized' average citizens or 'false' Muslims or unimaginably evil others.

15 The 2002 TRIA originally defined a terrorist attack as an attack committed by foreigners in the US with a total damage of more than $5 million. The 2007 extension expanded the definition of a certified act of terrorism to eliminate any distinction between domestic and foreign acts. At the same time, the triggering threshold for the programme to go in effect rose from $5 million under the original Act to $50 million after March 2006 and to $100 million in 2007. The elimination of the distinction between domestic and foreign terrorism has functioned as an impetus for the stand-alone market (Insurance Information Institute 2010).

5 Imagining catastrophes

1 See http://abcnews.go.com/Technology/Earth2100/story?id=7736882&page=1 (accessed 12 May 2010).

2 The 2004 report *Mapping the Global Future* offers a series of fictional scenarios – *Davos World, Pax Americana, A New Caliphate* and *Cycle of Fear* – which all, with the exception of *Pax Americana*, immediately read as worst case scenarios. They imagine the rise of China and India to fundamentally alter the rules of the international game, the demise of Western values under the spiritual sway of a new Caliphate and the dissolution of all values under a new anarchical state of weapons proliferation and illegal trade. On a closer reading, *Pax Americana*, the scenario of a world dominated by American power, is also revealed as a worst case scenario that plays itself out against the background of a continually divided world and a politics of resentment that stands in the way of the collective management of global issues such as climate change. Only four years later, a fourth instalment of the reports by the NIC significantly modified the unexpected events of the future and developed four different scenarios: *A World without the West, October Surprise, BRICs' Bust-up* and *Politics Is Not Always Local*. In spite of these differences, however, these scenarios are played out against the background of future catastrophes. In the final scenario, for instance, the optimistic tale of politics driven by networks of non-state actors that get important treaties agreed is only made possible against the background of catastrophe, as action is sparked by repeated environmental disasters: 'The environment was tailor-made because [of] the widespread commonality of interest in avoiding the Armageddon' (National Intelligence Council 2008: 91D).

3 For a notable exception, see Bougen and O'Malley (2009). The importance of images, either as supporting or resisting security frames, has been pointed out by M. C. Williams (2003) and Muller (2008). See also the 2007 special issue on 'Securitization, Militarization and Visual Culture in the Worlds of Post-9/11', *Security Dialogue*, 38(2).

4 As Richard Kearney has put it, imagination refers to a 'representational faculty which reproduces images of some pre-existing reality' or to a 'creative faculty which produces images which often lay claim to an original status on their own

right' (Kearney 1988: 15). Brann (1991), for example, takes spatial images to be defining of imagination.

5 See e.g. the World Economic Form *Global Risks* reports, which map global risks through the application of social network analysis to understand correlations between these risks (World Economic Forum 2008, 2009).

6 However, Daston (1984) has astutely pointed out that the use of analogy in exposition by Galileo is wedded to a theory of imagination that is seen as both implicated in the procedures of science and feared. Although the use of analogy was limited in Galileo's works due to his distrust of imagination, it was by no means absent.

7 The distinction between fantasy and imagination is established in Kant: 'In social conversation people sometimes leap from one subject to another, quite different one, following an empirical association of ideas ... This desultoriness is a kind of nonsense in terms of form, which disrupts and destroys a conversation. Only when one subject has been exhausted and a short pause follows can we properly launch another subject, if it is interesting. A lawless, vagrant imagination so disconcerts the mind by a succession of ideas having no objective connection that we leave a gathering of this kind wondering whether we have been dreaming' (quoted in Schulte-Sasse 1986).

8 The concept of imagination remains an elusive one, and has different and sometimes even contradictory meanings. In a philosophical review of the conception of imagination, Stevenson (2003) distinguishes no less than twelve different, albeit partly overlapping, definitions. Besides the two discussed here, Richard Kearney (1988) has identified a third paradigm of imagination in the psychoanalytic conception of 'imaginary', associated particularly with Lacan's work but also with philosophers such as Marcuse and Castoriadis. We have not engaged with psychoanalytic approaches given our interest in epistemology and knowledge rather than the relation between the imaginary and images.

9 Aristotle was the first to see imagination as an aspect of mental life (Cocking 1991: 17). For Aristotle, the various sensations are related and compared by the *sensus communis*, the common sense, which creates a unitary appearance, the *phantasia*.

10 Later on, Kant argued that it is important to consider imagination not just as reproducing perceptions for thought, but also as having productive capacity. In *Anthropology from a Pragmatic Point of View*, imagination is seen as part of sensibility alongside the senses (Kant 2006 [1798]). Thus, for Kant, 'sense is the power of intuiting in the presence of the object, imagination without its presence'.

11 Spivak has been similarly critical of Kant's analytic of the sublime for presupposing a 'cultured' subject able to bring the sublime under control because of their rational vocation (Spivak 1999). Lyotard on the other hand has reversed the relationship between imagination and reason in the spectator's perception of the sublime and has rendered the subject dependent upon the 'law of the other' See Rancière (2004b).

12 In *Anthropology from a Pragmatic Point of View*, Kant (2006 [1798]) also distinguishes productive and reproductive imagination or 'original' and 'derivative' imagination.

13 For ampler discussions of the role of the sublime in international politics, see the 2006 special issue on the Sublime, *Millennium*, 34(3).

14 The term 'technology of futurity' is borrowed from Lentzos and Rose (2009).

15 Collier and Lakoff (2008) have shown that many of the security technologies deployed in the post-9/11 era are traceable to ideas developed in the context of operations research, strategic bombing, civil defence and nuclear deterrence.

16 On the role of the senses in the governance of future catastrophes, see Chapter 6.

17 See http://graphicfacilitation.blogs.com/pages/2005/02/importance_of_s.html (accessed 20 December 2010).

18 Feminist scholars have drawn attention to the imbrications of reason and emotion in nuclear discourse. Carol Cohn's incursion in the world of defence intellectuals has revealed the 'rational' language of security as gendered and overflowing with violence. She also shows the ways in which the metaphors used by the community contribute to the domestication of nuclear weapons (Cohn 1987).

19 In *Thinking about the Unthinkable in the 1980s* (1984), Kahn directly refers to Schell's book, claiming that while the book's broad emotional appeal is to be welcomed, its portrayal of the future is flawed and too bleak. See Kahn (1984: 47, 207–208).

20 Interviews with Counter-Terrorism Security Advisers (CTSAs), UK, April-August 2009.

21 Project ARGUS 2009, Project Griffin and interviews with CTSAs.

22 See   http://www.cityoflondon.police.uk/citypolice/utility/redirection.htm (accessed 27 August 2008).

23 Research notes from ARGUS sessions in Doncaster, Cambridge, Guildford, Dunstable, Colchester and London (April-August 2009).

24 Research notes from ARGUS Hotels, Cambridge, 20 June 2009.

25 ARGUS event for retail, Doncaster, 4 June 2009; ARGUS event for hotels (pilot), Cambridge, 29 June 2009.

26 'Cover' is about hiding from view; 'confirm' concerns attention to exact location, number of gunmen and type of weapons; 'contact' is about calling the emergency number (999 in the UK) and 'control' about taking leadership in a situation. Research notes from ARGUS Hotels, Cambridge, 29 June 2009.

27 Research notes from ARGUS Retail, Doncaster, 4 June 2009.

28 Although this collective approach can be glimpsed in the work of Kant, it probably has found its most clear expression in the work of Arendt.

29 Chakrabarty (2000) rightly notes that Anderson does not theorize the concept of imagination despite the widespread use of the word.

30 'Stage Fright' exercise, 2000, UK Emergency Planning College Library archive.

31 Percival, Jenny (24 March 2009), 'New strategy will train shop and hotel managers to tackle terrorist threats', *Guardian*, available at http://www.guardian.co.uk/uk/2009/mar/24/anti-terror-al-qaida-weapons (accessed 20 December 2010).

32 Research notes from ARGUS exercises.

33 Joseph Bendersky (2007) has shown that Le Bon's psychology of the crowds was influential in US military thinking and practice through World War II.

34 For a discussion of different imaginations of the crowds in liberal thought, see Robin (2004).

6 Aesthetics of catastrophe

1 See for example the 2000 special issue of *Alternatives* on poetics and world politics, the 2006 special issue of *Millennium* on the sublime in international politics, the 2007 special issue of *Security Dialogue* on post-9/11 visual culture or the special issue of *Review of International Studies* on art and politics.

2 Yet, Rancière's answer is not as straightforward as he intimates in the conditions of (post-)modernity. As different theorists have pointed out, modernity is characterized by an overload of the senses through the multiplication and pervasiveness of sensorial stimuli (Buck-Morss 1992, Crary 2001).

3 According to Rancière (2005), art's possibility to invalidate existing hierarchies and cause ruptures in the distribution of time and space is at the heart of Plato's prohibition of theatre. His understanding of the republic as the organic embodiment of the collective could not tolerate an artistic stage where actors could assume a role other than their own. Avant-gardism, of course, is founded upon the notion that to be progressive, art must radicalize itself through a transgression of the rules of its production (Buckley 2009). Dadaists, for instance, played

with the distinction between art and non-art by portraying everyday objects on their canvases, and Andy Warhol later introduced mass-produced commodities such as soup tins into the secluded space of the museum.

4 Although climate change is seen to lag behind the fictional and popular culture propensity towards catastrophic terrorism, there is now a growing literature in the 'climate change sci-fi' genre. J. G. Ballard's *The Drowned World*, Bruce Sterling's *Heavy Weather* and Kim Stanley Robinson's *Science in the Capital* trilogy and many other sci-fi novels have tackled climate change. Board games now deploy apocalyptic scenarios of climate change: *Antarctica: Global WARming* by Savita Games pictures a world where leaders fight to gain access to the remaining land masses.

5 Projects in the UK have similarly used cartoons for preparedness purposes. Comic books and cartoon serials have attracted the imagination of the UN and other organizations involved in the prevention of climate change and its consequences. The UN has started a partnership with Marvel Comics (producers of *Spider Man* and *The Fantastic Four*) to produce a comic book about the UN fighting disease, poverty and conflict around the world. The book would be freely distributed to children in public schools in the US. *Captain Planet*, a comic character invented by CNN founder and strong UN supporter Ted Turner, has already played a similar role in making the public aware of problems like environmental degradation and pollution.

6 This is not to say that there isn't an aesthetics of risk assessment and calculability – graphs, statistical tables and so on are all aesthetic forms that foster particular affects and bodily reactions in the subjects deemed to be in control.

7 Ironically, the picture that accompanies the optimistic title 'the sky is the limit' is taken from Jonathan Swift's *Gulliver's Travels* and depicts Gulliver looking up at the floating city of Laputa, which is a male-dominated society characterized domestically by high inequality between rulers and servants and externally by a violent and tyrannical domination of cities on the mainland. Although floating cities have captured the human imagination since, for Swift the city of Laputa (apparently, Swift was well aware of its meaning in Spanish) represents the English government's repressive policies at home and abroad (Ireland).

8 See the Los Angeles Police Department, http://www.lapdonline.org/iwatchla/content_basic_view/42535 (accessed 13 October 2010).

9 Later, however, Jameson also cautioned against the spatialization of the social: '[W]e might be tempted to think that the social can be mapped that way, by following across a map insurance red lines and the electrified borders of private police and surveillance forces. Both images are, however, only caricatures of the mode of production itself (most often called late capitalism), whose mechanism and dynamics are not visible in that sense, cannot be detected on the surfaces scanned by satellites, and therefore stand as a fundamental representational problem – indeed a problem of a historically new and original type' (Jameson 1995: 2). In the next chapter, we discuss Marxist-inspired work that relies on an unearthing of the causes and mechanisms through which catastrophes are produced instead of conjectural mapping.

10 For a discussion of Lombardi's maps in relation to Jameson's cognitive mapping, see Toscano and Kinkle (2009).

11 See for instance the article 'Rampenoefening Euroborg loopt uit de hand' in *De Volkskrant* (11 November 2009), available at http://www.volkskrant.nl/sport/article1314704.ece/Rampenoefening_Euroborg_loopt_uit_de_hand (accessed 3 September 2010).

7 Catastrophe, exception, event

1   For a discussion of the spatialization of the exception in Schmitt's *Nomos of the Earth*, see Aradau (2007).
2   These processes of routinization, redeployment of knowledge and the governance of life have also been explored by drawing on Foucault's analysis of biopolitics. However, this is not without problems. On the one hand, in IR the shift from national to human security is often considered to be a post-Cold War development. On the other, the biopolitics of security as theorized by Foucault is an eighteenth-century development. How does one account for these different periodizations and transformations from securing territories to securing the life of populations? Although several authors have recently attempted to bring together sovereignty and biopolitics, either by considering life as the proper domain of sovereignty or by supplementing biopolitics with necropolitics, these periodizations make it difficult to understand the reiteration of the shift from sovereignty to biopolitics in current contexts (Agamben 1998).
3   This framing rejects a quasi-theological rendering of the event as 'pure' and ultimately transhistorical (as theories of the exception tend to do). If the event, by the emphasis on decision and sovereignty, appears to belong to the same theoretical and political species of exceptions (Wright 2008), there are important differences. Events are rupturing; they are interruptions rather than constitutive moments that reinforce and reproduce existing orders. Moreover, exceptions have been mainly considered in the juridical realm – even where exceptional practices appear to be more dispersed throughout the social – and tend to emphasize the sovereign decision at the expense of the event.
4   Obviously, the event is conceptualized differently in these works: Foucault – who never theorized the event as such – is close to Deleuze in his focus on the event as the invention of a singularity. By contrast, Badiou (2007) originally distanced himself explicitly from Deleuze and calls for a more radical understanding of the event as rupture. However, as several observers have noticed, Badiou's framework may share important traits with Deleuze's (and Foucault's) understanding of the event. See for instance Faber *et al.* (2010).

8 Conclusion

1   Research notes from ARGUS exercise, Dunstable, 18 April 2009.

References

ACE (2006), *ACE Terrorism Risk: Claim Scenarios*, http://www.aceterrorismrisk.com/claimsScen.asp (accessed August 2006).

Adam, Barbara (2003), 'Reflexive Modernization Temporalized', *Theory, Culture and Society* 20(2), pp. 59–78.

Adam, David (2008), 'Cartoonists Use Humour to Tackle Climate Change', *Guardian*, 23 July 2008.

Adorno, Theodor W. (1973 [1966]), *Negative Dialectics*, New York: Seabury Press.

___ (2004), *Aesthetic Theory*, London: Continuum Press.

___ (2005), *Critical Models: Interventions and Catchwords*, translated by Henry W. Pickford, New York: Columbia University Press.

Agamben, Giorgio (1998), *Homo Sacer: Sovereign Power and Bare Life*, translated by Daniel Heller-Roazen, Stanford: Stanford University Press.

Aldrich, Richard J. (2004), 'Transatlantic Intelligence and Security Cooperation', *International Affairs* 80(4), pp. 731–753.

Alexander, David (2002), 'Nature's Impartiality, Man's Inhumanity: Reflections on Terrorism and World Crisis in a Context of Historical Disaster', *Disasters* 26(1), pp. 1–9.

Allison, Graham T. (1971), *Essence of Decision: Explaining the Cuban Missile Crisis*, New York: Harper Collins Publishers.

___ (2005), *Nuclear Terrorism: The Ultimate Preventable Catastrophe*, New York: Henry Holt.

Amoore, Louise (2007), 'Vigilant Visualities: The Watchful Politics of the War on Terror', *Security Dialogue* 38(2), pp. 215–232.

___ (2009), 'Algorithmic War: Everyday Geographies of the War on Terror', *Antipode* 41(1), pp. 49–69.

Amoore, Louise and Marieke de Goede (2005), 'Governance, Risk and Dataveillance in the War on Terror', *Crime, Law and Social Change* 43, pp. 149–173.

___ (2008), 'Transactions after 9/11: The Banal Face of the Preemptive Strike', *Transactions of the Institute of British Geographers* 33(2), pp. 173–185.

Anders, Günther (1956), *Die Antiquiertheit des Menschen. Über die Seele im Zeitalter der Zweiten industriellen Revolution*, Munich: Verlag C.H. Beck.

___ (1981), *Die atomare Drohung. Radikale Überlegungen*, Munich: Verlag C.H. Beck.

Andersen, Niels Åkerstrom (2003), *Discursive Analytical Strategies: Understanding Foucault, Koselleck, Laclau, Luhmann*, Bristol: Policy Press.

Anderson, Ben (2007), 'Hope for Nanotechnology: Anticipatory Knowledge and the Governance of Affect', *Area* 39(2), pp. 156–165.

___ (2010a), 'Security and the Future: Anticipating the Event of Terror', *Geoforum* 41(2), pp. 227–235.

___ (2010b), 'Preemption, Precaution, Preparedness: Anticipatory Action and Future Geographies', *Progress in Human Geography*, 34(6) pp. 1–22.

Anderson, Benedict (1991), *Imagined Communities: Reflections on the Origin and Spread of Nationalism*, London: Verso.

Anderson, Chris (2008), 'The End of Theory: The Data Deluge Makes the Scientific Method Obsolete', *Wired Magazine*, http://www.wired.com/science/discoveries/magazine/16-07/pb_theory (accessed 20 December 2010).

Anghie, Antony (2004), *Imperialism, Sovereignty and the Making of International Law*, Cambridge: Cambridge University Press.

AON (2005), *An Integrated Counter-Terrorism Solution*, http://www.aon.com/uk/en/risk_management/insurance/terrorism.jsp (accessed August 2006).

___ (2010), *2010 Terrorism Threat Map*, http://www.aon.com/risk-services/terrorism-risk-map/index.html (accessed July 2010).

Appadurai, Arjun (2000), 'Grassroots Globalization and the Research Imagination', *Public Culture* 12(1), pp. 1–19.

Aradau, Claudia (2007), 'Law Transformed: Guantanamo and the "Other" Exception', *Third World Quarterly* 28(3): pp. 489–501.

___ (2008), *Rethinking Trafficking in Women: Politics out of Security*, Basingstoke: Palgrave.

Aradau, Claudia and Rens van Munster (2007), 'Governing Terrorism through Risk: Taking Precautions, (Un)knowing the Future', *European Journal of International Relations* 13(1), pp. 89–115.

___ (2008a), 'Insuring Terrorism, Assuring Subjects, Ensuring Normality: The Politics of Risk after 9/11', *Alternatives* 33(2), pp. 191–210.

___ (2008b), 'Taming the Future: The *Dispositif* of Risk in the "War on Terror"', in: Louise Amoore and Marieke de Goede (eds), *Risk and the War on Terror*, London: Routledge, pp. 23–40.

Arendt, Hannah (1958), *The Human Condition*, Chicago: Chicago University Press.

___ (1973), *The Origins of Totalitarianism*, San Diego: Harcourt Brace & Company.

___ (1978), *The Life of the Mind: One Volume Edition*, San Diego: Harcourt Brace & Company.

Badiou, Alain (1998), 'Politics and Philosophy. Interview with Peter Hallward', *Angelaki* 3(3), pp. 113–133.

___ (2004a), *Infinite Thought: Truth and the Return of Philosophy*, translated by Oliver Feltham and Justin Clemens, London: Continuum.

___ (2004b), *Theoretical Writings*, translated by Ray Brassier and Alberto Toscano, London: Continuum.

___ (2006), *Being and Event*, translated by Oliver Feltham, London: Continuum.

___ (2007), 'The Event in Deleuze', *Parrhesia* 2, pp. 37–44.

Badiou, Alain and Bruno Bosteels (2005), 'Can Change Be Thought? A Dialogue with Alain Badiou', in: Gabriel Riera (ed.), *Alain Badiou: Philosophy and Its Conditions*, New York: State University of New York, pp. 244–260.

Baker, Tom (2002), 'Liability and Insurance after September 11: Embracing Risk Meets the Precautionary Principle', *The Geneva Papers on Risk and Insurance* 27(3), pp. 349–357.

Baker, Tom and Jonathan Simon (eds) (2002), *Embracing Risk*, Chicago: Chicago University Press.

Balibar, Étienne (1994), *Masses, Classes, and Ideas: Studies on Politics and Philosophy before and after Marx*, London: Routledge.

___ (2005), 'Difference, Otherness, Exclusion', *Parallax* 11(1), pp. 19–34.

Balzacq, Thierry (2005), 'The Three Faces of Securitization: Political Agency, Audience and Context', *European Journal of International Relations* 11(2), pp. 171–201.

Beck, Ulrich (1992), *Risk Society: Towards a New Modernity*, London: Sage.

___ (1999), *World Risk Society*, Cambridge: Polity Press.

___ (2002), 'The Terrorist Threat: World Risk Society Revisited', *Theory, Culture and Society* 19(4), pp. 39–55.

___ (2005), 'Risk Society Revisited: Theory, Politics and Research Programmes', in: Barbara Adam, Ulrich Beck and Joost van Loon (eds), *The Risk Society and Beyond: Critical Issues for Social Theory*, London: Sage, pp. 211–229.

Becker, Markus (2009), 'Copenhagen Failure. Gunning Full Throttle into the Greenhouse', *Spiegel*, 19 December, http://www.spiegel.de/international/world/0,1518,668111,00.html (accessed 20 December 2010).

Bellman, Beryl L. (1981), 'The Paradox of Secrecy', *Human Studies* 4(1), pp. 1–24.

Bendersky, Joseph W. (2007), '"Panic": The Impact of Le Bon's Crowd Psychology on U.S. Military Thought', *Journal of the History of the Behavioral Sciences* 43(3), pp. 257–283.

Benjamin, Walter (1999), 'The Lisbon Earthquake', in: Michael W. Jennings, Howard Eiland and Gary Smith (eds), *Selected Writings (vol. 2: 1927–1934)*, Cambridge, MA: Belknap Press, pp. 536–540.

Bennett, Brian T. (2007), *Understanding, Assessing and Responding to Terrorism: Protecting Critical Infrastructure and Personnel*, Hoboken: John Wiley & Sons.

Best, Jacqueline (2009), 'Ambiguity, Uncertainty, and Risk: Rethinking Indeterminacy', *International Political Sociology* 2(4), pp. 355–374.

Bigo, Didier (2002), 'Security and Immigration: Toward a Critique of the Governmentality of Unease', *Alternatives* 27(Special Issue), pp. 63–92.

___ (2004), 'Global (In)security: The Field of the Professionals of Unease Management and the Ban-opticon', in: Jon Solomon and Sakai Naoki (eds), *Traces: A multilingual series of cultural theory*, No. 4 (Sovereign Police, Global Complicity), Hong Kong: University of Hong Kong Press, pp. 109–57.

Bigo, Didier and Anastassia Tsoukala (eds) (2006), *Illiberal Practices of Liberal Regimes: The Games of (in)security*, Paris: L'Harmattan.

___ (eds) (2008), *Terror, Insecurity and Liberty. Illiberal Practices of Liberal Regimes after 9/11*, London and New York: Routledge.

Bleiker, Roland (2001), 'The Aesthetic Turn in International Political Theory', *Millennium* 30(3), pp. 509–533.

___ (2009), *Aesthetics and World Politics*, Basingstoke: Palgrave.

Bloch, Ernst (1995 [1959]), *The Principle of Hope*, Cambridge, Massachusetts: MIT Press.

Boin, Arjen (2005), 'From Crisis to Disaster: Towards an Integrative Perspective', in: Ronald W. Perry and Enrico L. Quarantelli (eds), *What is a Disaster? New Answers to Old Questions*, Philadelphia: Xlibris, pp. 153–172.

Bonanno, G. A. (2004), 'Loss, Trauma, and Human Resilience: Have We Underestimated the Human Capacity to Thrive after Extremely Aversive Events?' *American Psychologist* 59, pp. 20–28.

Booth, Ken and Nicholas J. Wheeler (2007), *The Security Dilemma: Fear, Cooperation and Trust in World Politics*, Basingstoke: Palgrave.

Borodzicz, Edward P. (2005), *Risk, Crisis and Security Management*, Chichester: John Wiley & Sons.

Bougen, Philip D. (2003), 'Catastrophe Risk', *Economy and Society* 32(2), pp. 253–274.

Bougen, Philip D. and Patrick O'Malley (2009), 'Bureaucracy, Imagination and U.S. Domestic Security Policy', *Security Journal* 22(2), pp. 1–18.

Bowie, Andrew (2003), *Aesthetics and Subjectivity: From Kant to Nietzsche*, Manchester: Manchester University Press.

Bracken, Paul, Ian Bremmer and David Gordon (eds) (2008), *Managing Strategic Surprise: Lessons from Risk Management and Risk Assessment*, Cambridge: Cambridge University Press.

Brann, Eva T. H. (1991), *The World of the Imagination: Sum and Substance*, Lanham, MD: Rowman & Littlefield Publishers.

Braun, Bruce (2007), 'Biopolitics and the Molecularization of Life', *Cultural Geographies* 14(1), pp. 6–28.

British Council (1999), 'Shopping Centres', UK.

British Nuclear Group (2007), *Level 2 Exercise 'Aragon'*.

Brodie, Bernard (1949), 'Strategy as Science', *World Politics* 1(4), pp. 467–488.

Brown, Wendy (2003), 'Neo-liberalism and the End of Liberal Democracy', *Theory and Event* 7(1).

___ (2006), *Regulating Aversion: Tolerance in the Age of Identity and Empire*, Princeton: Princeton University Press, http://muse.jhu.edu/journals/theory_and_event/v007/7.1brown.html (accessed 28 February 2011).

Buck-Morss, Susan (1992), 'Aesthetics and Anaesthetics: Walter Benjamin's Artwork Essay Reconsidered', *October* 62, pp. 3–41.

___ (2007), 'Sovereign Right and the Global Left', *Rethinking Marxism* 19(4), pp. 432–451.

Buckley, Bernadette (2009), 'The Workshop of Filthy Creation: Or Do Not Be Alarmed, This Is Only a Test', *Review of International Studies* 35(4), pp. 835–857.

Burke, Anthony (2002), 'The Perverse Perseverance of Sovereignty', *Borderlands* 1(2), http://www.borderlands.net.au/vol1no2_2002/burke_perverse.html (accessed 20 December 2010).

Bush, George W. (2002), 'President Signs Terrorism Insurance Act', http://www.whitehouse.gov/news/releases/2002/11/20021126-1.html (accessed August 2007).

Butler, Judith (2004), *Precarious Life: The Power of Mourning and Violence*, London: Verso.

Buzan, Barry and Lene Hansen (2009), *The Evolution of Security Studies*, Cambridge: Cambridge University Press.

Buzan, Barry, Ole Wæver and Jaap de Wilde (1998), *Security. A New Framework for Analysis*, London: Rienner.

Cabinet Office (2004), 'Civil Contingencies Act', UK government, http://www.legislation.gov.uk/ukpga/2004/36/contents (accessed 20 December 2010).

Campbell, David (1998), *Writing Security: United States Foreign Policy and the Politics of Identity*, Manchester: Manchester University Press.

Carter, Ashton B. (1987), 'Sources of Error and Uncertainty', in: Ashton B. Carter, John D. Steinbruner and Charles A. Zraket (eds), *Managing Nuclear Operations*, Washington: The Brookings Institution, pp. 611–640.

Carter, Ashton B., John M. Deutch and Philip D. Zelikow (1998), *Catastrophic Terrorism: Elements of a National Policy*, Visions of Governance in the 21st Century Project, Cambridge, MA: Harvard University, http://www.hks.harvard.edu/visions/publication/terrorism.htm (accessed 20 December 2010).

Case collective (2006), 'Critical Approaches to Security in Europe: A Networked Manifesto', *Security Dialogue* 37(4), pp. 443–487.

Castel, Robert (2002), 'The Emergence of Social Property', *Constellations* 9(3), pp. 318–334.

Castoriadis, Cornelius (1997), 'Imagination, imaginaire, réflexion', *Fait et à faire. Les carrefours du labyrinthe V*, pp. 227–281.

Centre for the Protection of National Infrastructure (CPNI) (2009), 'What We Do', London, http://www.cpni.gov.uk/About/whatWeDo.aspx (accessed 20 December 2010).

___ (2010), *Guide for Producing Operational Requirements for Security Measures*, http://www.cpni.gov.uk/Docs/measures-operational-requirements-guide.pdf (accessed 20 December 2010).

Cerny, Philip G. (2000), 'The New Security Dilemma: Divisibility, Defection and Disorder in the Global Era', *Review of International Studies* 26(4), pp. 623–646.

Chakrabarty, Dipesh (2000), *Provincializing Europe: Postcolonial Thought and Historical Difference*, Princeton: Princeton University Press.

Cheney, Richard B. (2001) "*Vice President Cheney Delivers Remarks to the Republican Governors Association*", October 25, 2001. Washington, Office of the White House.

Chermack, Thomas J. and Tiffani D. Payne (2006), 'Process Level Scenario Planning', *Academy of Strategic Management Journal* 5, pp. 115–131.

Chester, David (2001), 'The 1755 Lisbon Earthquake', *Progress in Physical Geography* 25(3), pp. 363–383.

Civil Contingencies Secretariat (2009), 'Exercises', London: Cabinet Office, http://interim.cabinetoffice.gov.uk/ukresilience/preparedness/exercises.aspx (accessed 26 January 2011).

Clarke, Lee B. (2005), *Worst Cases: Terror and Catastrophe in the Popular Imagination*, Chicago: University of Chicago Press.

Cocking, J. M. (1991), *Imagination: A Study in the History of Ideas*, London: Routledge.

Cohn, Carol (1987), 'Sex and Death in the Rational World of Defense Intellectuals', *Signs* 12(4), pp. 687–718.

Coker, Christopher (2009), *War in an Age of Risk*, Cambridge: Polity.

Collier, Stephen J. (2008), 'Enacting Catastrophe: Preparedness, Insurance, Budgetary Rationalization', *Economy and Society* 37(2), pp. 224–250.

Collier, Stephen J. and Andrew Lakoff (2008), 'Distributed Preparedness: The Spatial Logic of Domestic Security in the United States', *Environment and Planning D* 26(1), pp. 7–28.

Colwell, C. (1997), 'Deleuze and Foucault: Series, Event, Genealogy', *Theory and Event* 1(2), http://muse.jhu.edu/journals/theory_and_event/v001/1.2colwell.html (accessed 28 February 2011).

Comaroff, Jean and John Comaroff (2000), 'Millennial Capitalism: First Thoughts on a Second Coming', *Public Culture* 12(2), pp. 291–343.

Comfort, Louise K. (2005), 'Risk, Security, and Disaster Management', *Annual Review of Political Science* 8, pp. 335–356.

Communities and Local Government and Home Office (2010), *Crowded Places: The planning system and counter-terrorism*, http://www.communities.gov.uk/publications/planningandbuilding/crowdedplacesplanning (accessed 20 December 2010).

Cooper, Melinda (2004), 'On the Brink: From Mutual Deterrence to Uncontrollable War', *Contretemps* 4, pp. 2–18.

___ (2006), 'Pre-empting Emergence: The Biological Turn in the War on Terror', *Theory, Culture and Society* 23(4), pp. 113–135.

___ (2008), *Life as Surplus: Biotechnology and Capitalism in the Neoliberal Era*, Washington, DC: University of Washington Press.

Cote, John A. (2007), 'Are We Ready for the Next Terrorist Attack', in: *Homeland Security. News & Analysis of Critical Issues in Terrorism & Homeland Defense*, available at http://inhomelandsecurity.com/2007/02/are_we_ready_for_the_next_atta. html (accessed 26 January 2011).

Council of the European Union (2005), 'The European Union Counter-Terrorism Strategy', http://register.consilium.europa.eu/pdf/en/05/st14/st14469-re04. en05.pdf (accessed 20 December 2010).

___ (2010), 'Draft Internal Security Strategy for the European Union: "Towards a European Security Model"', Brussels, http://register.consilium.europa.eu/pdf/ en/10/st05/st05842-re02.en10.pdf (accessed 20 December 2010).

Crary, Jonathan (2001), *Suspensions of Perception: Attention, Spectacle, and Modern Culture*, Cambridge, MA: MIT Press.

Crisis Solutions (2008), *Exercising for Excellence: Delivering Successful Business Continuity Management Exercises*, London: British Standards Institute.

Danchev, Alex and Debbie Lisle (2009), 'Introduction: Art, Politics, Purpose', *Review of International Studies* 35(4), pp. 775–779.

Daston, Lorraine J. (1984), 'Galilean Analogies: Imagination at the Bounds of Sense', *Isis* 75(2), pp. 302–310.

___ (2005), 'Fear and Loathing of the Imagination in Science', *Daedalus* 134(4), pp. 16–30.

Dauphinée, Elizabeth and Cristina Masters (2007), 'Introduction: Living, Dying, Surviving I', in: Elizabeth Dauphinée and Cristina Masters (eds), *The Logics of Biopower and the War on Terror: Living, Dying, Surviving*, Basingstoke: Palgrave Macmillan, pp. vii–xix.

Davidson, Arnold (2004), *The Emergence of Sexuality: Historical Epistemology and the Formation of Concepts*, Cambridge, MA: Harvard University Press.

Davis, Mike (2001), *Late Victorian Holocausts, El Nino Famines and the Making of the Third World*, London: Verso.

Davis, Tracy C. (2007), *Stages of Emergency: Cold War Nuclear Civil Defence*, Durham: Duke University Press.

de Goede, Marieke (2008a), 'The Politics of Preemption and the War on Terror in Europe', *European Journal of International Relations* 14(1), pp. 161–185.

___ (2008b), 'Beyond Risk: Premediation and the Post-9/11 Security Imagination', *Security Dialogue* 39(2/3), pp. 155–176.

de Goede, Marieke and Samuel Randalls (2009), 'Precaution, Preemption: Arts and Technologies of the Actionable Future', *Environment and Planning D* 27(5), pp. 859–878.

Dean, Mitchell (1999), *Governmentality: Power and Rule in Modern Society*, London: Sage.

___ (2007), *Governing Societies: Political Perspectives on Domestic and International Rule*, Maidenhead: Open University Press.

Deleuze, Gilles (1992), 'What is a *Dispositif?*', in: T. J. Armstrong (ed.), *Michel Foucault: Philosopher*, Hemel Hempstead: Harvester Wheatsheaf.

Department of Homeland Security (2004), *Are You Ready? An In-depth Guide to Citizen Preparedness*, http://www.fema.gov/areyouready/ (accessed 12 May 2010).

Derrida, Jacques (1984), 'No Apocalypse, Not Now (Full Speed Ahead, Seven Missiles, Seven Missives)', *Diacritics* 14(2), pp. 20–31.

___ (2005), *Rogues: Two Essays on Reason*, Palo Alto: Stanford University Press.

Digby, James, Marc Dean Millot and William L. Schwabe (1988), *How Nuclear War Might Start: Scenarios from the Early 21st Century*, RAND Note N-2614-NA, October 1988.

Diken, Bülent and Carsten Bagge Laustsen (2005), *The Culture of Exception: Sociology Facing the Camp*, London: Routledge.

Dillon, Michael (1996), *Politics of Security: Towards a Political Philosophy of Continental Thought*, London and New York: Routledge.

Dillon, Michael and Julian Reid (2001), 'Global Liberal Governance: Biopolitics, Security and War', *Millennium* 30(1), pp. 41–66.

Donzelot, Jacques (1988), 'The Promotion of the Social', *Economy and Society* 17(3), pp. 395–427.

Drabek, Thomas E. (2004), 'Sociology, Disasters and Emergency Management: History, Contributions, and Future Agenda', *Disciplines, Disasters and Emergency Management Textbook*, Emmitsburg, MD: FEMA. Available online at http://training.fema.gov/EMIWeb/edu/ddemtextbook.asp (accessed 25 January 2011).

Dreyfus, Hubert L. and Paul Rabinow (1983), *Michel Foucault: Beyond Structuralism and Hermeneutics*, Chicago: Chicago University Press.

Duffield, Mark (2008), 'Global Civil War: The Non-Insured, International Containment and Post-Interventionary Society', *Journal of Refugee Studies* 21(2), pp. 145–165.

Duncan, Ronald and Miranda Weston-Smith (eds) (1977), *The Encyclopaedia of Ignorance: Everything You Ever Wanted to Know about the Unknown*, Oxford: Pergamon Press.

Dupuy, Jean-Pierre (2002a), *Pour un catastrophisme éclairé. Quand l'impossible est certain*, Paris: Seuil.

___ (2002b), *Avions-nous oublié le mal? Penser la politique après le 11 septembre*, Paris: Bayard.

___ (2005), *Petite Métaphysique des Tsunamis*, Paris: Seuil.

___ (2008), 'Postface: Notre Dernier Siècle', in: Anne-Marie Mercier-Faivre and Chantal Thomas (eds), *L'Invention de la Catastrophe au XVIIIe Siècle. Du Châtiment divin au désastre naturel*, Génève: Libraire Droz, pp. 481–494.

Durodie, Bill (2004), 'The Social Basis for Fears about Science', London, http://www.durodie.net/pdf/SocialBasisforScienceFears.pdf (accessed 20 December 2010).

Dynes, Russel R. (2005), 'The Lisbon Earthquake in 1755: The First Modern Disaster', in: Theodore E. D. Braun and John B. Radner (eds), *The Lisbon Earthquake of 1755: Representations and Reactions*, Oxford: Voltaire Foundation, pp. 34–49.

Daase, Christopher and Oliver Kessler (2007), 'Knowns and Unknowns in the War on Terror and the Political Construction of Danger', *Security Dialogue* 38(4), pp. 401–425.

Eagleton, Terry (1990), *The Ideology of the Aesthetic*, Malden, MA: Blackwell.

East Riding of Yorkshire (2010), 'Crime and Law Enforcement', http://www.eastriding.gov.uk/cr/support-and-procurement-services/humber-emergency-planning/antiterrorism/ (accessed 20 December 2010).

Edkins, Jenny, Véronique Pin-Fat and Michael J. Shapiro (eds) (2004), *Sovereign Lives: Power in Global Politics*, London: Routledge.

Elkus, Adam (2007), 'Resilience and American Security', *Huffington Post*, http://www.huffingtonpost.com/adam-elkus/resilience-and-american-s_b_72502.html (accessed 20 December 2010).

Elliott, Anthony (1995), 'Symptoms of Globalization: Or, Mapping Reflexivity in the Postmodern Age', *Political Psychology* 16(4), pp. 719–736.

Emergency Management and Safety Solutions (2010), 'Emergency Exercises', San Francisco, CA, http://www.ems-solutionsinc.com/emr_exercises.html (accessed 20 December 2010).

Engmann, Joyce (1976), 'Imagination and Truth in Aristotle', *Journal of the History of Philosophy* 14(3), pp. 259–265.

Eqecat (2002), 'Eqecat releases probabilistic terrorism model', http://www.eqecat.com/resources/terrorism97.pdf#search=%22Eqecat%20modelling%20terrorism%22 (accessed July 2010).

Erickson, Christian W. (2007), 'Counter-Terror Culture: Ambiguity, Subversion, or Legitimization?' *Security Dialogue* 38(2), pp. 197–214.

Erickson, Christian W. and Bethany A. Barratt (2004), 'Prudence or Panic? Preparedness Exercises, Counterterror Mobilization, and Media Coverage – Dark Winter, TOPOFF 1 and 2', *Journal of Homeland Security and Emergency Management* 1(4), pp. 1–21.

Ericson, Richard V. (1989), 'Patrolling the Facts: Secrecy and Publicity in Police Work', *The British Journal of Sociology* 40(2), pp. 205–226.

____ (2007), *Crime in an Insecure World*, Cambridge: Polity Press.

Ericson, Richard V. and Aaron Doyle (2004a), 'Catastrophe Risk, Insurance and Terrorism', *Economy and Society* 33(2), pp. 135–173.

____ (2004b), *Uncertain Business: Risk, Insurance, and the Limits of Knowledge*, Toronto: University of Toronto Press.

Ericson, Richard V., Aaron Doyle and Dean Barry (2003), *Insurance as Governance*, Toronto: University of Toronto Press.

Ericson, Richard V. and Kevin Haggerty (1997), *Policing the Risk Society*, Oxford: Clarendon Press.

European Commission (2000), 'Communication from the Commission on the Precautionary Principle', Brussels, 2 February, COM(2000) 1, http://ec.europa.eu/environment/docum/20001_en.htm (accessed 20 December 2010).

____ (2004), 'Communication from the Commission to the Council and the European Parliament: Critical Infrastructure Protection in the Fight against Terrorism', Brussels, 20 October, COM(2004) 702, http://europa.eu/legislation_summaries/justice_freedom_security/fight_against_terrorism/l33259_en.htm (accessed 20 December 2010).

____ (2006), 'Crisis Management and the Fight against Terrorism', Brussels: Freedom, Security and Justice. Available online at http://ec.europa.eu/justice_home/fsj/terrorism/fsj_terrorism_intro_en.htm (accessed 04 February 2011).

Ewald, François (1986), *L'état providence*, Paris: Editions Grasset.

____ (2002), 'The Return of Descartes's Malicious Demon: An Outline of a Philosophy of Precaution', in: Tom Baker and Jonathan Simon (eds), *Embracing Risk*, Chicago: Chicago University Press, pp. 273–301.

Faber, Roland, Henry Krips and Daniel Pettus (eds) (2010), *Event and Decision: Ontology and Politics in Badiou, Deleuze, and Whitehead*, Newcastle upon Tyne: Cambridge Scholars Publishing.

Feldbæk, Ole, Anne Løkke and Steen Leth Jeppesen (2007), *Drømmen om tryghed. Tusind års dansk forsikring*, København: Gads Forlag.

Ferguson, Frances (1984), 'The Nuclear Sublime', *Diacritics* 14(2), pp. 4–10.

Fierke, Karin M. (2007), *Critical Approaches to International Security*, Cambridge: Polity.

Fischer, Henry W. III (2003), 'The Sociology of Disaster: Definitions, Research Questions, and Measurements. Continuation of the Discussion in a Post-September 11

Environment', *International Journal of Mass Emergencies and Disasters* 21(1), pp. 91–107.

Foucault, Michel (1973), *The Birth of the Clinic*, London and New York: Routledge.

___ (1980), 'The Confessions of the Flesh', in: Colin Gordon (ed.), *Power/Knowledge: Selected Interviews and Other Writings 1972–1977*, New York: Pantheon Books, pp. 194–228.

___ (1984), 'Nietzsche, Genealogy, History', in: Paul Rabinow (ed.), *The Foucault Reader*, London: Penguin Books, pp. 76–100.

___ (1991), 'Questions of Method', in: Graham Burchell, Colin Gordon and Peter Miller (eds), *The Foucault Effect: Studies in Governmentaity*, Chicago: University of Chicago Press, pp. 63–86.

___ (1998 [1976]), *The History of Sexuality I. The Will to Knowledge*, London: Penguin Books.

___ (2000), 'The Risks of Security', in: James D. Faubion (ed.), *Essential Works of Foucault 1954–1984: Volume 3, Power*, London: Penguin Books, pp. 365–381.

___ (2002 [1969]), *The Archaeology of Knowledge*, translated by A. M. Sheridan Smith, London: Routledge.

___ (2003), *Society Must Be Defended*, translated by David Macey, London: Allen Lane.

___ (2004a), *Abnormal: Lectures at the College de France, 1974–1975*, translated by Graham Burchell, Basingstoke: Palgrave Macmillan.

___ (2004b), *Naissance de la biopolitique. Cours au Collège de France, 1978–1979*, Paris: Gallimard/Seuil.

___ (2007), *Security, Territory, Population*, Basingstoke: Palgrave.

França, José-Augusto (1988), *Une ville des lumieres. La Lisbonne de Pombal*, Paris: Fondation Calouste Gulbenkian.

Frawley, William J., Gregory Piatetsky-Shapiro and Christopher J. Matheus (1992), 'Knowledge discovery in databases: An overview', *AI Magazine* 13(3), pp. 57–70.

Freedman, Lawrence (2003), *The Evolution of Nuclear Strategy*, Basingstoke: Palgrave.

Galison, Peter (2001), 'War against the Center', *Grey Room* 4, pp. 5–33.

Galison, Peter and Rob Moss (2008), 'Secrecy', http://www.secrecyfilm.com/about. html (accessed 20 December 2010).

Ghamari-Tabrizi, Sharon (2005), *The Worlds of Herman Kahn: The Intuitive Science of Thermonuclear War*, Cambridge, MA: Harvard University Press.

Gilbert, Claude (1998), 'Studying Disaster: Changes in the Main Conceptual Tools', in: Enrico L. Quarantelli (ed.), *What is a Disaster? Perspectives on the Question*, London and New York: Routledge, pp. 11–18.

Ginzburg, Carlo (1979), 'Clues: Roots of a Scientific Paradigm', *Theory and Society* 7(3), pp. 273–288.

___ (1980), 'Morelli, Freud and Sherlock Holmes: Clues and Scientific Method', *History Workshop Journal* 9(Spring), pp. 5–35.

___ (1991), 'Checking the Evidence: The Judge and the Historian', *Critical Inquiry*, pp. 79–92.

Glaser, Charles L. (1997), 'The Security Dilemma Revisited', *World Politics* 50(1), pp. 171–201.

Godet, Michel and Fabrice Roubelat (1996), 'Creating the Future: The Use and Misuse of Scenarios', *Long Range Planning* 29(2), pp. 164–171.

Goldhamer, Herbert and Hans Speier (1959), 'Some Observations on Political Gaming', *World Politics* 12(1), pp. 71–83.

Goldin, Abe J. (1943), 'War Damage Insurance', *Journal of the American Association of University Teachers of Insurance* 10(1), pp. 69–75.

Gross, Matthias (2007), 'The Unknown in Process: Dynamic Connections of Ignorance, Non-Knowledge and Related Concepts', *Current Sociology* 55(5), pp. 742–759.

Grotrian, Simon, Thomas Krogsbøl and Mariane Larsen (2008), *Hallo – jeg er vejret. 12 digte om klima og miljø*, Copenhagen: Borgen.

Grusin, Richard (2010), *Premediation: Affect and Mediality after 9/11*, New York: Palgrave.

Guldberg, Helene (2003), 'Challenging the Precautionary Principle', *Spiked-Online*, http://www.spiked-online.com/Printable/00000006DE2F.htm (accessed 20 December 2010).

Gunset, Joe (2006), *Statement of Lloyd's of London to the Terrorism Risk Working Group Meeting, March 29, 2006*, http://www.naic.org/documents/topics_tria_testimony 0603_lloyds.pdf (accessed 20 December 2010).

Hacking, Ian (1990), *The Taming of Chance*, Cambridge: Cambridge University Press.

___ (1992), 'Statistical Language, Statistical Truth and Statistical Reason: The Self-Authentication of a Style of Scientific Reasoning', *The Social Dimensions of Science* 3, pp. 130–157.

___ (1995), *Rewriting the Soul: Multiple Personality and the Sciences of Memory*, Princeton: Princeton University Press.

___ (2004), *Historical Ontology*, Cambridge, MA: Harvard University Press.

___ (2007), 'Kinds of People: Moving Targets', Paper for Proceedings of the British Academy, Oxford University Press.

Hall, Mimi (2007), 'Sci-fi Writers Join War on Terror', *USA Today*, http://www.usa today.com/tech/science/2007-05-29-deviant-thinkers-security_N.htm (accessed 20 December 2010).

Han, Béatrice (2002), *Foucault's Critical Project: Between the Transcedental and the Historical*, Stanford: Stanford University Press.

Hannah, Matthew (2010), '(Mis)adventures in Rumsfeld Space', *GeoJournal* 75(4), pp. 397–406.

Hansen, Lene (2006), *Security as Practice: Discourse Analysis and the Bosnian War*, London and New York: Routledge.

Harkin, James (9 July 2005), 'What Is … "Resilience"?', *The Times*, http://www.times online.co.uk/tol/comment/columnists/guest_contributors/article541958.ece (accessed 28 February 2011).

Hay, Colin (1996), 'From Crisis to Catastrophe? The Ecological Pathologies of the Liberal-Democratic State Form', *Innovation* 9(4), pp. 421–434.

Healy, Richard J. (1969), *Emergency and Disaster Planning*, New York: John Wiley & Sons.

Heartney, Eleanor (2003), 'The Sinister Beauty of Global Conspiracies', *New York Times*, 26 October, http://www.nytimes.com/2003/10/26/arts/design/26HEAR. html (accessed 20 December 2010).

Hengehold, Laura (2007), *The Body Problematic: Political Imagination in Kant and Foucault*, University Park, PA: Pennsylvania State University Press.

Henry, Doug (2005), 'Anthropological Contributions to the Study of Disasters', in: D. McEntire and W. Blanchard (eds), *Disciplines, Disasters and Emergency Management: The Convergence of Concepts Issues and Trends from the Research Literature*, Emittsburg, MD: FEMA.

Hirshleifer, Jack (1955), 'Compensation for War Damage: An Economic View', *Columbia Law Review* 55(2), pp. 180–194.

Hobart, Mark (1993), *An Anthropological Critique of Development: The Growth of Ignorance*, London: Routledge.

Hobsbawn, Eric (1996), *The Age of Extremes: A History of the World, 1914–1991*, New York: Pantheon Books.

Holling, C. S. (1973), 'Resilience and Stability of Ecological Systems', *Annual Review of Ecology and Systematics* 4(1), pp. 1–23.

Home Office (2006), 'Addressing Lessons from the Emergency Response to 7 July Bombings', London, http://www.londonprepared.gov.uk/downloads/home office_lessonslearned.pdf (accessed 26 January 2011).

___ (2009a), 'Working Together to Protect Crowded Places. A Consultation Document', London, https://vsat.nactso.gov.uk/SiteCollectionDocuments/ AreasOfRisk/working-together-crowded-places.pdf (accessed 26 January 2011).

___ (2009b), 'The UK Counter-Terrorism Strategy', London: Office for Security and Counter-Terrorism, http://tna.europarchive.org/20100419081706/http:// security.homeoffice.gov.uk/news-publications/publication-search/contest/contest-strategy/contest-strategy-2009?view=Binary (accessed 26 January 2011).

Honig, Bonnie (2009), *Emergency Politics: Paradox, Law, Democracy*, Princeton: Princeton University Press.

Horn, Eva and Sara Ogger (2003), 'Knowing the Enemy: The Epistemology of Secret Intelligence', *Grey Room* 11, pp. 58–85.

Hoskins, Andrew (2006), 'Temporality, Proximity and Security: Terror in a Media-Drenched Age', *International Relations* 20(4), pp. 453–466.

House of Lords (2008), 'Counterterrorism', London: Lords Hansard.

Hussain, N. (2003), *The Jurisprudence of Emergency: Colonialism and the Rule of Law*, Ann Arbor, MI: University of Michigan Press.

Huysmans, Jef (1998), 'Security! What Do You Mean? From Concept to Thick Signifier', *European Journal of International Relations* 4(2), pp. 226–255.

___ (2004), 'Minding Exceptions: Politics of Insecurity and Liberal Democracy', *Contemporary Political Theory* 3(3), pp. 321–341.

___ (2006), *The Politics of Insecurity: Fear, Migration and Asylum in the EU*, London and New York: Routledge.

___ (2008), 'The Jargon of the Exception: On Schmitt, Agamben and the Absence of Political Society', *International Political Sociology* 2(2), pp. 165–183.

Huysmans, Jef, Andrew Dobson and Raia Prokhovnik (eds) (2006), *The Politics of Protection: Sites of Insecurity and Political Agency*, London: Routledge.

Insurance Information Institute (2010), *Terrorism Risk: A Reemergent Threat. Impacts for Property/Casualty Insurers*, April, http://insurancemarketreport.com/Portals/131/ TerrorismThreat_042010.pdf (accessed 20 December 2010).

Intelligence and Security Committee (2006), 'Report into the London Terrorist Attacks on 7 July 2005', London, http://www.official-documents.gov.uk/document/ cm67/6785/6785.pdf (accessed 20 December 2010).

International Risk and Disaster Conference (2008), 'Diseases and Pandemics, Expect the Unexpected', Davos, http://www.preventionweb.net/english/professional/ news/v.php?id=3465 (accessed 20 December 2010).

Isin, Engin (2004), 'The Neurotic Citizen', *Citizenship Studies* 8(3), pp. 217–235.

Jabri, Vivienne (2006), 'Shock and Awe: Power and the Resistance of Art', *Millennium* 34(3), pp. 819–839.

___ (2007), *War and the Transformation of Global Politics*, Basingstoke: Palgrave Macmillan.

Jacobson, Sid and Ernie Colon (2006), *The Illustrated 9/11 Commission Report: A Graphic Adaptation*, New York: Hill & Wang.

Jakes Jordan, Lara (2006), 'Officials: Next Terrorist Attack on U.S. Not Matter of If, But When', *Insurance Journal*, http://www.insurancejournal.com/news/national/2006/09/10/72260.htm (accessed 20 December 2010).

Jameson, Frederic (1982), 'Progress versus Utopia; Or, Can We Imagine the Future? (Progrès contre Utopie, ou: Pouvons-nous imaginer l'avenir)', *Science Fiction Studies*, pp. 147–158.

___ (1988), 'Cognitive Mapping', in: Cary Nelson and Lawrence Grossberg (eds), *Marxism and the Interpretation of Culture*, Champaign: University of Illinois Press, pp. 347–360.

___ (1991), *Postmodernism. Or, The Cultural Logic of Late Capitalism*, Durham and London: Duke University Press.

___ (1995), *The Geopolitical Aesthetic: Cinema and Space in the World System*, Bloomington, IN: Indiana University Press.

___ (2005), *Archaeologies of the Future: The Desire Called Utopia and Other Science Fictions*, London: Verso.

Jardine Lloyd Thompson (2009), *Political Violence and Terrorism*, London: Jardine Lloyd Thompson Ltd.

Johns, Fleur (2005), 'Guantanamo Bay and the Annihilation of the Exception', *The European Journal of International Law* 16(4), pp. 613–635.

Johnston, Rob (2005), *Analytical Culture in the U.S. Intelligence Community: An Ethnographic Study*, http://www.dtic.mil/cgi-bin/GetTRDoc?AD=ADA507369&Location=U2&doc=GetTRDoc.pdf (accessed 20 December 2010).

Juengel, Scott J. (2009), 'The Early Novel and Catastrophe', *Novel* 42(3), pp. 443–450.

Jurgensen, John and Jamin Brophy-Warren (2009), 'Hollywood Destroys the World', *Wall Street Journal*, 31 July, http://online.wsj.com/article/SB10001424052970204619004574318630585925804.html (accessed 20 December 2010).

Kahn, Herman (1958), *Some Specific Suggestions for Achieving Early Non-Military Defense Capabilities and Initiating Long-Range Programs*, RAND Research Memorandum, RM-2206-RC.

___ (1960), *On Thermonuclear War*, New Brunswick: Transaction Publishers.

___ (1962), *Thinking about the Unthinkable*, New York: Horizon Press.

___ (1965), *On Escalation: Metaphors and Scenarios*, New York: Praeger.

___ (1984), *Thinking about the Unthinkable in the 1980s*, New York Simon and Schuster.

Kant, Immanuel (1999 [1781]), *Critique of Pure Reason*, translated by P. Guyer and A. W. Wood, Cambridge: Cambridge University Press.

___ (1951 [1790]), *Critique of Judgement*, New York: Hafner Press.

___ (2006 [1798]), *Anthropology from a Pragmatic Point of View*, Robert B. Louden, translated by Manfred Kuehn, Cambridge: Cambridge University Press.

Kaplan, Fred (1983), *The Wizards of Armageddon*, New York: Simon and Schuster.

Katznelson, Ira (2003), *Desolation and Enlightenment: Political Knowledge after Total War, Totalitarianism and the Holocaust*, New York: Columbia University Press.

Kearney, Richard (1988), *The Wake of Imagination: Ideas of Creativity in Western Culture*, London: Hutchinson.

Kessler, Oliver and Wouter G. Werner (2008), 'Extrajudicial Killing as Risk Management', *Security Dialogue* 39(2&3), pp. 289–308.

Keynes, John Maynard (1964), *The General Theory of Employment, Interest and Money*, New York: Harcourt Brace.

Kissinger, Henry A. (1977), *American Foreign Policy*, New York: W.W. Norton & Company.

Klein, Naomi (2007), *The Shock Doctrine: The Rise of Disaster Capitalism*, London: Allen Lane.

Klinke, Andreas and Ortwinn Renn (2002), 'A New Approach to Risk Evaluation and Management: Risk-Based, Precaution-Based, and Discourse-Based Strategies', *Risk Analysis* 22(6), pp. 1071–1094.

Knight, Frank H. (1946), *Risk, Uncertainty and Profit*, Boston: Houghton Mifflin Company.

Koselleck, Reinhart (1982), 'Krise', in: Otto Brunner, Werner Conze and Reinhart Koselleck (eds), *Geschichtliche Grundbegriffe. Historisches Lexikon zur politisch-sozialen Sprache in Deutschland*, Stuttgart: Klett-Cotta.

___ (2004), *Futures Past: On the Semantics of Historical Time*, translated by Keith Tribe, New York: Columbia University Press.

Krause, Keith and Michael C. Williams (eds) (1997), *Critical Security Studies: Concepts and Cases*, London: UCL Press.

Krauthammer, Charles (2010), 'Obama – Crisis, Catastrophe: Are These Words of Hope?', Washington, DC: CNN, http://www.ireport.com/docs/DOC-208679 (accessed 20 December 2010).

Kuklick, Bruce (2007), *Blind Oracles: Intellectuals and War from Kennan to Kissinger*, Princeton: Princeton University Press.

Kunreuther, Howard (2002), 'The Role of Insurance in Managing Extreme Events: Implications for Terrorism Coverage', *Risk Analysis* 22(3), pp. 427–437.

Kunreuther, Howard and Erwan Michel-Kerjan (2004), 'Dealing with Extreme Events: Challenges for Terrorism Risk Coverage in the United States', Cahier n° 2004-018, http://hal.archives-ouvertes.fr/docs/00/24/29/30/PDF/2004-12-16-187.pdf (accessed 20 December 2010).

___ (2005), 'Terrorism Insurance 2005', *Regulation*, pp. 44–51, http://www.cato.org/pubs/regulation/regv28n1/v28n1-8.pdf (accessed 28 February 2011).

Kunreuther, Howard and Mark Pauly (2009), 'Insuring against Catastrophes', Risk Management and Decision Processes Center, The Wharton School of the University of Pennsylvania, http://opim.wharton.upenn.edu/risk/library/WP20090413_HK,MP_KuU.pdf (accessed 20 December 2010).

Lafer, Gordon (2005), 'Neoliberalism by Other Means: The "War on Terror" at Home and Abroad', *New Political Science* 26(3), pp. 323–346.

Laffey, Mark and Jutta Weldes (2008), 'Decolonizing the Cuban Missile Crisis', *International Studies Quarterly* 52(3), pp. 555–577.

Lakoff, Andrew (2006), 'From Disaster to Catastrophe: The Limits of Preparedness', Social Science Research Council, http://understandingkatrina.ssrc.org/Lakoff/ (accessed 3 September 2010).

___ (2007), 'Preparing for the Next Emergency', *Public Culture* 19(2), pp. 247–271.

Larabee, Ann (1999), *Decade of Disaster*, Chicago: University of Illinois.

Larrère, Catherine (2008), 'Catastrophe ou Révolution: les catastrophes naturelles ont-elles une histoire?', in: Anne-Marie Mercier-Faivre and Chantal Thomas (eds), *L'Invention de la Catastrophe au XVIIIe Siècle. Du Châtiment divin au désastre naturel*, Génève: Libraire Droz, pp. 133–156.

le Bon, Gustave (1995), *The Crowd*, Charleston: BiblioBazaar.

Leahy, Stephen (2008), 'Artists Desperately Needed to Inspire Change', http://stephenleahy.net/2007/06/02/artists-desperately-needed-to-inspire-change/ (accessed 20 December 2010).

Lee, Benjamin and Edward LiPuma (2002), 'Cultures of Circulation: The Imaginations of Modernity', *Public Culture* 14(1), pp. 191–213.

Lentzos, Filippa and Nikolas Rose (2009), 'Governing Insecurity: Contingency Planning, Protection, Resilience', *Economy and Society* 38(2), pp. 230–254.

Leslie, Esther (2000), *Walter Benjamin: Overpowering Conformism*, London: Pluto Press.

Levmore, Saul and Kyle D. Logue (2003), 'Insuring against Terrorism-and Crime', *Michigan Law Review* 102(2), pp. 268–327.

Lifton, Robert J. (1986), 'Imagining the Real: Beyond the Nuclear "End"', in: Lester Grinspoon (ed.), *The Long Darkness: Psychological and Moral Perspectives on Nuclear Winter*, New York: Yale University, pp. 79–100.

Lisle, Debbie (2006), 'Sublime Lessons: Education and Ambivalence in War Exhibitions', *Millennium* 34(3), pp. 841–862.

Litman, Todd (2006), 'Lessons from Katrina and Rita: What Major Disasters Can Teach Transportation Planners', *Journal of Transportation Engineering* 132(1), pp. 11–18.

Lloyds (2008), 'Poetry Commissions: Trees in the City', London: Lloyds.

Lobo-Guerrero, Luis (2007), 'Biopolitics of Specialised Risk: An Analysis of Kidnap and Ransom Insurance', *Security Dialogue* 38(3), pp. 315–334.

___ (2010), *Insuring Security: Biopolitics, Security and Risk*, London and New York: Routledge.

London Fire Brigade (2010), 'London Community Risk Register', London, http://www.london-fire.gov.uk/Documents/LondonCommunityRiskRegister.pdf (accessed 20 December 2010).

Looney, Robert (2004), 'Darpa's Policy Analysis Market for Intelligence: Outside the Box or Off the Wall?', *International Journal of Intelligence and Counterintelligence* 17(3), pp. 405–419.

Lyotard, Jean-François (1994), *Lessons on the Analytic of the Sublime: Kant's Critique of Judgment*, Stanford: Stanford University Press.

Major, John A. (2002), 'Advanced Techniques for Modeling Terrorism Risk', *The Journal of Risk Finance* 4(1), pp. 15–24.

Makkreel, Rudolf A. (1984), 'Imagination and Temporality in Kant's Theory of the Sublime', *Journal of Aesthetics and Art Criticism* 42(3), pp. 303–315.

Mamdani, Mahmood (1985), 'Disaster Prevention: Defining the Problem', *Review of African Political Economy* 12(33), pp. 92–96.

Manyena, Siambabala Bernard (2006), 'The Concept of Resilience Revisited', *Disasters* 30(4), pp. 434–450.

Marsh (2009), 'Terrorism Reinsurance Act (TRIA) is Extended by Congress', Marsh, http://global.marsh.com/documents/TRIA_Is_Extended_2nd_Edition.pdf

Massumi, Brian (2005), 'Fear (The Spectrum Said)', *Positions: East Asia Cultures Critique* 13(1), pp. 31–48.

Maxwell, Kenneth (1965), *Pombal, Paradox of the Enlightenment*, Cambridge: Cambridge University Press.

Mayer, Aric (2008), 'Aesthetics of Catastrophe', *Public Culture* 20(2), pp. 177–191.

McConnell, Michael J. (2007), 'Annual Threat Assessment of the Director of National Intelligence', http://www.dni.gov/testimonies/20070227_testimony.pdf (accessed 20 December 2010).

McCue, Colleen (2005), 'Data Mining and Predictive Analytics: Battlespace Awareness for the War on Terrorism', *Defense Intelligence Journal* 13(1&2), pp. 47–63.

McDonald, Matt (2008), 'Securitization and the Construction of Security', *European Journal of International Relations* 14(4), pp. 563–587.

McEwan, Ian (2010), *Solar*, London: Jonathan Cape.

McKellar, Elizabeth (1999), *The Birth of Modern London: The Development and Design of the City 1660–1720*, Manchester: Manchester University Press.

Mercier-Faivre, Anne-Marie and Chantal Thomas (2008), 'Préface: Ecrire la catastrophe', in: Anne-Marie Mercier-Faivre and Chantal Thomas (eds), *L'Invention de la Catastrophe au XVIIIe Siècle. Du Châtiment divin au désastre naturel*, Génève: Libraire Droz, pp. 7–34.

Metropolitan Police (2006), 'If You Suspect It, Report It. Latest News', London, http://cms.met.police.uk/news/policy_organisational_news_and_general_information/partnerships/if_you_suspect_it_report_it (accessed 20 December 2010).

___ (2008), 'Major Incident Response Plan Standard Operating Procedure', http://www.met.police.uk/foi/pdfs/policies/health_and_well_being_sop_major_incident_response_plan.pdf (accessed 20 December 2010).

Miller, Peter and Nikolas Rose (1990), 'Governing Economic Life', *Economy and Society* 19(1), pp. 1–31.

Mitchell, Robert (2008), '"Beings that have existence only in ye minds of men": State Finance and the Origins of the Collective Imagination', *The Eighteenth Century* 49(2), pp. 117–139.

Moylan, Tom (1982), 'The Locus of Hope: Utopia versus Ideology (Le lieu de l'espoir: utopie vs idéologie)', *Science Fiction Studies*, 9(2) pp. 159–166.

Mueller, John (1994), 'The Catastrophe Quota: Trouble after the Cold War', *The Journal of Conflict Resolution* 38(3), pp. 355–375.

Muller, Benjamin J. (2008), 'Securing the Political Imagination: Popular Culture, the Security *Dispositif* and the Biometric State', *Security Dialogue* 39(2&3), pp. 199–220.

Myers, Norman (1993), 'Biodiversity and the Precautionary Principle', *Ambio* 22(2&3), pp. 74–79.

Müller, Jan Werner (2006), '"An Irregularity that Cannot be Regulated": Carl Schmitt's Theory of the Partisan and the "War on Terror"', *Notizie di Politeia: Rivista di Etica e Scelte Pubbliche* XXII(84), pp. 65–78.

National Commission on Terrorist Attacks upon the United States (2004), *The 9/11 Commission Report*, http://govinfo.library.unt.edu/911/report/index.htm (accessed 26 January 2011).

National Counter Terrorism Security Office (2003), 'Expecting the Unexpected', https://vsat.nactso.gov.uk/SiteCollectionDocuments/expecting.pdf (accessed 04 February 2011).

National Intelligence Council (2004), *Mapping the Global Future*, Washington: National Intelligence Council, http://www.foia.cia.gov/2020/2020.pdf (accessed 20 December 2010).

___ (2008), 'Global Trends 2025: A Transformed World', http://www.dni.gov/nic/NIC_2025_project.html (accessed 20 December 2010).

Neal, Andrew W. (2006), 'Foucault in Guantanamo: Towards an Archaeology of the Exception', *Security Dialogue* 37(1), pp. 31–46.

Neiman, Susan (2002), *Evil in Modern Thought: An Alternative History of Philosophy*, Princeton: Princeton University Press.

Neocleous, Mark (2003), *Imagining the State*, Maidenhead: Open University Press.

___ (2006), 'From Social to National Security: On the Fabrication of Economic Order', *Security Dialogue* 37(3), pp. 363–384.

___ (2008), *Critique of Security*, Edinburgh: Edinburgh University Press.

New York Consortium for Emergency Planning Continuing Education (2007),

'Public Health Emergency Exercise Toolkit', New York, http://www.nycepce.org/Documents/PHEmergencyExerciseToolkit.pdf (accessed 20 December 2010).

Neyrat, Frederic (2008), *Biopolitique des catastrophes*, Paris: Editions MF.

Noll, Gregor (2003), 'Visions of the Exceptional: Legal and Theoretical Issues Raised by Transit Processing Centres and Protection Zones', *European Journal of Migration and Law* 5(3), pp. 303–342.

Norfolk Constabulary (2008), 'Your Right to Be Suspicious', Norfolk, http://www.norfolk.police.uk/safetyadvice/preventingterrorism/yourrighttobesuspicious.aspx (accessed 20 December 2010).

Nowotny, Helga (1985), 'From the Future to the Extended Present: Time in Social Systems', in: G. Kirsch, P. Nijkamp and K. Zimmermann (eds), *Time Preferences: An Interdisciplinary Theoretical and Empirical Approach*, Aldershot: Avebury, pp. 1–21.

O'Connor, James (1943), 'Fire Insurance in War Time', *Journal of the American Association of University Teachers of Insurance* 10(1), pp. 41–45.

___ (1987), *The Meaning of Crisis. A Theoretical Introduction*, Oxford: Blackwell.

O'Malley, Patrick (2003), 'Governable Catastrophes: A Comment on Bougen', *Economy and Society* 32(2), pp. 275–279.

___ (2004), *Risk, Uncertainty and Government*, London: GlassHouse.

OECD (2005), *Catastrophic Risk and Insurance*, Policy Issues in Insurance No. 8, OECD.

___ (2008), *Concepts and Dilemmas of State-Building in Fragile Situations: From fragility to resilience*, OECD.

OECD Council (2004), 'OECD Check-List of Criteria to Define Terrorism for the Purpose of Compensation', OECD, http://www.oecdchina.org/OECDpdf/34065606.pdf (accessed 20 December 2010).

Okashah, L. A. and P. M. Goldwater (1994), 'Unknown Unknowns: Modeling Unanticipated Events', *Simulation Conference Proceedings*, 11–14 December, pp. 689–694.

Oliver-Smith, A. (1996), 'Anthropological Research on Hazards and Disasters', *Annual Review of Anthropology* 25, pp. 303–328.

Online Etymology Dictionary, available at http://www.etymonline.com/index.php?search=catastrophe&searchmode=none (accessed 25 January 2011).

Oregon OSHA (n.d.), *Expecting the Unexpected. What to Consider in Planning for Workplace Emergencies*. OSHA, Available from http://www.orosha.org/pdf/pubs/3356.pdf (accessed 9 August 2010).

Osborne, Peter (1995), *The Politics of Time: Modernity and Avant-Garde*, London: Verso.

Osborne, Thomas (1999), 'The Ordinariness of the Archive', *History of the Human Sciences* 12(2), pp. 51–64.

Page, Gina (2006), 'Another Terrorist Attack Coming Soon?', CBS News, http://www.cbsnews.com/stories/2006/06/05/terror/main1683852.shtml (accessed 20 December 2010).

Palladino, Paolo (2008), 'Ginzburg in Harlem: History, Structure and the Politics of Primitivism', *Culture, Theory and Critique* 49(2), pp. 203–217.

Pearson, Robin (2004), *Insuring the Industrial Revolution: Fire Insurance in Great Britain, 1700–1850*, Aldershot: Ashgate.

Pelling, Mark and Kathleen Dill (2009), 'Disaster Politics: Tipping Points for Change in the Adaptation of Socio-Political Regimes', *Progress in Human Geography* 34(1), pp. 21–37.

Pereira, Alvaro S. (2009), 'The Opportunity of a Disaster: The Economic Impact of the 1755 Lisbon Earthquake', *The Journal of Economic History* 69(2), pp. 466–499.

Perrow, Charles (2007), *The Next Catastrophe: Reducing Our Vulnerabilities to Natural, Industrial, and Terrorist Disasters*, Princeton, NJ: Princeton University Press.

Perry, Ronald W. (2007), 'What Is a Disaster?', in: Havidan Rodriguez, Enrico L. Quarantelli and Russel R. Dynes (eds), *Handbook of Disaster Research*, New York: Springer, pp. 1–15.

Petersen, Karen Lund (2008), 'Terrorism: When Risk Meets Security', *Alternatives* 33(2), pp. 173–190.

Petersen, Per Serritslev (2005), '9/11 and the "Problem of Imagination": *Fight Club* and *Glamorama* as Terrorist Pretexts', *Orbis Litterarum* 60(2), pp. 133–144.

Pimm, Stuart L. (1984), 'The Complexity and Stability of Ecosystems', *Nature* 307(5949), pp. 321–326.

Pizer, John (1993), 'Jameson's Adorno, or, The Persistence of the Utopian', *New German Critique* 58(Winter), pp. 127–151.

Polanyi, Karl (1944), *The Great Transformation*, Boston: Beacon Press.

Police Jobs (2010), 'Permanent and Temporary Emergency Planning Jobs', http://www.police-jobs.co.uk/emergency-planning-jobs/ (accessed 20 December 2010).

Pool Re (2010), 'Definition of an Act of Terrorism', London: Pool Re, http://www.poolre.co.uk/Definition.html (accessed 20 December 2010).

Poovey, Mary (1993), 'Figures of Arithmetic, Figures of Speech: The Discourse of Statistics in the 1830s', *Critical Inquiry* 19(2), pp. 256–276.

Popp, Robert, Thomas Armour, Ted Senator and Kristen Numrych (2004), 'Countering Terrorism through Information Technology', Communications of the ACM, 36–43, http://information-retrieval.info/taipale/papers/p36-popp.pdf (accessed 20 December 2010).

Purpura, Philip P. (2007), *Terrorism and Homeland Security: An Introduction with Applications*, Burlington: Elsevier.

Quarantelli, Enrico L. (2006), 'Catastrophes are Different from Disasters: Some Implications for Crisis Planning and Managing Drawn from Katrina', http://understandingkatrina.ssrc.org/Quarantelli/ (accessed 12 May 2010).

Ralston, Bill and Ian Wilson (2006), *The Scenario-Planning Handbook: A Practitioner's Guide to Developing and Using Scenarios to Direct Strategy in Today's Uncertain Times*, Crawfordsville, IN: Thomson/South-Western, p. 102.

Rancière, Jacques (2004a), 'Entretien avec Jacques Rancière', *Multitudes*, http://multitudes.samizdat.net/article.php3?id_article=1416 (accessed 20 December 2010).

___ (2004b), *Malaise dans l'esthétique*, Paris: Galilée.

___ (2005), 'From Politics to Aesthetics?' *Paragraph* 28(1), pp. 13–25.

___ (2006), 'Democracy, Republic, Representation', *Constellations* 13(3), pp. 297–307.

___ (2009), *Aesthetics and Its Discontents*, Cambridge: Polity Press.

Rasmussen, Mikkel Vedby (2004), '"It Sounds Like a Riddle": Security Studies, the War on Terror and Risk', *Millennium* 33(2), pp. 381–395.

___ (2006), *The Risk Society at War*, Cambridge: Cambridge University Press.

Ray, Gene (2004), 'Reading the Lisbon Earthquake: Adorno, Lyotard and the Contemporary Sublime', *The Yale Journal of Criticism* 17(1), pp. 1–18.

Reddaway, Thomas Fiddian (1940), *The Rebuilding of London after the Great Fire*, London: J. Cape.

Reid, Edna, Jialun Qin, Wingyan Chung, Jennifer Xu, Yilu Zhou, Rob Schumaker, Marc Sageman and Hsinchun Chen (2004), 'Terrorism Knowledge Discovery

Project: A Knowledge Discovery Approach to Addressing the Threats of Terrorism', *Intelligence and Security Informatics* 3073, pp. 125–145.

Rich, Michael (2010), 'Catastrophe Risk Management in the Public Sector. Keynote Speech.' Inaugural International Symposium on Catastrophe Risk Management, Nanyang Technological University, Singapore, http://www.rand.org/content/dam/rand/pubs/corporate_pubs/2010/RAND_CP598.pdf (accessed 20 December 2010).

Risk Management Solutions (2004), *Terrorism Risk*, Newark: Risk Management Solutions.

___ (2005), *A Risk-Based Approach for Extending TRIA*, http://www.rms.com/Publications/A%20Risk%20Based%20Approach%20for%20Extending%20TRIA.pdf (accessed October 2007).

___ (2008a), 'Terrorism Risk: 7-Year Retrospective, 7-Year Future Perspective', RMS White Paper, available from <http://www.rms.com/publications/Seven_Years_of_Terrorism_Risk.pdf> (accessed 7 March 2011).

___ (2008b), 'Advanced Mapping Capabilities', Risk Manager Brochure, available from <http://www.rms.com/Publications/RiskManager_brochure.pdf> (accessed 8 August 2010).

Ritter, Harry (1986), *Dictionary of Concepts in History*, Westport: Greenwood Press.

Roberts, Yvonne (2010), 'If Only We Can Teach Resilience to Those Who Need It', *Independent*, 16 January, http://www.independent.co.uk/opinion/commentators/yvonne-roberts-if-only-we-can-teach-resilience-to-those-who-need-it-1869545.html (accessed 20 December 2010).

Robin, Corey (2004), *Fear: The History of a Political Idea*, Oxford: Oxford University Press.

Roe, Paul (1999), 'The Intrastate Security Dilemma: Ethnic Conflict as a "Tragedy"?' *Journal of Peace Research* 36(2), pp. 183–202.

Rose, Nikolas (1999), *Powers of Freedom: Reframing Political Thought*, Cambridge: Cambridge University Press.

___ (2001), 'The Politics of Life Itself', *Theory, Culture and Society* 28(6), pp. 1–30.

Rosenthal, Uriel (1998), 'Future Disasters, Future Definitions', in: Enrico L. Quarantelli (ed.), *What is a Disaster? Perspectives on the Question*, London and New York: Routledge, pp. 146–159.

Rosenthal, Uriel, Michael T. Charles and Paul 't Hart (eds) (1989), *Coping with Crises: The Management of Disasters, Riots, and Terrorism*, Springfield, IL: Charles C. Thomas.

Rousseau, Jean-Jacques (1992 [1756]), 'Letter from J.J. Rousseau to Mr. de Voltaire', in: Roger D. Masters and Christopher Kelly (eds), *Collected Writings of Rousseau (Vol. 3)*, Hanover: University Press of New England, pp. 108–121.

Rozario, Kevin (2007), *Disaster and the Making of Modern America*, Chicago: Chicago University Press.

Rozen, Laura (2009), 'The Fatalist. The Man Reshaping How U.S. Intelligence Views the Future', *Foreign Policy*, http://www.foreignpolicy.com/articles/2009/04/15/the_fatalist (accessed 20 December 2010).

Rumsfeld, Donald (2002), 'Secretary Rumsfeld Press Conference at NATO Headquarters, Brussels, Belgium', 6 June, http://www.defense.gov/transcripts/transcript.aspx?transcriptid=3490 (accessed 20 December 2010).

Sallis, John (2000), *Force of Imagination: The Sense of the Elemental*, Bloomington, IN: Indiana University Press.

Salter, Mark B. (2008a), 'When the Exception Becomes the Rule: Borders, Sovereignty, and Citizenship', *Citizenship Studies* 12(4), pp. 365–380.

___ (2008b), 'Risk and Imagination in the War on Terror', in: Louise Amoore and Marieke de Goede (eds), *Risk and the War on Terror*, London: Routledge.

Sanger, David E. (2010), 'Obama Vows Fresh Proliferation Push as Summit Ends', *New York Times*, 13 April, http://www.nytimes.com/2010/04/14/world/14summit. html (accessed 20 December 2010).

Schell, Jonathan (1982), *The Fate of the Earth*, New York: Alfred A. Knopf.

Schelling, Thomas (1960), *The Strategy of Conflict*, Cambridge, MA: Harvard University Press.

Scheuerman, William E. (2006), 'Carl Schmitt and the Road to Abu Ghraib', *Constellations* 13(1), pp. 108–124.

Schiappa, Edward (1989), 'The Rhetoric of Nukespeak', *Communication Monographs* 56(3), pp. 253–273.

Schmitt, Carl (1996), *The Concept of the Political*, translated by Tracy B. Strong, Chicago: University of Chicago Press.

___ (2003), *The* Nomos *of the Earth in the International Law of the* Jus Publicum Europaeum, translated by G. L. Ulmen, London: Telos Press.

Schulte-Sasse, Jochen (1986), 'Imagination and Modernity: Or the Taming of the Human Mind', *Cultural Critique* 5, pp. 23–48.

Schweber, S. Sylvan (2009), 'Science without Laws', *Perspectives in Biology and Medicine* 52(1), pp. 141–152.

Secure Futures (2010), 'What are Crowded Places?', London, http://www.crowded-places.com/index.php (accessed 20 December 2010).

Sedgwick, Eve Kosofsky (1990), *Epistemology of the Closet*, Berkeley, CA: University of California Press.

Seifert, Jeffrey W. (2007), *Data Mining and Homeland Security: An Overview*, http://www.ipmall.piercelaw.edu/hosted_resources/crs/RL31798_071205.pdf (accessed 20 December 2010).

Shell (2003), *Scenarios: An Explorer's Guide*, London: Shell Centre, http://www-static. shell.com/static/aboutshell/downloads/our_strategy/shell_global_scenarios/ scenario_explorersguide.pdf (accessed 20 December 2010).

Smithson, Michael (1989), *Ignorance and Uncertainty: Emerging Paradigms*, New York: Springer.

Sontag, Susan (2004), 'The Imagination of Disaster', *The Science Fiction Film Reader*, New York: Limelight Editions, pp. 98–113.

Spivak, Gayatri Chakravorty (1999), *A Critique of Postcolonial Reason: Toward a History of the Vanishing Present*, Cambridge, MA: Harvard University Press.

Stark, Werner (2003 [1947]), *America: Ideal and Reality: The United States of 1776 in Contemporary European Philosophy*, London: Routledge.

Stern, Eric K. (2003), 'Crisis Studies and Foreign Policy Analysis: Insights, Synergies, and Challenges', *International Studies Review* 5(2), pp. 183–191.

Stern, Warren and Elena Buglova (2007), 'Expecting the Unexpected. The IAEA's Incident and Emergency Centre Helps Prepare States to Face Radiological Emergencies', *IAEA Bulletin* 48(2), pp. 66–68.

Stevenson, Leslie (2003), 'Twelve Conceptions of Imagination', *British Journal of Aesthetics* 43(3), pp. 238–259.

Stritzel, Holger (2007), 'Towards a Theory of Securitization: Copenhagen and Beyond', *European Journal of International Relations* 13(3), pp. 357–383.

Sullivan, John P. and Alan Bauer (2008), 'Terrorism Early Warning. 10 Years of Achievement in Fighting Terrorism and Crime', Los Angeles County Sheriff's

Department, http://www.lasd.org/tew/TEW2009.pdf (accessed 20 December 2010).

Sunstein, Cass R. (2002), *Risk and Reason*, Cambridge: Cambridge University Press.

___ (2005), *Laws of Fear: Beyond the Precautionary Principle*, Cambridge: Cambridge University Press.

Swiss Re (2002), *Terrorism Risks in Property Insurance and Their Insurability after 11 September 2001*, http://www.swissre.com/resources/cd7d5100462fcc2183dcd3300190b89f-Terror_Risks_Prop_en.pdf (accessed October 2007).

___ (2004), *The Risk Landscape of the Future*, Zurich: Swiss Reinsurance Company.

___ (2005), *A Shake in Insurance History: The 1906 San Francisco Earthquake*, Zurich: Swiss Reinsurance Company.

___ (2009), *Fire Insurance*, Zurich: Swiss Reinsurance Company.

Sylvester, Christine (2001), 'Art, Abstraction, and International Relations', *Millennium* 30(3), pp. 535–554.

Tait, Joyce (2001), 'More Faust than Frankenstein: the European Debate about the Precautionary Principle and Risk Regulation for Genetically Modified Crops', *Journal of Risk Research* 4(2), pp. 175–189.

Thackrah, John Richard (2003), *Dictionary of Terrorism*, Abingdon: Routledge.

The Complete University Guide (2010), 'Disaster Management', http://www.thecomplete universityguide.co.uk/single.htm?ipg=9177 (accessed 20 December 2010).

The Times (1803), 'Coroner's Inquest', 29 September 1803.

___ (1805a), 'Shocking Catastrophe', 6425, p. 3.

___ (1805b), 'Melancholy Catastrophe', 1 October 1805.

___ (1848), 'An Unexpected Catastrophe', 3 May 1848.

___ (1974), 'Nuclear Catastrophe', 24 September 1974.

Tiedemann, Rolf (2003), 'Introduction', in: Rolf Tiedemann (ed.), *Can One Live after Auschwitz? A Philosophical Reader*, Stanford: Stanford University Press.

Tierney, Kathleen J. (2007), 'From the Margins to the Mainstream? Disaster Research at the Crossroads', *Annual Review of Sociology* 33, pp. 503–525.

Trachtenberg, Marc (1991), *History and Strategy*, Princeton: Princeton University Press.

Toscano, Alberto and Jeff Kinkle (2009), 'Baltimore as World and Representation: Cognitive Mapping and Capitalism in *The Wire*', *Dossier Journal*, http://dossierjournal.com/read/theory/baltimore-as-world-and-representation-cognitive-mapping-and-capitalism-in-the-wire/ (accessed 20 December 2010).

Tuana, Nancy (2004), 'Coming to Understand: Orgasm and the Epistemology of Ignorance', *Hypatia* 19(1), pp. 194–232.

Tucker, Ben (2010), 'Media Release. Marsh, 23 June 2010', New York, http://www.marsh.co.uk/mediacentre/2010/pr20100623b.php (accessed 20 December 2010).

Tuomi, Ilkka (1999), 'Data Is More than Knowledge: Implications of the Reversed Knowledge Hierarchy for Knowledge Management and Organizational Memory', *Journal of Management Information Systems* 16(3), pp. 107–121.

UK Foresight Programme (2010), 'Foresight', London: Department for Business Innovation and Skills, http://www.bis.gov.uk/foresight/about-us (accessed 20 December 2010).

United Nations (1992), *Rio Declaration on Environment and Development*, General Assembly, 12 August, http://www.un.org/documents/ga/conf151/aconf15126-1annex1.htm (accessed 20 December 2010).

United Nations International Strategy for Disaster Reduction (UNISDR) (2009), *2009 UNISDR Terminology on Disaster Risk Reduction*, Geneva: United Nations.

US Congress (2002), *Terrorism Risk Insurance Act 2002*, Washington, DC.

US Department of Homeland Security (2008), *National Response Framework*, http://www.fema.gov/pdf/emergency/nrf/nrf-core.pdf (accessed 20 December 2010).

van der Sluijs, Jeroen P. (2007), 'Uncertainty and Precaution in Environmental Management: Insights from the UPEM Conference', *Environmental Modelling and Software* 22(5), pp. 590–598.

van Munster, Rens (2004), 'The War on Terrorism: When the Exception Becomes the Rule', *International Journal for the Semiotics of Law* 17(2), pp. 141–153.

___ (2009), *Securitizing Immigration: The Politics of Risk in the EU*, Basingstoke: Palgrave.

Vaughan-Williams, Nick (2007), 'The Shooting of Jean Charles de Menezes: New Border Politics?', *Alternatives: Global, Local, Political* 32(2), pp. 177–195.

Vetter, Daniel (2010), 'Swiss Re Hosts the First Knowledge Seminar of 2010', London: Swiss Re, http://www.swissre.com/clients/corporations_businesses/events/london_knowledge_seminar.html (accessed 20 December 2010).

Vijayan, Jaikumar (2010), 'N.Y. Bomb Plot Highlights Limitations of Data Mining', http://www.computerworld.com/s/article/9176317/N.Y._bomb_plot_highlights_limitations_of_data_mining (accessed 20 December 2010).

Walker, B., C. S. Holling, S. R. Carpenter and A. Kinzig (2004), 'Resilience, Adaptability and Transformability in Social-Ecological Systems', *Ecology and Society* 5, http://www.ecologyandsociety.org/vol9/iss2/art5/ (accessed 20 December 2010).

Walker, R. B. J. (2006), 'Lines of Insecurity: International, Imperial, Exceptional', *Security Dialogue* 37(1), pp. 65–82.

Walklate, Sandra and Gabe Mythen (2010), 'Agency, Reflexivity and Risk: Cosmopolitan, Neurotic or Prudential Citizen?', *The British Journal of Sociology* 61(1), pp. 45–62.

Warnock, M. (1994), *Imagination and Time*, Oxford: Blackwell.

Warren, Carol and Barbara Laslett (2010), 'Privacy and Secrecy: A Conceptual Comparison', *Journal of Social Issues* 33(3), pp. 43–51.

Watts, Michael (1983), 'Hazards and Crisis: A Political Economy of Drought and Famine in Northern Nigeria', *Antipode* 15(1), pp. 24–34.

Weick, K. E. and K. M. Sutcliffe (2001), *Managing the Unexpected: Assuring High Performance in an Age of Complexity*, San Francisco: Jossey-Bass.

Wessel, A. E. (1962), *The American Peace Movement: A Study of Its Themes and Political Potential*, RAND, http://www.rand.org/pubs/papers/2008/P2679.pdf (accessed 20 December 2010).

Wight, Martin (1991), *International Theory: The Three Traditions*, Leicester: Leicester University Press.

Williams, Michael C. (2003), 'Words, Images, Enemies: Securitization and International Politics', *International Studies Quarterly* 47(4), pp. 511–531.

___ (2007), *Culture and Security: Symbolic Power and the Politics of International Security*, London and New York: Routledge.

Williams, Michael J. (2008), '(In)Security Studies, Reflexive Modernization and the Risk Society', *Cooperation and Conflict* 43(1), pp. 57–79.

Wohlstetter, Albert (1958), *The Delicate Balance of Terror*, RAND Paper P-1472, 6 November, revised December 1958.

Wolff, Kurt H. (ed.) (1950), *The Sociology of Georg Simmel*, New York: The Free Press.

Wolff, Sula (1995), 'The Concept of Resilience', *Australasian Psychiatry* 29(4), pp. 565–574.

Woo, Gordon (2002a), 'Quantitative Terrorism Risk Assessment', *The Journal of Risk Finance* 4(1), pp. 7–14.

___ (2002b), *The Art of Terror*, http://www.rms.com/NewsPress/NEWS_GW_RT_101702.asp (accessed August 2006).

World Economic Forum (2008), *Global Risks 2008. A Global Risk Network Report*, Cologny/Geneva: World Economic Forum.

___ (2009), *Global Risks 2009. A Global Risk Network Report*, Cologny/Geneva: World Economic Forum.

Wright, Colin (2008), 'Event or Exception? Disentangling Badiou from Schmitt, or, Towards a Politics of the Void', *Theory and Event* 11(2), http://muse.jhu.edu/journals/theory_and_event/v011/11.2.wright.html (accessed 28 February 2011).

Wuthnow, Robert (2010), *Be Very Afraid: The Cultural Response to Terror, Pandemics, Environmental Devastation, Nuclear Annihilation, and Other Threats*, Oxford: Oxford University Press.

Young, Iris Marion (2003), 'The Logic of Masculinist Protection: Reflections on the Current Security State', *Signs* 29(1), pp. 1–25.

Zerilli, Linda M.G. (2005), '"We Feel Our Freedom": Imagination and Judgment in the Thought of Hannah Arendt', *Political Theory* 33(2), pp. 158–188.

Zins, Daniel L. (1991), 'Strategic "Thought" in Arthur Kopit's *End of the World*', in: Nancy Anisfield (ed.), *The Nightmare Considered: Critical Essays on Nuclear War Literature*, Bowling Green, OH: Bowling Green State University Popular Press, pp. 129–139.

Žižek, Slavoj (1999), *The Ticklish Subject: The Absent Centre of Political Ontology*, New York and London: Verso.

___ (2004), *Iraq: The Borrowed Kettle*, London: Verso.

___ (2006), 'The Depraved Heroes of 24 Are the Himmlers of Hollywood', *Guardian*, 10 January, http://www.guardian.co.uk/media/2006/jan/10/usnews.comment (accessed 20 December 2010).

Index

economy 5, 17, 21, 54, 58–60, 66, 73,
97, 103, 115, 124, 133, 142, 143, 145,
146, 152–154, 159
emergence 1, 14, 15, 29, 33, 71, 81, 91,
104, 110, 118, 124, 125, 129, 132, 133,
143, 144
emergency 2–5, 7–9, 20, 28, 29, 44–47,
58, 74, 78, 79, 81, 95, 96, 102, 107,
108, 121, 123, 128, 130, 136, 144–146,
148, 149, 151, 153–155, 157, 159;
emergency planning 8, 46, 74, 78, 81,
96, 102, 128, 136, 153, 155
enactment 29, 30, 69, 80, 91, 92, 95–97,
123
Enlightenment 37, 38, 56, 119, 121,
124, 150, 152
environment 3, 5, 7, 17, 37, 41–43, 48,
54, 65, 74, 89, 90, 102, 103, 114, 134,
137, 143, 144, 146, 147, 158–160
epistemic regime 14, 15, 28, 112, 122
epistemology 8, 47, 71, 86, 131, 135,
144, 149, 157, 158
escalation 24–26, 74–76, 150; escalation
ladder 24, 75
European Commission 27 37 40 41
42
European Union (EU) 27, 33, 37, 144,
149, 159
event catastrophic vii, 1–16, 17, 19, 25,
26, 28, 29, 31, 32, 33, 40, 41, 44, 46,
51, 52, 54, 55, 56, 57, 58, 65, 73, 78,
81, 82, 85, 92, 95, 99, 104, 106, 107,
108, 109, 112, 118, 120, 122, 124,
125, 126, 127; concept of 118–120;
eventfulness 9, 17, 27, 44; politics of
117–122; unexpected 15, 29, 31, 45,
56, 75, 80, 123, 134n2; unknown 95,
119
evidence 14, 15, 31, 32, 39, 41, 42, 49,
51, 111, 117, 119, 131, 132, 147
Éwald, Francois 20, 41, 55, 65, 69, 72
exception 3, 11, 12, 16, 29, 48, 82,
106–124, 126, 127, 130, 132, 134, 138,
140, 145, 149, 150, 153, 154, 157, 159,
160; exceptionalism 3, 11, 108, 109,
113, 116–118, 126
exercise 8, 9, 11, 13, 20, 22, 23, 25, 26,
42, 44, 45, 46, 49, 50, 62, 67, 69, 75,
76, 78–83, 85, 95–100, 102, 104–106,
126, 136, 138, 142–144, 146, 154
experience 2, 5, 8, 9, 10, 15, 22, 26, 31,
60, 74, 76, 77, 82, 84, 87–89, 98, 105,
106, 111, 113, 126, 131; experiential
knowledge 26, 47

experiment 14, 25, 39, 46, 47, 50, 89,
104
exploitation 57, 115

famine 4, 28, 115, 144, 159
fantasy 18, 31, 70–73, 135
fear 1, 6, 11, 17, 39, 57, 62, 71, 83, 85,
86, 89, 91, 109–112, 134, 135, 141,
144, 145, 149, 152, 156, 158
Federal Emergency Management
Agency (FEMA) 5, 27, 28, 82, 98, 128,
144, 145, 148, 159
Federation of European Risk
Management (FERMA) 66
fiction 2, 9, 12, 18, 68, 69, 71, 89, 134,
137, 150, 153, 157
Foucault, Michel 10, 12–15, 20, 32–34,
51, 55, 71, 91, 106, 108, 119, 120, 124,
126, 127, 129–132, 138, 139, 143–145,
147, 148, 153
future 64, 66, 67, 68, 69, 71 72 74 75
76 77 78 79 82 84 85 86 89 900 91
92 94 95 96 97 99 101 107 112, 115,
118–123, 125, 127, 128, 130, 134–136,
140, 144, 145, 147, 150, 153 future
history 74, 84; futures studies 8

Galison, Peter 26, 38, 147
game theory 54, 76, 84
genealogy 12, 13, 19, 55, 56, 126, 130,
143, 147
Ginzburg, Carlo 30–32, 51, 71, 125,
131, 132, 147, 154
global warming *see* climate change
God 24, 56, 95, 113, 147
governance 1, 5, 7, 10, 11, 13, 14, 16, 17,
19, 20, 23, 29–31, 36, 38, 41, 42, 49, 70,
71, 92, 95, 103, 109, 112, 123–125, 132,
135, 138, 139, 142, 145, 146
governmentality 9, 15, 20, 56, 112, 126,
141, 144
Great Fire of London 57, 59
Guantanamo Bay 150

Hacking, Ian 13, 14, 32, 50, 54, 55, 125,
131, 134, 148
Haiti Earthquake 126
hazard 19, 25, 27, 33, 40, 44, 53, 74, 79,
90, 107, 133, 154, 159
hint 2, 32
Hiroshima 113, 114
history 1, 8, 11, 12, 14, 16–18, 22, 23,
32, 33, 53, 60, 71, 72, 74, 84, 123, 127,
129, 130–133, 145, 147, 154

neoliberalism 65, 133, 151 *see also* capitalism
novelty 2, 10, 11, 13, 18, 33, 44, 47, 50, 51, 66, 68, 70, 95, 97, 99, 103, 104, 107, 117, 118, 122–124, 127, 128, 131
nuclear strategy 23, 147
nuclear war 7, 16, 18, 19, 21–24, 60, 74–77, 84, 129, 131, 145, 147, 150, 160 *see also* anti-nuclear movement

OECD 49, 62, 66, 154
Office for Security and Counter-Terrorism 36, 149
O'Malley, Patrick 21, 29, 71, 129, 134, 142, 154
Osborne, Peter 10, 51, 129, 154
organizational studies 130

pandemics 2, 13, 78, 103, 127, 149, 160
Paris School of security studies 14
pattern 6, 25, 35, 36, 43, 51, 88, 102
perception 24, 70, 72, 75, 79, 80, 82, 84–90, 92, 94, 98, 101, 111, 114, 115, 126, 135, 144
performance 45
planning 7–9, 22, 23, 25, 35, 43, 45, 46, 57, 72, 74, 76, 81, 96, 97, 102, 107, 113, 116, 128, 136, 143–145, 147, 148, 152–155 *see also* disaster planning, emergency planning
plausibility 22, 120, 125, 127
Polanyi, Karl 121, 155
police 4, 7, 9, 14, 20, 46, 65, 79, 97–102, 106, 109, 130, 131, 136, 137, 141, 146, 153–155
politics 3, 11, 12, 16, 18, 21, 33, 42, 86, 95, 98, 107, 116–118, 120, 122, 123, 125–127, 129, 132, 134–136, 139–142, 144–146, 149, 154, 155–157, 159, 160; at the limit 107–112,; politicization; depoliticization *see also* metapolitics
Pool Re 61, 133, 155
possibility 8, 10, 13, 15, 19, 20, 22, 24, 28, 30, 35, 38, 43, 64, 67, 69, 77, 78, 80, 88, 101, 104, 108–110, 116, 118–121, 123, 125, 127, 129, 136
postulate 39, 43, 49
power 9, 10, 13–15, 18, 20, 29, 34, 41, 47, 49, 56, 62, 69–71, 73, 74, 76, 77, 80, 87–89, 95, 98, 106–112, 116, 117, 119–121, 123, 126, 129, 130, 134, 135, 139, 142, 144, 145, 147, 149, 152, 156, 159

precaution 7, 23, 32, 33, 35, 41–45, 50, 51, 78, 127, 130, 132, 140, 144, 146, 148, 151, 153, 158, 159
predictive analytics 38, 152
pre-emption 42, 140, 144
premediation 20, 31, 144, 148
preparedness 11, 25–27, 32, 33, 44–46, 49–51, 69, 75, 78–80, 82, 85, 86, 95–97, 100, 101, 104, 106, 108, 115, 116, 126, 137, 140, 143, 144, 146, 151
prevention 4, 11, 17, 20, 22, 26, 29, 30, 32, 33, 35, 37, 38, 45, 53, 78, 104, 108, 133, 137, 149, 152
privacy 39, 132, 159
probability 10, 22, 23, 35, 41, 54, 55, 76, 92, 94
problematization 2, 3, 5, 9, 16, 17–19, 23, 30–32, 34, 39, 44, 49, 50, 53, 68, 74, 78, 123–125, 131
Project ARGUS 67, 79–80, 83, 96–101, 126, 136, 138
property 8, 22, 25, 48, 55, 57–62, 64–67, 74, 111, 113, 133, 143, 149, 158
protection 27, 32, 33, 35, 40–43, 53, 55, 58, 66, 67, 82, 132, 133, 143, 146, 149, 152, 154, 160
psychiatry 34, 82, 132
psychoanalysis 32, 51
psychology 47, 50, 82, 83, 132, 136, 141, 145
pursuit 16, 32, 33, 35, 50, 69

Quarantelli, Enrico 5, 28, 29, 141, 147, 155, 156

radicalization 37, 49
Rancière, Jacques 39, 88, 89, 135, 136, 155
RAND Corporation 5, 74, 77
rational choice 75
reality 26, 32, 36, 39, 45, 47, 48, 51, 53, 72, 77, 84, 86, 92, 101, 113, 132, 134, 157
recovery 22, 25, 33, 44, 49, 58, 60
resilience 25, 46–49, 67, 107, 132, 141, 143, 145, 148, 149, 152, 154, 156, 159, 160
revolution 2, 114, 119, 127, 129, 139, 151, 154
risk 2–11, 15–30, 33, 35, 39, 40–48, 50–66, 69, 74, 78, 79, 84, 86, 90–96, 99, 102–104, 107–109, 111, 113, 117, 123, 124, 129–133, 135, 137, 139–144, 146–152, 154–160;